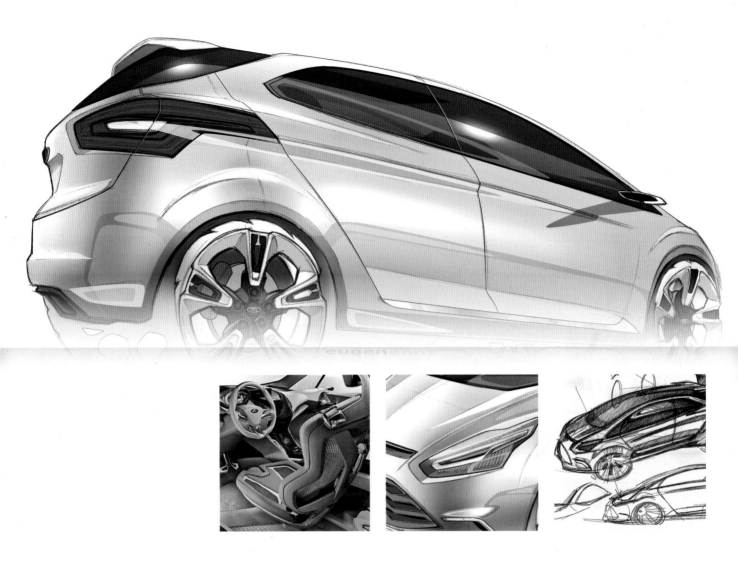

HOW TO **DESIGN** cars
LIKE A PRO

New Edition

Tony Lewin

Ryan Borroff

Foreword by Ian Callum
Design Director, Jaguar

Quarto is the authority on a wide range of topics.

Quarto educates, entertains and enriches the lives of
our readers—enthusiasts and lovers of hands-on living.

www.quartoknows.com

First published in 2010 by Motorbooks, an imprint of Quarto Publishing Group USA Inc., 400 First Avenue
North, Suite 400, Minneapolis, MN 55401 USA. Telephone: (612) 344-8100 Fax: (612) 344-8692

quartoknows.com
Visit our blogs at quartoknows.com

Motorbooks titles are also available at discounts in bulk quantity for industrial or sales-promotional use. For
details contact the Special Sales Manager at Quarto Publishing Group USA Inc., 400 First Avenue North,
Suite 400, Minneapolis, MN 55401 USA.

ISBN 978-0-7603-3695-3

Library of Congress Cataloging-in-Publication Data

Lewin, Tony.
How to design cars like a pro / Tony Lewin, Ryan Borroff.
    p. cm.
Includes bibliographical references.
ISBN 978-0-7603-3695-3 (sb w/ flaps)
1. Automobiles—Design and construction. I. Borroff, Ryan. II. Title.
TL240.L445 2010
629.2'31—dc22

                    2010013742

Editor: Jeffrey Zuehlke
Design Manager: Kou Lor
Designed by: Simon Larkin

Printed in China

On the front cover and the title pages:
Sketches of the Ford Iosis Max concept. *Ford of Europe Design*
On the back cover:
Original design art by Paul Nichols.
On the frontis:
The Nissan Nuvu concept car (2008). *Nissan Motor (GB) Limited*

contents

foreword
by Ian Callum Design Director, Jaguar Cars

I really can't imagine a more exciting time to become a car designer. New challenges and demands on the motor car are going to change the comfortable assumptions we have had for many years. Challenges include safety, resources, and, of course, sustainability.

The process of anticipating trends in technology and customer needs is now a primary focus. We need to question the whole aspect of how we package components, because components are changing. Where there is now a large V-8 engine, one day it may house a battery or electric motor. What was once acceptable for aerodynamics is no longer the norm. What was once crashworthy is now dangerous. All these aspects affect the way we will design future cars. Not just incrementally, but dramatically.

Designers starting their careers during the coming decade will need to grapple with questions like these, and will have the unique opportunity to shape a new design direction for the industry.

So, more than ever before, car design is a profession where motivated, talented young people can make a real difference to the world around them.

For many, this can be the fulfilment of a lifelong dream. As a teenager, classic shapes like the Jaguar Mk II and the XJ fuelled my passion for automotive design, and inspired me to send my first application letter to Jaguar as a 14-year-old!

Even during the 1970s, however, car design was a competitive world, and it took over a decade of hard work and persistence to secure a position within the industry.

Fast-forward over 30 years, and I have had the privilege of overseeing the re-invention of the Jaguar brand, returning to the original values of innovative, modern design which Sir William Lyons established during Jaguar's heyday.

This revolutionary change was not achieved overnight. It was a long, ten-year journey, and highlights that the talent to create attractive shapes is not enough: Designers need to have real tenacity and the ability to communicate the vision behind their ideas.

At Jaguar, we embraced this change from heritage-led design in three stages. Each successive model–the XK coupé, the XF sedan, and the **flagship XJ**–moved the design language forward, combining distinctly modern appearance with the purity of line and sense of proportion which underpins all classic Jaguars.

The exceptionally favourable reception for these vehicles has been a strong vindication that our approach was the right one, and is a good example of the unique rewards which this profession can offer.

Young people who share a similar passion for automotive design, and who are keen to establish a foothold in what remains a highly sought-after and competitive profession, will find this book a valuable resource.

Providing a detailed insight into the world of car design, it also profiles the work of a number of young, up-and-coming designers.

Fresh, modern ideas which capture the imagination, and which get customers enthralled, are the lifeblood of our profession, and I look forward to seeing the next generation of talented car designers entering the industry.

THE FAST MOVING WORLD OF
design

A lot can happen in the space of seven years, especially in a world as fast moving as the automobile industry. Why seven years? Because that's how long it has been since the publication of the first edition of *How to Design Cars Like a Pro,* and because seven years gives a handy perspective from which to take stock of the changes that have affected the lives of everyone involved in the auto industry, not least those people working in the design business.

In the space of those seven years the cars in the showrooms and on our streets became faster, fatter and more fabulous—only to shrink back to more responsible proportions as tighter environmental regulations became a certainty rather than just an idle threat. Styles such as the big, bullying SUV have come and gone in that short space of time, and buyers are becoming increasingly intolerant of any product that smacks of easy profit rather than personality. At model level, the struggles of grandiose super-rich projects such as Maybach and Bugatti contrast starkly with the rise of new entry-level models such as Renault's Logan and Tata's ambitious new $1500 people's car, the Nano. All are differentiated by good design.

Even greater convulsions have shaken the companies that build our cars. Financial pressures leading to the breakup of several of the major carmaking empires have liberated brands such as Jaguar, Volvo, Aston Martin, and Saab from centralised corporate control, but also put them at the mercy of harsh market forces; equally, once-famous marques like Oldsmobile, Pontiac, and Rover have

already succumbed and now languish on the scrapheap.

Even more noteworthy has been the rise of two Asian nations. Korea's Hyundai and Kia brands are now a global force to be reckoned with, and China is emphatically on the map as the biggest car market in the world as well as the nation with the greatest number of automakers—and perhaps also the greatest hunger for all things automotive.

But what does this all mean for designers, especially aspiring young designers who are full of ideas but who have yet to train or find a job? Fortunately, most of the news is good news. The profusion of newer, smaller and more independently minded companies means easier access to design professionals for design hopefuls. In fact, there is something of a renaissance in car design going on. Never has the design and styling of automobiles been so fundamentally important to a carmaker as it is now. Design is at the forefront of how cars are perceived and directly affects consumers' purchase decisions. And as time moves forward, consumers are becoming more demanding. They want the cars they drive to have character, suggest individuality, to communicate to the world their lifestyles, status, even their values and ideals. In fact, though environmental and safety regulations now place tight constraints on how cars are shaped, the era of the anonymous family sedan is over: carmakers are desperate to differentiate their ranges from those of their competitors, and all of them realise that design is much the most effective tool with which to achieve such

differentiation. And for that reason most studios welcome the spark and fresh inspiration that young talent can bring.

It could be argued, too, that it has never been easier to get started. Professional digital design programs are now available at affordable prices so that anyone with competence and a computer can produce impressive, near studio quality results. Back in 2003, when the first edition of this book appeared, such programs cost several thousand dollars per user. Yet such an obvious democratisation of design tools brings with it one enormous challenge: Anyone seeking to make their career in design is now in competition with like-minded people all around the globe, from Chile to China and from South Africa to Sweden.

Rest assured, however, that studios and colleges know that true talent will always shine through. The job of this book is to fire up your interest in car design: It will guide you through the initial part of the process, help you understand what makes a good design, celebrate the true classics of design, and guide your own first steps in putting pen to paper or mouse to keyboard and screen. It's then that, all being well, inspiration will take over and it becomes time to consult our list of design colleges at the back of the book. And beyond that? It's all up to you, your inspiration and your talent.

TONY LEWIN
RYAN BORROFF
Spring 2010

CHAPTER 1

DESIGN
defined

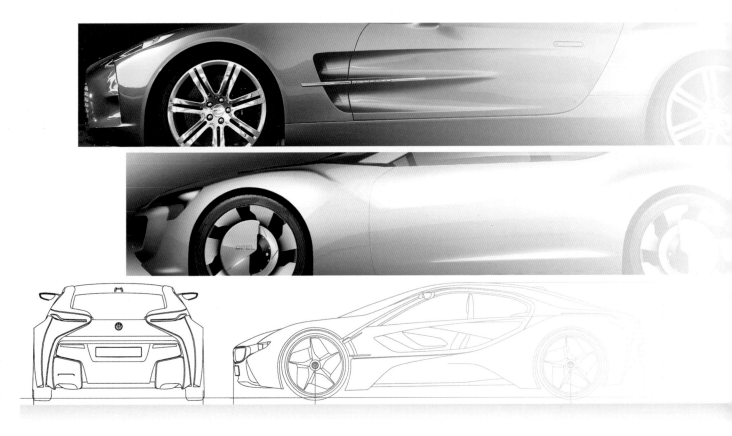

We asked four leading designers what attracted them to car design, what influences them, and which of their designs best encapsulates their design approach.

Marek Reichman, director of design, Aston Martin

Marek Reichman has overseen the most prolific period of design for Aston Martin and has led the creation of the four-door Rapide coupé, DBS, and One-77, as well as the Cygnet city car.

My fascination with cars and design began from a very early age. My dad was a car fan and my older brother a fanatic. We spent many hours at family and friends' garages repairing and messing about with cars, hearing stories about cars of the 1940s and 1950s—so I guess that really rubbed off on me as the youngest member of the all-male Reichman household. I became very interested in design as my brother began his education as a designer. I was of a very impressionable age and remember always hearing about the cool stuff that design students became involved with.

I was also a fan of all boys' toys, such as Meccano, Lego, Hornby trains, and Scalextric, but it was design that really captured

my imagination. Reading about the Bauhaus school, Le Corbusier, and the modern design movement, I started to sketch various crazy ideas. I wanted a very rounded design education, which is why I decided to study industrial design. This proved to be a great foundation as I studied material science, form, function, and manufacturing technologies. I was always asking the question "how and why?" I think every designer wants to analyse and take apart objects to discover . . . how they are made. The goal? The art of the impossible, along with purity and simple refinement. Designers are essentially geeks who are into things, always attempting to make the world a better, more interesting place.

All of the designs I have been involved in creating follow this ethos in principle: It is always about defining the elements of a car or brand in order to design. As an example, a recently submitted design for a new generation of London bus used this approach to deliver a functionally better bus with a characterful exterior. At the heart of design should be beauty *and* functionality. The best examples of this approach are the **Aston Martin Rapide** and **One-77** cars.

Peter Schreyer, chief design officer, Kia Motor Company

One of the world's most influential car designers, Peter Schreyer is best known for his work at Audi in the 1990s, most notably the TT, which is already considered one of the twentieth century's most iconic designs. He has been chief design officer at Kia Motor Company since 2006.

I think my fascination with car design was fired by one particular car that I saw when I was quite young. It was a white 1950s Mercedes 300 SL, with a red-leather interior. It belonged to a guy who was a motorcycle racer in my hometown in Bavaria. Even now I still have a screensaver of a photograph of myself and my brother standing next to it.

My father had a great passion for cars, and I recall one day he came home saying there was a great new car—the Jaguar E-Type. He said it cost 23,000 Deutschmarks and to me that sounded like millions—like a lottery win. But it was a great car and it was so beautiful.

I believe concept is so very important to making a good car. Another vehicle I have always admired is the Rumpler Tropfenwagen—strange perhaps to some people—and it was in some ways like the old horse-drawn carriages that preceded the modern car. But the concept of the Rumpler was that it should provide space for people in comfort in a very aerodynamic body. Its teardrop shape was remarkable in a vehicle that so perfectly provided convenience and function—perhaps the first case of form following function in the motor car. In fact until the 1980s, it still had the best drag coefficient figure of any vehicle.

Of course, it is not just car design that influences car designers. For example, most people might not imagine that the P51 Mustang influenced the cabin design of the last model Volkswagen Passat. However, if you look at the cockpit canopy of the Mustang and the cabin of the Passat, there is a great similarity. Both are organic forms that sit on top of the respective bodies in a fluent manner—and the Passat cabin, like the Mustang, does not have lines that are merely parallel with the body of the car; it narrows towards the rear—just like the Mustang.

I was particularly proud of the **Audi A2**. I saw several on a recent visit to London, and the car still looks right on the streets today. That is because it fulfills its concept—an aerodynamic, lightweight,

fuel consumption-conscious package that provides a good space package, a commanding driving position, and an attractive shape; it is still a great-looking car.

My design approach at Kia is the same. Our new **Venga**, like the A2, is compact yet it provides excellent space and a good driving position. It has good looks—it is almost like a cute little frog sat on the road—but inside it surprises its occupants with impressive space, comfort, and style. The **Soul** was all about character—despite the fact that it is very much a B-segment car, but it stands out and makes its owners smile. And our just-launched Cadenza takes that arc of tension, that direct design link, a stage further. It is a lighthouse car—it will stand out in showrooms and attract people to the brand. It has consistency of design, and even if someone comes in to look at the car but goes away in something more humble, they will know that the design of the car they have chosen is connected directly to the Cadenza. Communicating a consistent brand identity is the key challenge as Kia design moves forward. We must have one language and communicate it clearly and understandably to our customers.

Concept Interior Geneva 2008

Anthony Lo, vice president, exterior design, Renault

Anthony Lo *is vice president of exterior design at Renault. Previously Lo was director of advanced design at General Motors Europe. Designer of the Saab Aero X, Lo led the design of GM cars for the Saab, Opel, and Vauxhall brands, including the Saab 9-X, 9-3X, and 2006 Opel GTC, 2007 Opel Flextreme, and 2009 Opel Flextreme GT/E concepts.*

Wedge-shaped car design of the late 1960s and early 1970s has greatly influenced my design philosophy. The idea of a slim silhouette, minimal cross sectional area, wide stance, and the "no excess" efficient package fascinates me. Among many great examples from this era (Maserati Bora, BMW M1, Lamborghini Countach, Lotus Esprit), the **Lamborghini Espada** stood out for me. This is a proper four-seater sports car with a supercar performance. The proportions are classical front engine, rear drive,

with long dash-to-axle distance and a relatively long wheelbase. There is something particularly appealing about a four-seater GT because of the combination of style, elegance, performance, and function. The sleek profile was a result of having both front and rear passengers sit very close to the ground, where seating comfort was questionable over long distance trips. But then again, if comfort is your highest priority, there are plenty of other options out there. The Espada is a GT with the strong visual drama of a mid-engine supercar and an ultimate driving experience for four travelling at supercar speed centimetres above ground. Designing a sports car with four decent-size seats is a real challenge, especially with safety, comfort, entry, and exit in mind. Proportions on the Espada are well managed, with a sleek profile that stretches over the rear passengers' head without a hump.

The **Flextreme GTC Concept** encompassed a similar highly optimised design. It expressed Opel's design philosophy of sculptural artistry and German precision. The overall proportion of this sleek coupé was exaggerated with large wheel and tyre diameters, pronounced fender flares, and a tight, fitted body with a sloping profile. Unlike supercars, mainstream cars have to meet the needs of a bigger cross section of the population. Safety standards, performance measures, and customer-oriented improvements have changed the landscape of car design radically since the 1970s. The design process has become much more complex and involves many more variables than it used to. Apart from establishing a design vision for a given concept and developing models, designers are working hand in hand with their counterparts in engineering to find the best solutions that are aesthetically pleasing and offer maximum benefit to the customers. This is the challenge that makes car design so exciting.

Adrian van Hooydonk, head of BMW group design

Adrian van Hooydonk, director of BMW Group Design, is responsible for design development for the BMW, Rolls-Royce, and MINI brands. Hooydonk created the Z9 Gran Turismo prototype, which introduced the brand's sculptured design idea that was to inform BMW body design for more than a decade. The BMW 6 and 7 Series cars, as well as the BMW Concept CS M1 Homage Study and Z4 all bear his influence.

Drawing, first of all, fascinated me. As a kid, I was sketching in every book, in every school paper I had. At some point, I was thinking about what I could do to turn that into a profession. The other thing I was always interested in was how things are built, how things are produced. So this is why I studied industrial design and later came to car design.

We at the BMW Group always talk about proportion, surface, and detail, and we deal with them in that order. It means that we spend a lot of time getting the proportions right. The way the car sits on its wheels, the relation of length to width and height. These are things that we study at great length. We study proportion models before we decide what the right proportion is. After that, we deal with the surface. Now we are dealing with light and shadow. And in our surface design, we know we are able to generate a lot of emotion. Finally, of course, we deal with the detail. We have a great love of detail. This means that in a premium product like a BMW, a Rolls-Royce, or a MINI, we want to make sure that the customer

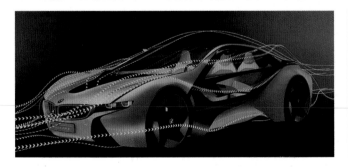

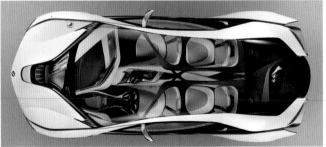

will discover more and more great details the longer they look at the car, the longer they own the car. This is how we can keep our designs relevant for a long time and can give customers a very strong personal and emotional relationship to their vehicles for a long time.

In recent times, a show car and a production car encapsulate this approach. The show car is the **BMW Vision EfficientDynamics** concept car that we showed in Frankfurt in 2009. This is a car that is actually not only about design. It addresses the biggest issues in the car industry today: entirely new drivetrains—such as electric drive or smaller engines—and much lower fuel consumption and emissions. With the BMW Vision EfficientDynamics, we did all that by making a car that is very light and very aerodynamic. And those two elements, lightweight and aerodynamics, are expressed through the design. They are given a shape that I would call highly emotional, and I believe that is very desirable. So in a nutshell, the design philosophy at BMW is that we want to do design that is authentic, that expresses what the vehicle is capable of, and what the customer will experience while driving the car. A recent production car example of that philosophy is the new BMW 5 Series.

CHAPTER 2

SKETCH TO
showroom

Great showmanship is about walking the tightrope between the real and the fantastical—too much of either and you risk alienating your audience through boredom or disbelief. This certainly applies to carmakers exhibiting at motor shows, who in years past were pilloried for using conceptual flights of fancy to deflect attention from the disappointingly homogeneous production designs with which they shared the stage.

Whether through mounting pressure to make every development dollar count—some manufacturers, like Audi, don't really do concepts at all, applying the name to thinly veiled preproduction prototypes instead—or simply a greater aptitude for bending the rules, we're seeing an increasing number of dramatic concepts reach production virtually unmolested, and in record time. Here we trace the development of seven key models from the drawing board to the street, successfully running the gauntlet of safety legislation, plummeting budgets, and focus groups to emerge with their essence intact. Each one is a tribute to the vision, skill, and dedication of the designers who created them.

Jaguar XJ

The story of the new Jaguar XJ is not the standard one of a bold and futuristic concept car wheeled out at a glitzy motor show and only later re-emerging, barely recognisable, as a bland production model, toned down to chime in with conservative focus groups and awkward regulations.

A year ahead of the XJ's unveiling in summer 2009, design director Ian Callum was clear that this was a car that could go straight to market, without a concept version ahead of the launch. The smaller XF, introduced in 2008, had already done all the softening-up work normally accomplished by a show car, reasoned Callum—and in any case the XF had been preceded by its own concept, the **C-XF**, whose impact was still fresh in the customer's mind.

"As I get older, I find I get braver," commented Callum as he discussed the XJ's shape at the unveiling. Given that the XJ had hardly evolved over its many generations since the William Lyons original of 1968, the bravery Callum was referring to must have been two-fold: first, in daring to put a new face to a sacred Jaguar icon that no one had dared to touch and, secondly, in making that new face such a radical and progressive one.

Though the XF had already signalled the bringing of Jaguar sedan design into the modern era, Callum wanted to go further with the XJ and make a real impact. Self evidently, the design would be thoroughly modern, but instead of a cut and paste of familiar XJ design cues the team looked at the proportions and the architecture of the original and applied these lessons to a modern Jaguar.

One of the most striking aspects of the XJ is the visually very stretched window profile, with the rear quarter light taking the waistline to the trailing edge of the rear wheel arch. "This is a pure teardrop shape, a strong graphic that gives the car a lot of virtual length," says Callum. Indeed, the XJ looks very long and graceful, even in the shorter of its two wheelbases. As with the original, the rear overhang is long and the roof slender and graceful, aided at the rear by glazed-over C-pillars that add visual width to the rear window. Perhaps the boldest aspect of the XJ—and certainly the most discussed—is the pure surface of the trunk lid, framed by elegantly striated vertical rear lights and with only the leaping Jaguar symbol for decoration. Again, Callum asserts the need for some formality in the design.

Reiterating the statement first attributed to Ford's head of design, J Mays, Jaguar managing director Mike O'Driscoll insists the British brand is in the business of entertainment rather than transport. With its exterior exuding a real sense of occasion and its interior living up to that promise with state-of-the-art audio-visual systems and a programmed welcome sequence as you enter, the new XJ convinces as automotive entertainment of the classiest possible kind.

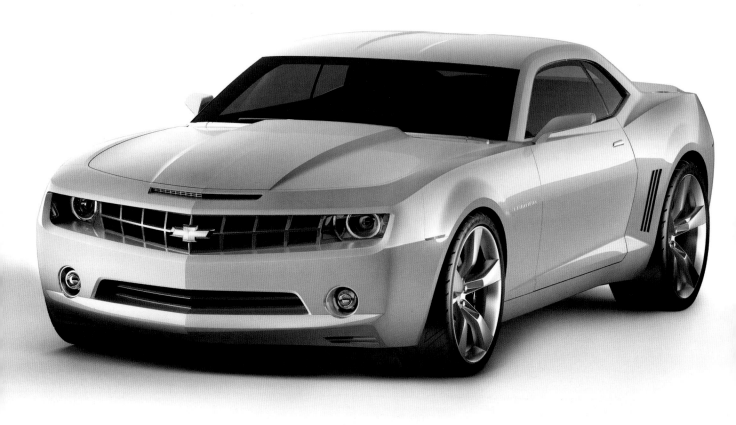

Chevrolet Camaro

Ford may have kicked off the process two years earlier with its successful reinterpretation of the Mustang, but it is 2006—with the unveiling of the Chevrolet Camaro and Dodge Challenger concepts at the NAIAS in Detroit—that will always be remembered as the year that the American muscle car made its triumphant return to the world stage.

The motoring blogs had been awash with speculative images of these cars in the months preceding their unveiling, what seemed like the world and his dog getting busy with photo and design software to provide their own take on the future of the pony car. If anything, the two official cars exceeded expectations—in particular the Camaro, which combined proportions and graphical elements inspired by the iconic **1969 version** with a progressive twenty-first century surface treatment.

This, though, was the culmination of what was by all accounts a very short (just seven months) but tumultuous design process. One

auto journal talks of a last-minute walk-through by then-GM CEO Rick Wagoner resulting in a finished concept being scrapped on the grounds of being too faithful to the original. A second team was then drafted in to work alongside the existing designers and come up with a more progressive design under the direction of newly appointed VP of global design, Ed Welburn. The two rival designs were created by Simon Cox's studio in the UK and Frank Saucedo's West Coast Advanced Design team in California—we may never know which outfit's design made the cut.

Regardless, the final design not only garnered almost universal praise at its launch the following year, but also required remarkably few alterations in order to meet the demands of mass production. From the outside, the 2010 Camaro (top) is a dead ringer for the concept that previewed it; only the closest of examinations reveals the difference between the two. The intakes in the rear fenders have been replaced with decorative slits for aerodynamic reasons;

the rear-view mirrors have swelled to a more practical size; the side indicator and reversing lights have been repositioned to meet legislation requirements; and the lower parts of the front and rear bumpers are subtly reprofiled to optimise airflow. And that's it. The "Coke-bottle" rear, short front and rear overhangs, and muscular hood that characterised the concept are very much present and correct on the showroom model (top).

While some of the glitzy cockpit detailing has been lost, the spirit of the **concept interior** has also survived remarkably intact in the **production version**. The instrument panel (IP) is wide and unusually open for a sports car, and interior design manager Jeff Perkins succeeded in keeping the recessed twin driver's dials, a deep-dished steering wheel, and distinctive (albeit less colourful) four-pack gauges behind the gearshifter that gave the design study such a strong aesthetic link to the 1960s version. In terms of both concept and execution, the Camaro is something of a masterpiece.

Citroën C3 Picasso

Born in 2004 under the codename A58, the C3 Picasso's design and development was overseen by Citroën's head of concept cars, Carlo Bonzanigo. The goal was to translate the cutting-edge design language developed on cars like the C-SportLounge and apply it to a mainstream production minivan (MPV). In doing so, Bonzanigo and his team created a car that totally subverts expectations of what a small, affordable minivan should look like, both inside and out.

Led by Miles Nurnberger and Frédéric Duvernier, the exterior design kicked off with the traditional PSA two-week sketching phase, after which the initial themes were translated into 3D computer-aided design (CAD) renderings for assessment by the entire team. Two of these proposals were then milled in full scale from polystyrene; this allowed the designers to refine the volumes and surfaces prior to the

management presentation a few months later.

Both themes shared a two-box profile and a stubby, high-set hood reminiscent of the Audi A2's, plus a voluminous rear with more rounded surfaces than previously seen on compact minivans. Duvernier's initial sketches featured window lines that sank down between the A- and C-pillars—an element that featured in one of the proposals but was later adapted so that the visual "kick" into the rear fender is achieved via the shoulder line rather than the side glass. Like the car's three-part windshield, which allowed the A-pillar to be drawn back to minimise driver blind spots, this went on to become one of the production C3 Picasso's most distinctive features.

A full-scale clay model was created in Spring 2005 for final surface development. It was at this point that the designers came up with the car's complex three-tiered front graphic, which combines

some of the dramatic elements explored on previous Citroën show cars with a benign, almost friendly down-the-road graphic (DRG).

The interior development process ran in parallel with that of the exterior and was led by Pascal Grappey and Andreas Stump, who came up with a diverse range of themes. It was Stump's "opera" IP theme that was taken to the hard model phase, as he proposed an IP whose upper panel fans out and away from the centre, creating a natural recess between the two sections that becomes more prominent at either end of the dashboard. As on the finished version, the digital instrument binnacle was also mounted centrally, at eye level, on top of the upper dash panel and the gearshift located high on a simple, relatively clutter-free console.

A few more changes had taken place by the time the interior design clinic was held in June 2006, most notably the replacement of circular air vents with bevelled rectangular items that echo the exterior theme.

By any standards, the C3 Picasso is a roaring success. Compact, characterful, and extremely versatile, it deserves to rank alongside the DS and 2CV in Citroën's illustrious hall of fame.

Toyota iQ

It is perhaps only fitting that the next evolutionary step in vehicle packaging should have emerged from the spiritual home of miniaturisation, Japan. Slightly wider and longer than a Smart ForTwo, Toyota's iQ nevertheless takes up less than three metres of road space. Within this length (less than even the original Mini's), Toyota's design and engineering team have managed to create accommodation for three adults and a child (or luggage)—no small feat given the airbags, crumple zones, and pedestrian impact protection that each new car must offer.

Work on the iQ began at Toyota's European design centre, ED2, in 2006. Design boss Wahei Hirai's brief was to create a "dynamic and on-the-edge design" that would move the goalposts in terms of "size, functionality, and CO_2 emissions." The project's real roots can be traced back to 2004, however, when ED2 first experimented with the square, wheel-at-each-corner city car format for its Endo concept, which was launched at the 2005 Frankfurt show.

Toyota cited the manta ray as inspiration for the **2007 iQ concept's** unusual side profile, specifically the unusual cut-back "wave" in the

rear side glass and the distinctive curved character line that runs between the front and rear fenders. The car's DRG, meanwhile, was dominated by geometric lines that ran diagonally from the bottom of the A-pillars and the outer corners of the bumper, intersecting deep into the hood area to form the innermost points of the triangular, faired-in headlights.

Like the character line, this dramatic graphic was toned down a little for production. But the prototype that appeared at Geneva in 2008, just six months after the Frankfurt design study, retained a surprising proportion of the concept's more unusual design elements, presenting an altogether more aggressive face than its city car rivals. The **high beltline, V-shaped crease** leading to a slit-like grille intake, and wide, wheel-at-each-corner stance give the iQ an abnormally large amount of visual attitude for its size.

The car's radical interior design made the transition from concept to showroom equally unscathed. Gone is the sculptural, manta ray–inspired IP that flowed along the top of the instrument cluster, folding like a layer of silver-lined purple silk to form a sharp point and a natural home for the car's infotainment screen, HVAC controls, and perforated air vent design. But the very architectural, **T-shaped dashboard architecture** remains, as does the V-shaped console effect.

Arguably the IQ's biggest selling point could be seen as its pioneering **3+1 seating configuration**. This had, in fact, appeared before, on the 2004 Opel Trixx and Fiat Trepiuno concepts. But Toyota was the first to bring it to the showroom, thanks largely to a series of engineering innovations. A new way of packaging the differential and steering rack allowed the front wheels to be moved to the outer extreme of the body; an ultra-thin underfloor fuel tank and seating design combine to maximise rear headroom; and squeezing the air-conditioning system into the confines of that vertical console allowed the passenger-side dash to be pushed back several inches. The end result provides physical proof of the great things that can be achieved when design and engineering work collaboratively towards a single goal.

Volkswagen Scirocco

With the Scirocco firmly established as one of the most desirable coupés of modern times, it's perhaps easy to forget the troubled start that it had to life. Created by then-design boss of Volkswagen, Murat Günak, and launched with the name **IROC** at the 2006 Paris show, the concept (above) was a big hit with a public tantalised by the prospect of a stylish, practical Volkswagen four-seat coupé.

The following year, however, saw the departure of Günak in favour of former Seat design boss Walter de'Silva—and with it substantial revisions to the design of the already-in-development Scirocco production car. The most notable of these was carried out to the car's face.

The **street-ready version** unveiled at Geneva in 2008 bore a much less aggressive down-the-road graphic (DRG) than the concept—not exactly unusual in automotive design. The reasons behind this change were more profound than a simple loss of nerve on the part of VW, however. The production Scirocco's geometric front end—a collaboration between de'Silva, VW Potsdam studio chief Klaus Bischoff, and former creative director of the VW Group

Flavio Manzoni—was to provide a template for the new face of VW.

The gently flared-out headlights connected by a narrow grille is a theme that has since been adapted for both the new Golf and Polo, but which will reach its zenith (for now at least) on the production version of the BlueSport roadster concept shown at Detroit in 2009. Another key element pioneered on the Scirocco and destined for other models is the symmetry shared by the front and rear lights, both of which are linked by a horizontal line (the grille at the front, and the tailgate shut line at the rear) and flare outwards towards the fenders.

The rest of the exterior, overseen by head of exterior design Mark Lichte, has remained remarkably faithful to the concept. The flat windscreen and wide body hark back to the original Giugiaro-designed 1974 model, while the strong shoulder line that flows from headllight to taillight, widening as the glasshouse tapers at the rear, creates a very pronounced tumblehome—a cue long used to communicate power and aggression.

Less of Ulrich Lammel's IROC interior design (below left) made it onto the final product (below right). The triangular door pulls and centre console side structures provide some link with the more exaggeratedly geometric concept interior, and the car's low seating position and pillarbox-style windscreen reinforce the feeling that you're in a proper sports coupé. But the dashboard is lifted straight from the Eos and the seats from the Passat CC—handsome enough elements in their own right, but perhaps an opportunity lost for VW to reassert its position at the cutting edge of interior design.

Nissan Juke

It was 2006 when Nissan delivered the surprise that would rocket the brand back into the limelight and have its UK factory struggling to build enough cars to keep up with demand. Ingeniously and imaginatively, Nissan had seized the name, the crossover feel, and some of the design cues of the 2004 Qashqai concept to provide a Golf-class competitor with a crucial difference. By giving the Qashqai the high stance, four-wheel-drive option, and urban cool of a 4x4 whilst keeping its price down and its running costs reasonable, Nissan elevated itself above the mainstream competition, preserving its profit margins and cultivating a superior image whilst also appealing to customers who might normally have shopped for a Ford Focus or an Opel Astra.

It was a gamble, but it worked—and the Qashqai has been a huge success. The company realised that it could benefit from a similar energy boost in the smaller B segment, where the Micra was lost in a sea of low-cost hatchbacks. Yet, says Alfonso Albaisa, former London-based vice president of Nissan Design Europe, the approach would be bolder still: "We wanted it to be both masculine and agile, something that would be unique in the B segment. It needed to be less cautious than the Qashqai, as that model has a wider range of customers. It's not so rebellious as the B-car world."

The early target qualities were defined as sports plus tough plus cute, though the latter was later dropped. Four years away from its planned showroom debut of September 2010, teams

in several Nissan design centres began sketching; soon, a key sketch emerged, one which everyone could buy in to as the way ahead. Crucially, the aim was to target a person, a type of customer, rather than an attribute such as roominess. With Matt Weaver in the NDE London studio appointed lead designer, a dramatic but small shape began to develop, with a heavy emphasis on its large wheels and wheel arches, tall build, rally-car style spotlights, and unusual high-set headlights mounted further back on the hood.

"We pushed in the area between the doors so that the wheel forms became even more dominant," says Albaisa. Patrick Reimer, meanwhile, had led an innovative, very sculptural interior treatment, which included a centre console shaped like a motorcycle fuel tank and flipper-shaped forms on the door casings to reflect the model's adventurous, outdoor role.

Aware that the Juke would represent a major leap in style for the consumer, part of the plan had always been a warm-up act in the shape of a concept car at the 2009 Geneva show. Presented as the Qazana—a name chosen only just before the show—the model shocked, stunned, and baffled showgoers and commentators, but was judged bold and exciting.

"The brief for the show car was to hint, but not to reveal specifics," says Albaisa. "We didn't need to show the size or the roominess, but all the key elements were included."

Riding on massive 19-inch wheels, the Qazana came across as powerful and impressive, just as Albaisa had intended, and a suicide-door arrangement allowed photographers a usefully clear view into the cabin. "We wanted to celebrate the interior as much as the exterior," commented the design team. The feedback, says Albaisa, was so overwhelmingly positive that nothing was changed on the production car—which, ironically, was being tested in clinics at around the same time as the concept was being shown.

Few believed that Nissan would have the bottle to go into production with something as dramatic as the Qazana concept. Yes, some of the more fancy details have been toned down, but the radical proportions and the aggressive urban funkiness of the concept have been kept intact for the showroom Juke, evidence of the trust in design shown by Nissan's senior managers.

On the strength of the Juke, Nissan's residual image as a cautious brand may at last be overturned. "This car needs to attract people who aren't even paying attention," notes Albaisa, tellingly.

CHAPTER 3

interiors

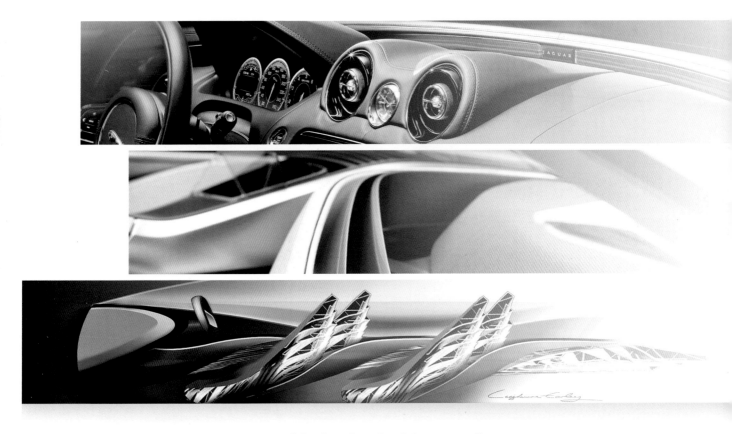

And so here we are at the end of the first decade of the twenty-first century, some years since the automotive design community collectively woke up to the importance of interior design to its increasingly design-literate customer base. So, just how far have we come since those dark days of plastic black cockpits built down to a price?

Pretty far, it seems. The inexorable cross-pollination between the world of automotive interiors and other design spheres such as architecture, fashion, and product design, has been steadily gathering pace. Car designers are openly acknowledging the influence exerted by the products on display at exhibitions, such as the Milan Furniture Fair and Tokyo's 100% Design, as well as the gadgets they carry around in their pockets to play music and make phone calls with. The result is a blurring of the boundaries between the car and other everyday products.

We're not just talking about exotic prestige sedans or luxury grand tourers here, either. A quiet revolution has been going on at some of the mainstream manufacturers, whose small cars now boast some very progressive interior designs. The drive to lift cabin quality

without breaking the bank is pushing them to explore new material applications, to play with lacquered and matte surfaces in ways that would have seemed unimaginable before this decade began.

Combined with the arrival of hybrid and plug-in electric drivetrain technology, this trend is creating a paradigm shift in the way that designers approach car interiors. Far from the undervalued space it once was, the interior is now a playground for exploring new packaging solutions and aesthetics and create interactive mobile sculptures that engage and delight the occupants. None exemplify this forward momentum better than the cars explored here.

Citroën Hypnos

When historians look back over Citroën's long and illustrious career, it is probably the 2008 Paris Motor Show that will be singled out as its finest hour of recent years. Packed into the same stand as the stunning GTbyCitroën (a concept designed entirely in the virtual realm and—prefacing an emerging trend—specifically for a video game) and the game-changing C3 Picasso compact minivan, the more conventionally styled Hypnos concept was understandably

overlooked by many at first. But as its barn-style doors opened up, the car lit up like an aurora borealis; its arresting, otherworldly interior was bathed in rainbow-coloured ribbons of light that left the viewer entranced as to their nature and origin.

The main focus of the interior is the exploration of three-dimensional spiral forms. Starting at the left, the upper IP—interrupted only by a diamond-shaped recess for the car's crystalline instrument cluster—runs to meet the right-hand door before folding back on itself to form the lower dash panel. This then twists out from the centre in a cylindrical turbine shape, fanning out as it goes to form asymmetrical, staggered seating. The latter unfolds from the centre like the petals of a flower, creating private spaces for all four passengers, while the rainbow gradation lighting effect comes from a mix of coloured leather panels and roof-mounted projectors.

Another major theme is the prism, which was inspired by Citroën's C42 building in Paris. It appears on the instrument cluster, seats, dashboard, doors, and even the trunk. Art, sculpture, and drama—the Hypnos takes the automotive interior in an utterly unexpected yet highly convincing direction.

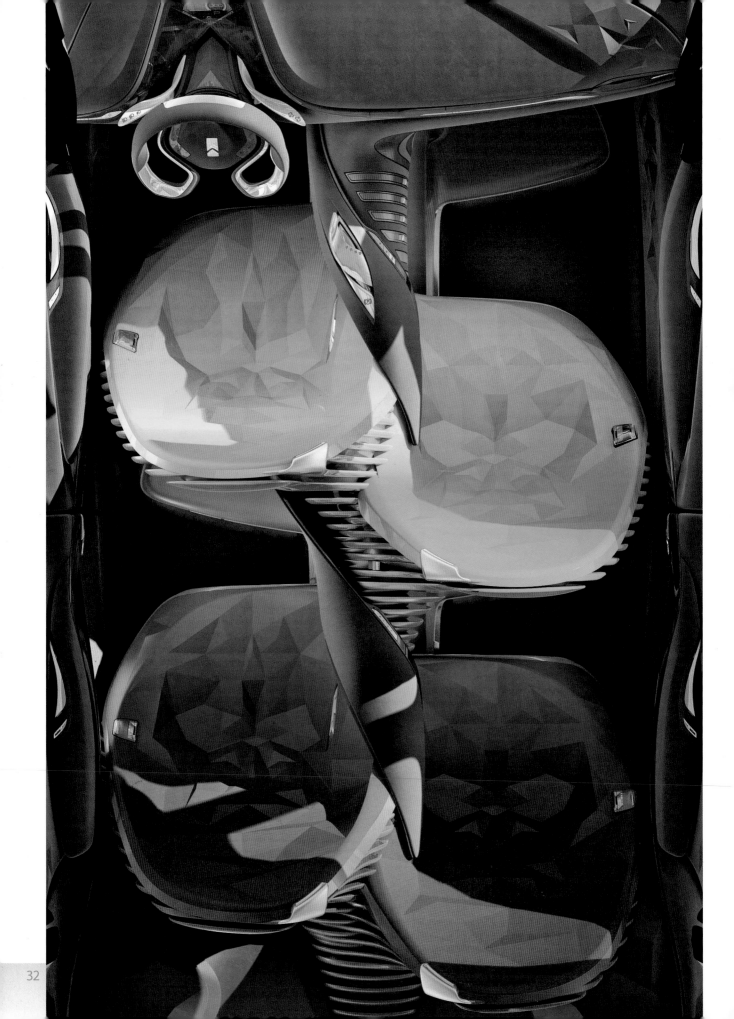

Fiat 500

If there's one car that reflects the recent change in fortunes at Fiat—and, indeed, the new social climate we find ourselves in—it's the 500. Previewed by the much-loved Trepiuno concept at the 2004 Geneva show (a year in which many pundits were forecasting bankruptcy for the Italian manufacturer), the production car that appeared three years later simultaneously tapped into the native charm of the 1957 original and the public's appetite for cute, friendly cars that mix retro elements with touches inspired by product design.

Developed in just 17 months by Fiat design boss Roberto Giolito and the same people that created the Trepiuno, the 500 echoes the MINI before it in presenting information such as speed, revs, and trip data, in a large, analogue dial, although here it's mounted conventionally behind the wheel rather than in the centre of the IP. In a nod to the original 500, the full-width lower dash surface consists

of a metal-effect panel finished in the same colour as the exterior, while Bakelite-style air conditioning and stereo controls below add a high-quality, tactile feel.

Another classic 500 cue is the disc-shaped headrests that sit atop the car's four seats, which can be upholstered in a staggering array of colours and materials—many of which would be considered too garish by rival manufacturers, but which fit the 500's playful personality to a tee. In addition to the four trim levels and 15 upholstery choices, buyers can select numerous key case colours to match the exterior bodywork, just as they might switch the cover of their Nokia mobile phone.

After years of kitting out their small cars with sombre, workmanlike interiors built down to a price, cars like the 500 mark a realisation among carmakers that young, particularly female, buyers don't equate size with quality.

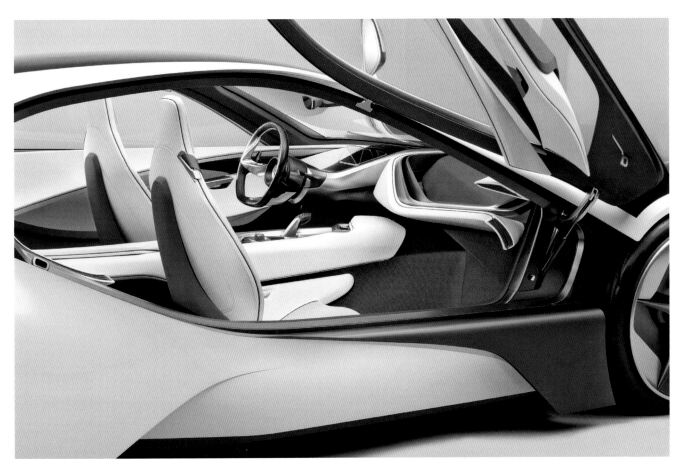

BMW Vision EfficientDynamics

Design often lags at least a couple of steps behind engineering; after all, the ability to store music on a portable hard drive had been around for years by the time Apple invented the iPod. So it has proven with "green" vehicle technologies.

At the 2009 Frankfurt Auto Show, however, we finally witnessed the arrival of the automotive iPod—or at least a very convincing blueprint for one. The EfficientDynamics concept was born out of a desire on the part of design director Adrian van Hooydonk and his team to communicate BMW's "low-weight, maximum efficiency" engineering philosophy in physical form. The end result transcends even that ambitious goal, presenting a holistic, dynamic sports car design that embraces the concept of sustainability at every level.

Prior to the design process, interior design director Marc Girard urged his team to ignore the tenets of car design and experiment with sculpting, painting, and folding fabrics and metals. This became

the basis of the car's highly sculptural, layered form language—one that makes an art form of exposing the car's structural elements, paring weight down to the absolute minimum in the process.

The IP takes root on either side of the stamen-shaped integrated steering column and instrument cluster, dividing into upper and lower layers that highlight the negative spaces behind. The lower layer folds over and back to form the door armrests, while the other runs along the top of the doors and behind the "floating" rear seats to meet its twin, before twisting back and forming a natural cover for the central battery "spine" that divides the interior. The thin Kevlar seats are every bit as comfortable as the ones in a 7 Series, according to the car's designers.

Light, aerodynamic, fast, and clean—not to mention beautiful to sit in and look at—the EfficientDynamics represents a true intersection between sustainable design and engineering.

Jaguar XJ

While controversy still plagues the exterior design of the 2010 XJ (the first four-door Jaguar to truly break the mould set by the iconic 1968 model), the car's interior is busy refining expectations of prestige car design. Created by chief interior designer Mark Philips, the XJ interior brings the British concept of automotive luxury into the twenty-first century.

The clean, low-set dashboard (lower, even, than in the XK coupé) is visually separated from the windscreen by a veneer "curtain" that extends in an arc from the upper door panels, creating an environment that is at once both spacious and intimate. There are subtle links to Jaguar's past—the pair of eyeball vents that flank the centrally positioned dashboard clock, for one—but the overwhelming sense is of sitting in a contemporary lounge space. We've become accustomed to seeing this kind of thing in concepts (Jaguar's own RD6, for example), but this is the first time it's been pulled off in a production car. Philips cites the work of Hermes, Cartier, and Savile Row, among others, as sources of inspiration for the XJ's colour and trim.

There's a real sense of theatre to the XJ, too. Joining the XK-derived rising circular transmission control in creating a sense of occasion is a "virtual" instrument display that sees an animated leaping Jaguar morph into the driver's dials on start-up. The centre console is also a work of art, housing the gear shifter, an elegant touchscreen, and the HVAC interface in a slim, brushed metal surround inspired by Loewe's LCD TVs.

The convergence of fashion with automotive and product design has become something of a holy grail in interior design of late. It looks like Jaguar has got there first.

Audi R8

The R8 had a difficult childhood, first appearing as the 1991 Quattro Spyder concept before reportedly being killed off by then-CEO Ferdinand Piech for fear of competing with his family's beloved Porsche brand. The project resurfaced soon after Piech's departure in 2002, this time dubbed the Le Mans concept; rapturous praise ensued, and work soon began on a mid-engined sports car based on the Lamborghini Gallardo's ASF (Aluminium SpaceFrame) platform.

Those of us who expected the 2006 Paris show production car to resemble a remodelled Gallardo with an upscale TT interior were proved very wrong. While elements like the flat-bottomed steering wheel and the three-knob climate control system located just ahead of the gearlever were already familiar Audi fare—as was the concept of rotating the brand's trapezoidal grille by 90 degrees to form the

basis of the centre console, a theme first explored on the A6—the R8 is truly in a class of one in terms of sports car design.

The shroud that follows the arc of the binnacle cover down into the door and twists below the armrests is unusually sculptural by Audi standards, creating a sense of intimacy that offsets the rather clinical interplay between the car's primary surfaces and materials. Every inch of the interior is upholstered, and the *de rigueur* aluminium trim has made way for carbon and lacquered finishes that echo the exterior's side blades and paintwork in providing visual contrast.

Then there are those elliptical eye-shaped instruments, the cylindrical gear lever and the Batman-esque segmented bucket seats, all of which look and feel superb. Never before has the exotic and the ergonomic been so successfully combined.

CHAPTER 4

CONCEPT cars

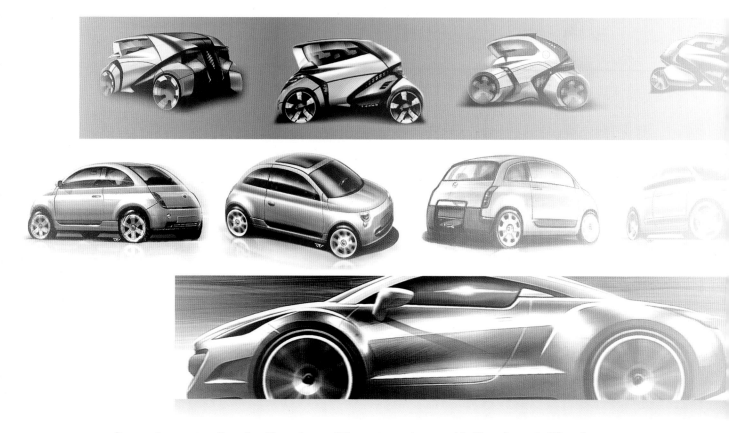

Concept cars are the shooting stars of the automotive world. They burn brilliantly but all too briefly before fizzling out and disappearing into the darkness—yet in those few instants, they surprise, startle, illuminate, and inspire.

Much the shortest-lived of a car company's products, their lifespan in the public eye is measured in days and weeks, rather than the years and decades of factory-built models. Yet even though they represent investments of thousands of man-hours and millions of dollars, they are soon forgotten after their brief flash of fame. After all, who remembers Metisse, Iosis, Napta, Eclectic, or IROC? No one but serious car buffs. By way of contrast, names such as R8, C4 Picasso, Qashqai, and Auris are much more familiar. Why the difference? All nine are models picked at random from the list of new designs launched at the 2006 Paris Motor Show—yet as production cars rather than concepts, the latter four have stayed in our consciousness rather than fading into obscurity.

Of course, no sensible car company wantonly wastes cash on an unproductive exercise. It is thus natural to question the logic of blowing millions on something as ephemeral and as a one-off special that only sees the light of day—or the showtime spotlight—for a couple of weeks. So why, then, do carmakers build concept cars? Different companies will give different answers, but most responses will share a common thread. By deciding to build a concept car, prototype, design study, research model—call it what you may—and putting it on a motor show turntable, an automaker is making a statement of intent. It is saying something about its future policy or the direction it intends to take; it could be signalling a new segment of the market it intends to enter, or it could be previewing new design themes or technical solutions. In the case of Renault at the 2009 Frankfurt show, an array of no fewer than four concepts for electric vehicles (including the Zoe ZE, above) left observers in no doubt whatsoever about the intention of the Renault-Nissan alliance to dominate future markets for zero-emission transportation.

Whatever the reason, there is a lot more strategy behind the appearance of a concept car than might at first seem to be the case. Renault, for instance, values concept cars not just for the external impact and the benefit they bring to the company's public image: They have an important internal function too, providing an outlet for the creativity and inventiveness of the company's designers, especially the younger designers, and boosting the morale of the company in general. At Renault a central plank of company policy is to generate a steady stream of design studies exploring new segments and putting out fresh design ideas.

"Since 1988 concept cars have always played a strong role at Renault," says its former design director Patrick le Quément, who steered Renault design for two decades from 1987 and who made design central to the marque's image and brand values. "I see them as a means of accelerating evolution. We take them very seriously. That's why we try to protect them from the external environment— things like rules, standards, and regulations. The concept car inspiration gives design direction and releases designers from the responsibility of knowing that the vehicle will be produced. We try to put the target as far ahead as possible."

Boosting morale at every level is one of the most important aspects of PSA Peugeot Citroën's design strategy, as design director Jean-Pierre Ploué made clear in an interview for this book: "I push a lot for concept cars," he says. "It feeds the production cars at the same time. It's a quick, efficient process: There's more freedom, less constraint, and it is good for morale."

Following a period of unadventurous and formulaic production car designs around the turn of the millennium, a series of creative concept designs beginning in the mid-2000s had put Citroën designers back in touch with the company's radical roots and built up a climate of confidence and optimism, said Ploué. The effect was now being felt in the latest production models, he noted.

A second and more commercially motivated tack is to bring a carefully timed concept car to discourage buyers from choosing a competitor's product—in effect staking a claim to a piece of real estate in the marketplace. Audi's 2003 Le Mans concept, which directly previewed the 2006 R8 supercar, was a message to elite sports car buyers to hold back from buying a Porsche; likewise, Audi had everything to gain by previewing its 2010 A1 small car some three years before launch with the 2007 Metroproject quattro. With no existing Audi in the compact segment, Audi could sustain interest with customers who might otherwise have bought a Mini or an Alfa Mito.

Jaguar, too, has succeeded in manipulating public opinion in a similar manner, though from a position of weakness rather than strength. With sales in a free fall and no significant new models for a painfully long time, Jaguar's very future was in doubt in 2005 and 2006. Investors needed reassurance that the company had the means to survive, and Jaguar customers needed to know there were exciting models in the pipeline that they could identify with. The solution was the radical **C-XF** concept car, unveiled to an emotional

welcome at the 2007 Detroit show; the production XF sedan, which followed a year later, got off to a strong start thanks to the publicity generated by the concept.

Jaguar's sister brand Land Rover provides a good example of the tactical use of concept cars to push public opinion in a desired direction. Land Rover rarely produces concept cars in advance of a production model. In 2008, however, it released the LRX concept for a compact, fuel-efficient SUV that still embodied premium design values. Not only was the LRX a signal of the company's intention to open up a new market segment, but its timing in the midst of the oil price spike provided Land Rover with a handy riposte to critics who accused it of having nothing but antisocial, gas-guzzling heavy SUVs in its lineup. Four years previously, Land Rover's first-ever concept vehicle, a more rakish version of the Range Rover known as Range Stormer, had been given an enthusiastic reception. The production model that ensued, the Range Rover Sport, went on to become the most profitable vehicle in the company's history.

The Range Stormer example touches on another of the most important roles of a concept car: to ask questions. The Stormer's mission was to ask if the buying public would be interested in a sporty Range Rover—and the response was a resounding yes. Other concepts from other automakers have asked different, and sometimes much more profound questions. A recent example is the **Infiniti Essence**, presented at the Geneva show in 2009. This plush, elaborate design in effect invited the public to pass judgement on the plausibility of Nissan's premium brand building a top-luxury GT sports car with the aura of an Aston Martin. Some years earlier, Lexus—the equivalent brand from Toyota—had posed exactly the same question with its LF-A series of concepts. The LF-A is now in limited volume production.

The unspoken question bundled in with the 2009 Volkswagen BlueSport, a compact mid-engined two-seater sports roadster, was whether VW could be a plausible contender in the market for

near-premium pure sports cars. In much the same way, **Nissan's Qazana** prototype (Geneva, 2009) sought to assess public reaction not just to the idea of a compact, aggressively styled urban crossover for young buyers, but to the potential credibility of Nissan as a hip youth brand.

More fundamentally, public reaction to a show car can assist management decision-making by helping an automaker gauge whether a planned move into a new segment will be right for the brand or whether it will be seen as too much of stretch to be credible. Peugeot's RCZ (next page, bottom) concept posed just such a question in 2008. Its mission was to establish whether a provocatively styled coupé from the French company could be seen as a credible direct rival for Audi's iconic TT premium sports coupé (which itself began life as a concept car). The verdict being judged positive, the RCZ went into production two years later.

Many such litmus-test moves have taken place over the years; some even try to explore the position of a whole brand rather than just an individual model. This exercise is not always as successful as managers have planned, however, especially when it comes to highly image-sensitive super-luxury brands. Aston Martin, globally

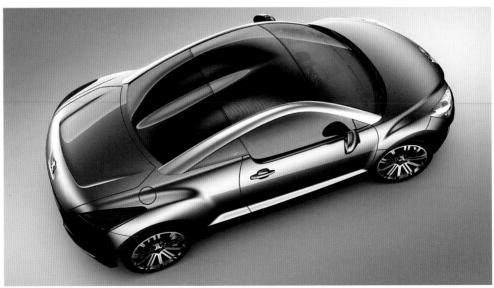

admired for the impeccable design of its luxury sports cars, found
out the hard way when, in March 2009, it tried the concept car route
to test its idea for a model to revive its dormant Lagonda marque, a
nameplate with a long history of large and elegant luxury limousines
for the aristocratic and wealthy. The **Lagonda** concept, unveiled in
the highly public forum of the Geneva motor show, proved to be
a bold and very imposing sport utility, as far removed from Aston
Martin's design purity as it was possible to imagine.

When an automaker is planning a major shift in style or a truly
game-changing move, such as Renault's 2009 shift into electric
vehicles, the wheeling out of a carefully targeted concept car
ahead of the launch can have an important role in softening up
consumer opinion and making buyers more familiar with—and,
hopefully, more open to—the new thinking. It is a fair bet that
prior to Renault's unveiling of its **Fluence**, **Twizy**, **Kangoo**, and
Zoe concepts at the 2009 Frankfurt show, few people had a clear
idea of what a modern mainstream electric car would look and
feel like. These prototypes, Renault says, are very close to the
final production models. With this reassurance, many previously

sceptical buyers may now be seriously considering the purchase of an electric model. Peugeot, for its part, would have had great difficulty explaining its BB1 (see page 61), an electric urban four-seater cross between two scooters and a small car, had it not had the concept car on hand to make the idea believable.

Historical examples abound of concept cars being used to pre-promote a step-change new product, much like a movie trailer previews a new film. One of the best documented is the Renault Scénic. Today, it is hard to imagine life without these practical, sensible, and good-value vehicles, but in the early 1990s they represented excitingly innovative thinking. The highly colourful and imaginative people carrier concept displayed in 1991 presented for the first time the idea of a medium-sized version of the Espace, which almost a decade earlier had begun to create the large minivan market in Europe. The versatile and imaginative concept's approach met with almost universal approval and a multipurpose Scénic version appeared as part of the mainstream Mégane line in 1997—though with very different styling to the show-car example.

Had the concept met with a lukewarm reaction from commentators and show visitors, Renault might have thought twice about volume production. But the company's confidence was fully vindicated and the Scénic went on to become an astonishing success, bankrolling Renault's resurgence as a major carmaker and sending rival carmakers into panic programmes to develop models that could compete.

Concept cars presented at international events can contain coded messages not always discernible to lay—or even expert—observers. Concepts are often used by designers and managers to trail new ideas—Peugeot's big-mouth grille, for instance, or the large rectangular air intake we are all now accustomed to on Audis. For Citroën, with its sudden flowering of creative activity following the appointment of Jean-Pierre Ploué as head of design in 2000, it is more than just configurations, technical solutions, and design details—such as the double chevron grille—that are being trailed:

"Take the **Hypnos** [Paris, 2008], for instance," he explains. "We picked a big SUV crossover, but that doesn't mean we are going to

build a model like this. It could have been anything else, a sedan even. The interior was an extreme design too. What we wanted to do with the Hypnos was to manifest the next form language for Citroën. It's much more about the language than the car."

The PSA design director's message is clear: Future Citroëns will draw the inspiration for their exterior surfacing from the complex and voluptuous interlinking sweeps of this key concept model. The interior design of the Hypnos deliberately pushes the boundaries even further with its rainbow colours and bold, interlocking shapes. Citroën has no particular production-car agenda with this interior— nor that of the smaller **Révolte** concept shown 12 months later— but the work is nevertheless valuable in positioning the brand as a leader when it comes to innovative thinking both inside and outside the car.

While French, Italian, and often British and US design studies tend to focus on innovation in the style and the actual format or role of the vehicle, concept models from German and Japanese automakers often concentrate their innovative power on the

technology under the skin and can place less emphasis on
aesthetics as a result. Mercedes-Benz is the perfect case in point.
The imposing **F700** from 2007, widely trumpeted as a blueprint for
a next-generation S-Class flagship, is hardly pretty by conventional
standards of aesthetics. Instead, its dramatic impact is due just
as much to the astonishing technologies built into the platform
as to the challenging shapes of its unconventional outer body.
Mercedes reasons that its future customers need just as much time
to understand and appreciate new technology concepts—such
as forward-looking radar that scans the ground to pre-adjust the
suspension for the bumps it detects—as to become accustomed to
fresh themes in exterior styling.

The same reasoning could also be applied to the smaller
Blue Zero, presented as a concept in January 2009. An
unremarkable body and a very standard-looking interior concealed
a remarkable electric-drive sandwich chassis configuration able to
run with either pure battery power, as a plug-in hybrid with a range-
extender engine, or with a hydrogen fuel cell for fully emissions-
free driving. The concept allows the same basic hardware and

packaging to be used for all three forms of propulsion, thus reducing the manufacturing costs of these next-generation powertrains—yet it would have been easy to walk straight past the exhibit because of its unremarkable exterior.

Citroën's C-Cactus of 1996 took a different tack to many French designs: Its mission was not to explore the outer limits of avant garde style or futuristic interiors, but to exploit the ingenuity of designers and engineers to produce a highly CO_2-efficient medium-sized family hatchback at a cost similar to current models. To this end, it dramatically simplified the design of both the body and interior, reducing the number of parts and the complexity of manufacture. There was no separate dashboard, for instance; the windows were fixed; and the unpainted doors had just two component parts instead of the usual 12. The resultant savings, said Citroën, would allow such a model to be offered with diesel-hybrid power—normally several thousand euros more costly—at the price of a conventional model.

This was a concept that, in the words of PSA design director Jean-Pierre Ploué, was born not from a design brief or an aesthetic vision, but which emanated from the philosophy of the design team

to re-examine simplification, recycling, and a minimisation to the necessary basics. True, with its bulging grille, goofy headlights, and bulky rear, it sat uneasily under the showtime spotlights, and its message was probably lost on the mass of casual show-goers filing past the Citroën booth. But for industry insiders, it was something to study and to savour: a set of ingenious solutions that, while not glamorous in the conventional sense of the word, certainly got everyone thinking.

While Citroën's Hypnos previews a new external style, the C-Cactus flags up clever minimalist technologies and the Mercedes F700 goes to the opposite extreme, Renault's Zoe and Twizy are the first ambassadors for the upcoming electric age. But it is perhaps left to BMW, a rare creator of genuine concept cars rather than simply production preview models, to provide a truly complete picture. Its 2009 **Vision EfficientDynamics** is a dramatic and compelling glimpse into a plausible near-future high-performance coupé, yet it incorporates lessons for smaller, cheaper models as well as flagging up a radical new surface language that could be rolled out across a wide range of mainstream BMW models. As such, the Vision EfficientDynamics is as much a manifesto for the likely *modus operandi* of BMW's new design director, Adrian van Hooydonk, as it is a technological mission statement for BMW's engineering division. As a concept car, it ticks all the boxes—from glamour and visual wow-factor to technical intrigue and design fascination; it is a breathtaking, tantalising taster for how we could be driving in a few years from now.

Here, we have touched on just a few examples of the concept car builder's art; a proper appreciation of the concept car output of even the past three years would take a book much larger than this. Nevertheless, there are many more designs that fairness dictates must be name-checked: the remarkable momentum of Nagare design studies from Mazda, which must surely presage breakthrough models in the production pipeline; the imaginative productions of Korea's Kia and Hyundai; the prolific past output of

designers at Chrysler Jeep, now in recovery mode from bankruptcy; and, by coincidence Chrysler's new controller, Fiat, with its occasional and brilliant concept designs such as the EcoBasic and the **Trepiuno**, which previewed the highly successful 500. While for Sweden's struggling Saab, now controlled by Spyker, concept cars like the **Aero X** were very much a matter of staking out new territory to advertise its track back to future survival, fellow countryman Volvo has used a series of imaginative design studies to preview the XC90, XC60, and S60 production models and trail important safety innovations such as pedestrian avoidance – again fulfilling a key concept car function.

Yet no one should be under any illusions that this is the finished product. A concept car under the floodlights on a motor show turntable is not like the catwalk during fashion week in Paris or Milan. Buyers cannot simply whip out their chequebooks the second they see a new style they like. Cars have gestation periods counted in years rather than weeks and are vastly more complex to put into production than even the fanciest hats, coats, or dresses. The million time-consuming, dollar-gobbling steps between salon spotlight and high-street showroom mean that automakers need all the help they can get in planning ahead, anticipating changes in consumer taste, and avoiding costly fashion blunders.

Strangely enough, it is precisely because it does cost so much money to develop and build a volume production car that the extra expense of a concept vehicle is worthwhile. With manufacturers often having to spend up to a billion dollars to put a new model series into the showroom, the financial stakes are so high that no one can afford to make a mistake. The concept car is a vital part of the strategy for, as we have seen, it is the perfect means of flagging up new ideas and assessing public reaction. The carmaker can then get a clearer picture of whether the new idea is likely to work well in volume production or whether it needs tweaking in order to capture the buyers' imagination; in this sense, the concept car provides the ideal high-profile, low-risk means of staking out territory and inviting comment.

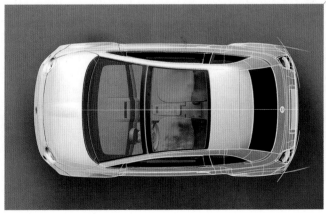

More than anything else in the firm's portfolio, the concept car is a powerful statement of a company's aims, ideals, and ambitions—a mirror to the visionary thinking going on in the boardroom. At its best, a concept car has the power to change the way the whole industry thinks—Giugiaro's Megagamma of 1978, Renault's 1991 Scénic concept, and GM's 2001 **Autonomy** "skateboard" spring to mind. The truly good ones can indirectly boost the fortunes of a company—think of how the Toyota RAV4, originally just a show concept, instantly caught on as soon as it hit the showrooms—while those that are merely very good, like Ford's original Ka or Audi's TT, translate straight into successful production cars.

At the opposite end of the scale, a mistaken choice of concept can send the wrong messages or spell out promises that may be impossible to fulfil. Cadillac's gargantuan **Sixteen**, a potshot at Rolls-Royce, now looks like the folly of overambitious managers, and all the high hopes surrounding Jaguar's beautiful F-Type of 2000 backfired on the company, then owned by Ford, when the project was cancelled. Even Dacia, Renault's value brand, might have raised expectations a few notches too high

with its stylish **2009 Duster concept**: the production car that followed was sensible and simple, rather than progressive in its language. Conversely, a too-conservative concept will signal a lack of corporate vision or ambition; worse still, concepts that are over-the-top, extravagant, or simply irrelevant are likely to fall embarrassingly out of fashion the moment the show closes, if not before. Nevertheless, a special mention should at this point go to the many weird and wonderful, and often totally outrageous, study models wheeled out by the mainstream Japanese manufacturers at the biennial Tokyo Motor Show.

Frequently baffling to Westerners but often wildly imaginative and invariably highly inventive, these concept models can be anything from discotheques or coffee bars on wheels to a mobile greenhouse with special health-giving light inside, or an all-terrain rescue 4x4 stowing both mountain bikes and surfboards in the rear. The very best, such as **Nissan's Pivo**, which can rotate on its own axis to eliminate the need for reversing, set other designers thinking; the others provide a sense of humour and an attention to detail—such

as the use of vegetable-derived plastics—that is often absent from Western designs.

Either way, however, concept cars provide a welcome freedom that designers positively revel in, a rule- and regulation-free environment that allows their creative powers to truly blossom. But, as the wilder excesses of too many "design-gone-mad" show cars so graphically illustrate, it needs the gentle hand of enlightened company management to ensure that those creative talents are channelled in the right direction and not wasted on superficial and inappropriate stand candy.

Risky? Only if imagination is lacking or management doesn't know where it's going. For sure, a concept car is always going to be the freeze-frame of future thinking at a particular instant, that shooting star whose light is destined to burn brilliantly for a few fleeting moments before it falls, expended, to earth. And its real value, as any designer imbued with wisdom as well as experience will testify, lies in the inspiration that can later be drawn from that brief first flash of brilliance.

On the following pages: The 2010 Lincoln C concept.

CHAPTER 5

DESIGNER
profile

Jean-Pierre Ploué
Director of design, PSA Peugeot-Citroën

Long since gone are the days when a single charismatic individual could dictate the style of a car company's products, shaping the models according to his instincts and intuitions. The last such designer-manager was perhaps Sir William Lyons, whose instinctive feel for style, poise, and proportion brought Jaguar a worldwide reputation for elegance and racy sophistication. It helped, of course, that Lyons founded, owned, and ran the company; in today's intricate multinational structure of car companies, it would be unthinkable to allow an individual, however brilliant, to exercise such unfettered control over the visual template and cultural aura of a brand and its models.

Yet since the last great icon of the Lyons era, the massively influential Jaguar XJ of 1968, there have been many individual design directors who have made an indelible mark on a brand or brands and who have influenced the history of car design as a result.

Italian Bruno Sacco quietly and confidently steered the design of Mercedes-Benz cars for the quarter century to 1999, establishing the rock-solid template that is the foundation of the brand's modern identity; just down the Autobahn at BMW, Wilhelm Hofmeister did an arguably even greater job in transforming the German company from a maker of bubble cars and old-fashioned limousines into a builder of distinctive sports sedans whose clear identification with success and dynamism eventually allowed BMW to overtake Mercedes as a premium car maker. At the turn of the millennium, another more controversial BMW design director, Chris Bangle, would once again take hold of the brand's identity and seek to reshape it.

Yet it is not purely in the premium segment that a clear and consistent design vision can help bring about change in the perception of a company. Right now, Asian automakers such as Mazda, Kia, and Hyundai, are working hard through design to forge a strong, positive message that will attract customers and help ratchet up the recognition of the firm's products. Behind this is a

clear design policy decided at the highest levels—and it is a fair bet that these companies are taking their lessons from the textbook example set by Renault and its recently retired design director, Patrick le Quément.

The Renault that le Quément joined in 1987 was an incoherent muddle, its models ranging from the quirky and confusing to the forgettable and bland. The only thing they had in common was that they did not sell well enough. His great determination, matched by strong buy-in from Renault's top management, allowed le Quément to begin by bringing the quality of Renault's products up to scratch; he built up a strong design team and shepherded a series of groundbreaking designs, such as the Twingo (whose designers included Jean-Pierre Ploué), into production. By the mid-1990s, a stylish and coherent range of well-accepted products was in place, and in 1997 le Quément came up with the Mégane Scénic, a segment-busting family minivan that became a huge success and left competitors struggling to catch up.

After two decades of le Quément's carefully planned brand building, Renault is now into its third generation of Méganes and Scénics and is widely respected as an innovator in the volume market. "If you don't want to do an anonymous car, you have to take a certain risk," he said at the launch of the Mégane II in 2003. "In the final analysis, our CEO takes the decisions—but I make the recommendations. It is quite normal that a [new] car should not necessarily be instantly likeable."

The keys to the success of his policy, said le Quément, were to use design as an instrument of product planning policy and to have design represented at board level.

The situation facing Jean-Pierre Ploué when he became design director of PSA Peugeot Citroën in 2008 was nowhere near as desperate as that of Renault in the 1980s—but that did not mean the role was any less challenging. Both of PSA's brands enjoyed a strong position in small-car sales, buoyed up by tax incentives

favouring models with low CO_2 emissions, yet sales outside of the core western European market remained weak and it had been a decade or more since either Citroën or Peugeot had had any success in the generally more-profitable market for larger cars. Citroën, in particular, had sustained steady criticism that its products had abandoned the marque's famed **futuristic feel** to become dull and anonymous, and both nameplates had been hit hard by the rise in market share of premium and near-premium brands, such as VW.

Ploué had something of an advantage in that he had previously worked at Renault, Audi, and Ford and already knew one side of the group, having been design director of Citroën since 2000; already, he had succeeded in remobilising some of the adventurous and avant garde design spirit that characterised Citroën products from the 1950s to the 1980s.

"Step by step, through concept cars, we have started to rebuild the design philosophy for Citroën," he said in an interview for this book. "Concept cars are a very important way of preparing the

future—they are a kind of accelerator, to speed everything up."

Design studies like the **C-Métisse**, **C-Cactus**, Hypnos, and Révolte have given full credence to the revolution that swept through Citroën's studios in the years following Ploué's arrival; earlier concepts such as the 2005 C-Sportlounge fed directly into the production C4 hatchback, which with its high-sweeping rear roofline and radical fixed-centre steering wheel went some way towards pleasing Citroën fans who had been waiting so long for a showroom model with a sense of the future to it. Much more is still to come, promises Ploué.

"We're getting there, but we haven't finished yet," he adds. "It takes time to understand the brand, to see what you can do within a big company like PSA, to find the right connections, and get to what you want to do. We're working step by step to improve our technology and our quality and determining what could be our future design language—grain, colour, harmony, all that. It takes time."

Now, however, with Peugeot added to his portfolio, the stakes have ratcheted up quite considerably. "Ever since I was given

responsibility for two brands, it has been more complicated," he confides. "When you are boss of a single brand, you put your heart and soul into it; it's a part of you. It's one baby to look after. But as soon as you have two brands, you have to step back a bit."

While Ploué is quick to concede that he is quite directive in the way he manages design for the two brands, he is also confident at the same time that the members of his teams are able to express themselves. "Of course, I have to guarantee the design at the end—it's what the [Peugeot] family and the people at the top expect from me. But at the same time, you have to have the right creativity and the right energy. You have to be able to allow people to do their own work and to propose their own solutions. It's a balance of control and freedom from control."

Asked if he still designs cars, Ploué bats the question away with a "far too busy organising" gesture. Instead, he says, it is brands he now designs. Like many in his position, he sees his role as someone who sets a framework and a climate in which the creativity of others can flourish and bloom. Only rarely will he sit down and sketch, he claims, even though a neat pocket-sized notebook soon belies this.

Amongst the notes of meetings, phone calls, and supplier contacts are dozens of neat design doodles sketched when he has a spare moment in meetings, in the back of a car, or on an aeroplane. Often small details rather than complete vehicles, Ploué's doodles show the mindset of an active and creative designer at work. They are the kind of detailed design solutions to issues, such as door seals, bodyside sections, and pillar profiles, that only a practising designer would realise are significant.

Characteristically modest, he declines to single out the design he is most proud of. Instead, he says each project is different, each one brings a new challenge and a new adventure. Inspired as a child by "the simplicity of a 2CV, the luxury of a Delage, or a Citroën ID19", he is nowadays motivated by an unceasing quest for renewal and creativity, drawing in ideas from art, architecture, sculpture, watchmaking—and, he is quick to point out, from everyday contact with his design teams.

One of the key responsibilities of a design director is to encourage and to inspire. "It's my task to motivate and help team members overcome any doubts that may crop up as a project takes shape," he says. "You really have to summon up all your determination to convince them. It's very high risk but at the same time extremely motivating."

Yet, faced with the lofty objectives set for the two brands, Ploué and his team will need every ounce of inspiration and motivation they can collectively muster. The aim, says Ploué cautiously, as if to assess the reaction it provokes, is an ambitious one—to make Peugeot a design benchmark for the auto industry and to reinvent Citroën even more.

"I don't think Citroën has done enough yet. In fact, it's just the beginning of the story—and my bosses probably agree too," he explains. "But I think I will have done a good job with my team if Peugeot becomes number one or number two in the world in automotive design and if Citroën reinvents itself."

Quite how these world standings will be evaluated is something Ploué does not explain, though he refrains from commenting on the design of current Peugeot models. Instead—and this comes as something of an indictment of recent Peugeot efforts—he cites as the true icons of the Peugeot brand the **205 hatchback**, which debuted in 1983, and the 406 coupé, dating from 1997.

"There were plenty of good designs before these, but in recent times these stand out. The 406 coupé displays all the good values of Peugeot—elegance, balance, freshness, harmony, and also robustness, as this was always a Peugeot quality. The 205 brought all the new values of Peugeot—dynamism, sportiness, youth, urban chic—all that."

Tellingly, both 205 and 406 were styled by Italian design house Pininfarina, which had had a long-standing relationship with the brand and which had shaped a whole host of elegant and influential models, including the 403, 404, 505, 406, and, of course, the spectacularly successful 205. Yet surprisingly, despite the historical success of these models, Ploué has no desire to return to the previous practice of shopping outside for its design work. "To build a solid and strong design philosophy, you need to do the work yourself. You have to understand where you are and what you want to do before you ask people outside. You can't share this philosophy with them—as a supplier they have their own philosophy. Pininfarina, especially, may more or less know what Peugeot is, but it doesn't

know where we want to go. If we want to get Peugeot to the top, it would be disruptive to call in someone from the outside."

Only when a brand is confident of its own values and clear in its direction would it be sensible to consider outsourcing the task of design; this, according to Ploué, is likely to occur sooner with Citroën, which has in the past used Bertone for models like the BX and Xantia.

Yet reinventing the Peugeot brand and elevating it to a high position in the design world could prove to be a tougher task than the same exercise with Citroën. Peugeot does not possess the same high profile in the popular imagination as does Citroën. The latter still commands immediate respect for its inventive engineering solutions, its futuristic body shapes, and its audacity to innovate. It is linked with artistic and intellectual types, whereas Peugeot's traditional place has been in the bourgeois realm, its sober but elegant styling housing robust mechanical components proven in rallies across Africa. Citroën has icons aplenty—the 2CV for bohemian minimalism, the DS for a breathtaking quantum leap in innovation, the GS for advanced engineering at an affordable price. The quintessential Peugeot, on the other hand, is probably the bulletproof 505 station wagon—plus, of course, the chic 205, cited by Ploué and which brought the brand a fresh urban audience.

Nevertheless, the Peugeot design team radiates the calm confidence that comes with the knowledge that there are strong ideas in the pipeline that will set the brand on its course towards regaining its design benchmark status. Gilles Vidal, architect of many breakthrough concepts at Citroën, was swiftly moved by Ploué, first to take charge of concept car design at Peugeot and soon afterwards to take on responsibility for the full brand. Like his boss, he maintains the party line of no advanced disclosure, but both hint heavily that a new Peugeot concept car to be unveiled at the 2010 Paris Motor Show will provide a very clear public display of the future direction the brand will take. Barely disguised among these hints is the feeling that the new design will somehow recapture the emotion of innovation and chic style that the 205 brought to the Peugeot brand in 1983, but cast in a much more modern context as retro is not a viable option.

Vidal has the added opportunity of bringing more focus to Peugeot's strategy, a policy which in recent years has seen a

confusing mixture of mundane close-to-production mainstream models, strange three-wheeled buggy-scooters, and outrageous supercar concepts that are so far disconnected from the core brand and the prevailing social climate as to be dismissed as irrelevant. What has been conspicuously lacking from Peugeot's output has been the kind of design the customer likes to see—designs which fire the popular imagination and provide a vision of what production models might be like in five or seven years' time. This is what Citroën has become so good at, and the signs are that this might change under Peugeot's new leadership.

An early indication of Peugeot's new thinking, though hardly mainstream, came in the unorthodox shape of the tiny **BB1** electric city car, first presented in September 2009 and then publicly demonstrated in five European capital cities over the course of the autumn. The genesis of this very well-received model is intriguing, says Ploué. Designers, especially those involved in concept work, pride themselves on being sensitive to what he describes as *"l'air du temps"*—the spirit of the times, the mood of the moment. "They're like sponges—they filter and soak up what's going on—it could

be a trend, an event, a book, a new architectural project; this is often where the ideas come from. Marketing people could have got information from social studies and so on, but this not how it is usually done. This is the difference between the designers and the commercial guys who sell the cars."

What became the BB1 started in two places, says Vidal. "We had a discussion about small cars like this, and we also had a sketch. We wanted something with a different attitude, a different posture—not just a new concept with new form language, but a new morphology and a new kind of mobility too."

There was already a model with three wheels, but this was not what Ploué wanted to pursue as it was something Peugeot had done before. "We had all these sketches, and we picked one of them [that] was very strong—but it was a two-seater and it had three wheels. So I said to the team: 'We need to do a car. But we need to do something compact and incredible, and I want four wheels.'"

As the design progressed step by step, Ploué upped the ante by insisting on it taking four people—at which point the engineers on the team began to protest that this was impossible within the specified length of 2.50 metres. Yet, recalls Ploué, those same engineers came back a week later with a solution that was effectively two scooters, with the four riders sitting astride twin side-by-side **motorcycle-style seats**. The breakthrough in accommodating the four people was to have them close together and leaning slightly forward, as on a motorcycle. This then led to the BB1's characteristic forward-sloping windscreen. For short urban trips, the level of comfort would be perfectly adequate, reasoned the team.

"It's true; that's how it was born," says Ploué with evident satisfaction. But, as Vidal points out, the normal pattern is to have a discussion on a concept prior to embarking on the sketches that lead to the designs and styles, which then determine the most suitable aesthetic to go with it. "The BB1 project was quite special because there was a reflection on mobility [beforehand] and there were a lot of sketches and morphologies, and the final definition of the concept came afterwards," he said.

Then, says Ploué, the marketing people were quick to understand the interest in the concept and the strength of its design, working on the idea of mobility, what kind of car this could become, and how to fine-tune it to suit the Peugeot brand.

Precisely how a BB1-like production car would be tuned in to a dedicated Peugeot wavelength might in the past have been the subject of intense and perhaps bitter discussion. But as an integral part of his remit as design director of the PSA group, it is one of Ploué's weightiest responsibilities to establish the strategic direction for each brand and to ensure that they are perceived as different and individual in the market place—while, of course, maximising the level of engineering commonality so as to keep costs and production complexity to a minimum.

To this end, the teams have drawn up a comprehensive philosophical presentation, linking Peugeot with the elements of earth and fire and the animal qualities of a lion—physical, feline, and active; Citroën is positioned in the space of air and water, with a touch of magic and the more intellectual, fluid qualities of a dolphin. Examples taken from everyday objects and activities help clarify the distinction. A Peugeot garment would be close-fitting, precise, and elegant with an haute-couture touch, while Citroën's style is softer, more extravagant, and more flamboyant, with a feeling of theatricality.

Summing up the differentiation as applied to individual car components—it is too early to see it materialised in actual vehicles—Ploué gives the example of seating. A Peugeot seat is a sporty bucket seat, close-fitting, and supportive; Citroën, meanwhile, might be characterised by a sumptuous lounging seat, much like the bench in the rear of the **Révolte** concept car, where the seat turns the corner and runs forward again. Peugeot drivers, likewise, are characterised by their desire to take active control of the dynamics of their vehicles; Citroën owners—perhaps with a more relaxed, more passive attitude to driving—are happy to let automatic systems prevail and for the car to make decisions without the driver having to intervene. An example is given in the future implementation of lane departure warning systems. In Peugeots, these will take the form of a warning vibration transmitted through the driver's seat, as in today's Citroëns; in next-generation Citroëns, however, the driver's course will be automatically corrected as the system intervenes directly on the steering wheel.

Yet the fact that inventiveness and Citroën can once again be uttered in the same breath is a great tribute to the vision and the perseverance of Jean-Pierre Ploué. Towards the end of the 1990s, when the creative spark seemed to have been snuffed out at the brand's design studios, Citroën had begun to flatline as a me-too marque, distinguished from its competitors only by a more aggressive price-cutting policy. He and his team were able to pick up that spark and run with it, producing a series of memorable concept cars over the space of a decade, launching five distinctive production models and building up a strong lineup of new designs for future release.

Looking towards the future, Ploué foresees a time when—with reliability, safety, and low emissions all taken for granted—the German solidity that everyone currently craves will begin to seem like something from the past. "We've got to the limit of this protective heaviness, this solidity, now," he declares. "People will come to expect designs that are more pure, more simple; the main trend will be towards simplicity, fluidity, and lightness. This is what people want, and it's what we feel too."

Yet, even with the advent of electric propulsion opening up the possibilities of totally different mechanical layouts and dramatic shifts in external proportions and appearance, Ploué is quick to rule out the temptation to be too much of a thought leader, to be too far ahead of

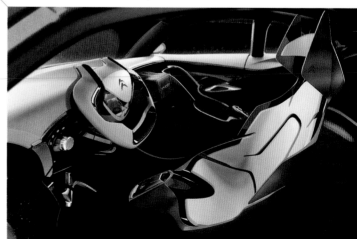

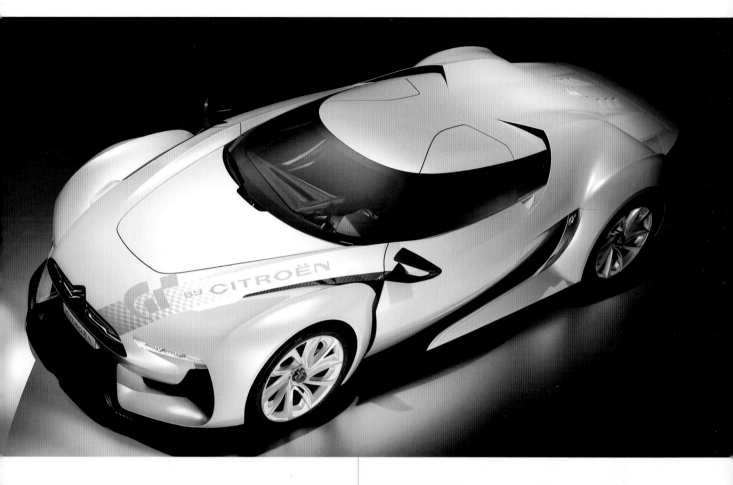

consumer tastes. "We are all working towards Citroën and Peugeot being the best in design, being a step ahead. But this is of no interest if we don't sell the car. After all, what's the point of bringing an extreme design to the market if we can't sell it?

"We should be able to aim our designs not for today's customers but for the customers' tastes in three or four years' time—and still be able to sell well in seven years' time," he continues. "Look at the recent history of Renault design. They have been very courageous with their designs—even the small Mégane, which I like. The previous Mégane was a good design, but people didn't like it—they bought it because of Renault's big dealer network in Europe."

When tested in Citroën's internal clinics against the C4, the Mégane's results were very poor, recalls Ploué. "I liked the design, but I wouldn't have done it. We are not just artists. We need to find a way of adapting to what the consumer and the company want—so no more bizarre designs!"

Thankfully, however, this does not mean that interesting designs are ruled out. Ploué promises that the DS5, the forthcoming big sister to the DS3 in Citroën's new semi-premium sub-brand, will have a "very strong design and an incredible package," and the go-ahead has been given for limited production of the very extreme **GTbyCitroën**, an outrageously low and wide supercar conceived for the Gran Turismo Sony PlayStation game and brought into physical reality for the crowds at the 2008 Paris Motor Show.

It is a measure of Citroën's newfound confidence and respect that such a wild and flamboyant design as the GT was seized on with alacrity and excitement by the show-going public rather than dismissed as irrelevant to a mainstream carmaker.

Now, all Ploué needs to do to complete the renaissance of PSA design is to repeat the trick with the Peugeot brand.

On the following pages: The Peugeot SR1 concept

CHAPTER 6

DESIGNER'S
diary

A week in the life of a designer

As chief designer at Land Rover's Advanced Design Studio, it is <u>Oliver le Grice's job to</u> anticipate future trends and come up with exciting designs to inspire the next generation of Land Rover and Range Rover products. Le Grice's recent credits include formative work on the groundbreaking LRX concept shown at Detroit and Geneva in 2008. This is his account of a busy week in—and out of—Land Rover's world-class studio in Gaydon, central England.

Monday

Monday morning. Time to engage the gears and plan for the week ahead. Nothing happens before morning coffee, which we share as a team—exchanging stories about our weekends.

Soon we are talking through some of the wider issues surrounding the products we are engaged in. Most of the team went for a visit to the Eden Project in Cornwall over the weekend and had a full day getting to understand the motivation behind the project. The person who made it happen, Tim Smit, was good enough to give a personal account of what inspired it, what its values are, as well as how they may be relevant to Land Rover. This subject is vitally important to our brand, as there is no doubt that the sustainability

agenda is going to be a huge one moving forward, especially for vehicle designers. Maybe we have an advantage in that Land Rover is already associated with the natural environment and is used by a variety of humanitarian organisations. Environmental integrity shouldn't be something to spray on a product; it must be intrinsic, integrated, and holistic. We discuss how we can communicate these aspirations in what we do on our latest project.

As for my weekend, London was a bit of a trip down memory lane. My time there at [Ford group design studio] Ingeni in Soho was so formative in terms of my development as a designer, and the vision that the team had there still informs what I do on a daily basis. It is absolutely true that as a designer you are a product of your experiences and what you surround yourself with. Therefore, where you are based and what you do in your free time will be a constant source of inspiration.

I'm lucky that the studio where I work is a highly motivating place in terms of facilities, environment, and team. I can reflect on my time working with this team and what we've achieved over the years, culminating with the LRX, which is going to be a fantastic product when launched. That's when the job is at its most rewarding, when a team creates a great piece of design, which is then implemented into production as unchanged and as true to the original vision as possible. Design really works best like this, uncompromised and fresh. It's what we all aspire to as we develop the products of the future.

We've moved on now from LRX; for designers there is always the next vehicle in line to deal with. As soon as one is done, the next is ready to be tackled. For the team in advanced design the aim is to really try to understand the requirements of the market five, ten, even fifteen years ahead. It is a process of defining the products people will want, how they want them to feel, and which features and technologies they will expect. It's about giving the products a compelling narrative, or a "story." Then it is time to start sketching

and giving life to the products, giving them form.

By 11 a.m. it is time for our team meeting. This is a forum where we discuss aspects of the coming week's work, as well as some wider plans for models stretching into the longer term. This is important planning time. All of what we decide will need to be programmed and resourced, so our programme managers will have to liaise with the modelling and prototyping teams. These are situated close to us within the building, and it is their job to bring our ideas to life. Without them we cannot communicate our designs to the wider business and beyond.

After lunch the team is sketching and developing designs, and I spend a bit of time working with the clay modellers refining a full-size clay that will become a vision property for one of our upcoming programmes. This model will indicate the size, proportions, and general feel of the product the design organisation believes we should make. This is a milestone model and will support all the ongoing events that surround the progress of a design into maturity. It will subsequently be handed over to the production design area to be refined, and a deeper level of feasibility incorporated, before signing off for production.

At this point, though, I have to develop the clay without its upper canopy—which means the entire roof and glazed area. This can be difficult and slightly risky. I have to rely on experience and judgement and hope that when the two halves of the model are united it will be what we want. Either way, I am totally dependent on our sculpting team to give me what I have in mind, communicated by words, gestures, and the sketchwork we've generated. These visuals are our "contract" with the modelling team and the design director, so they are vitally important to the process—as is the patience and good humour of the team. The aim is to get things right the first time, but in reality design is a process of development and there will always need to be changes and refinements.

Last thing today, we are meeting to discuss new design tools for the studio. This means computer software mainly, not pens and pencils these days. Part of what we do as advanced design is to test new tools and working methods and propose new ways of doing what we do. We have developed many new key skills over the last decade and now really rely upon designers to be able to develop in 3D on the computer, to visualise their design in real-time packages.

This is above and beyond the 2D Photoshop skills, which are now absolutely vital. Strange to think how little of this stuff existed when I started less than two decades ago! On Thursday evening I will travel to Germany to talk to a supplier about these new tools.

Leave the studio at about 5:30 and go to my gym for a workout, then home to the family. Watch an interesting (no, really!) programme about the design and corporate identity of the London Underground.

Tuesday

We start relatively early in the studio, so by the time most London creative agencies are coming to life at around 10 a.m., some of the modelling team have already put in three hours. Designers are in a little later, guiding their modelling teams, dealing with issues as they arise. Whilst working on a clay, the demands are constant: taping lines on surfaces, defining sections, engaging with engineers on packaging and technical issues; all of these have direct knock-on effects on the theme that is being developed. Working in the same space around the model (as happens in Gaydon) is a major benefit, as issues can be addressed as they arise. Surfacing, too, is part of the design team's work, and all of this helps greatly with communication and efficiency. Interaction can be the water cooler kind, which is then backed up then by more detailed meetings.

The clay development is totally iterative, with the onus on the designer to retain the spirit of the theme right through the feasibility process, preventing the life being boiled out of a design in the process of adhering to the wider demands of the project. These demands are significant and grow more difficult to reconcile every year. Safety standards, cost pressures, technical proliferation, supplier integration, product complexity, globalisation and increasing customer expectation are all making the process of creating a new vehicle incredibly demanding. Car design isn't getting any easier! Some older team members go misty eyed at the memory of how things used to be and how much fantasy there was in car design. Admittedly, this aspect has diminished, but within advanced design there is still the chance to dream, especially on a show-car project.

Later on I spend some time on Alias creating some surfaces that can be transferred directly on to the clay. This is another way of interacting with the model, and I personally find this way of working

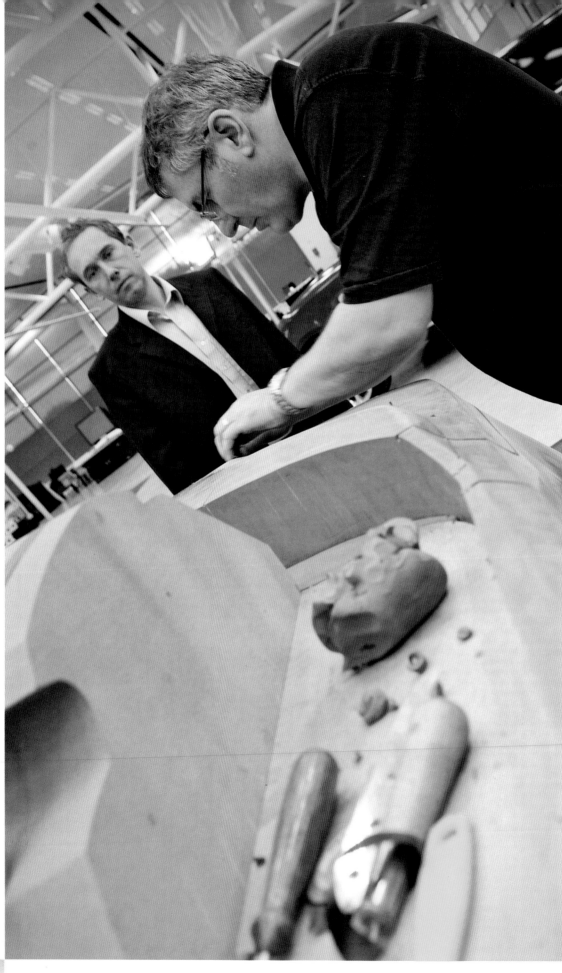

very effective. It is possible to be too "precious" when manually working a clay; you don't want to lose what you have and can become afraid of taking a wrong turn. Plus you don't want to mislead your modelling team, as this is both inefficient and can cause friction. These factors can work against experimentation with form, which is why it can be easier to default to what they know works or, worse still, copying from other brands.

Using digital form generating tools allows for experimentation, boldness, and what's more you never have to lose anything on the way. Plus there's the advantage that you can do what we are doing this afternoon: milling a clay on our five-axis machine, direct from design-generated data. This is a tried-and-trusted method now and is the most common method for starting a full-size model.

So I walk to our five-axis milling department and watch as the machines do their work virtually unaided, transforming a block of clay into a direct representation of the car I had on my screen only a few hours ago. For me this stuff is close to magic. I love being able to have this unmediated control, direct from my imagination to reality.

Late afternoon—coffee with the team and discuss last night's TV. While working, I listen to music from my computer. We do have music in the studio, but it has to be a bit lowest common denominator stuff. No one can relate to the music I like, so I put on headphones and retreat into my own private zone for a while. Looking around at the team members, they are mostly doing the same. In fact, many in the studio are bathed in the glow of their "tube," staring into their own private, but shared, space. If it wasn't for the clay models, there would be a danger it could look like a call centre. . . .

Get home earlier tonight for some family time. European football's on, which I'm afraid I watch avidly.

Wednesday

Review with the team today to talk about the Eden trip and the progress of our major project of the moment. We are concentrating on the exterior proposals and will be comparing the work done by the main team with the results of some recent graduates who are working in the studio for a short period. They are gaining an insight into working

in a major studio while giving us the benefit of some really fresh new ideas, untainted by the baggage of too much real-world experience. It is noticeable how long it takes to really get a grip on the importance of the history and intrinsic values of a brand like Land Rover. After some years, knowing what constitutes a Range Rover or a Land Rover becomes second nature, but at first most students or graduates tend to design for themselves, or for some generic brand.

Most young designers want to do low, sporting cars with open wheels and loads of sculpture, but soon understand the real challenges of designing for a brand like Land Rover and for real-world requirements. I think a designer becomes really useful after a couple of years and is at their peak creatively from this point on. How long it lasts is all down to the individual and his or her circumstances. Some designers naturally slot in to more organisational and managerial roles, whilst others are only comfortable exercising their creativity. The key is to play to people's strengths and where possible trust their judgement. Back to the football: It's like a team, some are born defenders, while others like the glory roles, scoring all the goals. The Land Rover team thankfully has a good mix of all these types.

The review goes well and there are some promising routes to go down. I think we will build a number of Alias models illustrating a variety of product concepts. These we will animate and test in market research clinics. Doing these digitally has proved to be a very good way of testing the reactions of future customers; it is cheaper than shipping models around, and you can try lots of different things. Market research on design solutions and aesthetics is much less productive; designers need to be ahead of the market and need to be trusted to get this equation right. This is all vital to the process of product planning, and we now work very closely with the marketing, strategy, and research areas in the company to get the right products into our cycle plan.

Today involves a mixture of other things, a lot of taping again on the clay model, which will be reviewed tomorrow. Also some Alias work on a top secret "under the radar" project we are doing. I put in about an hour's work on this a day—I pick it up and put it down when I have time. I meet with our IT guys and the advanced project manager to discuss the new design tools we want to try out. These people are fully integrated with us and take away some of the administrative work that

needs to be done alongside the creative stuff. I am very glad of this support: Without it we really couldn't do our jobs.

Checked the dry fit of the upper canopy of the vision clay model last thing. It fits precisely, which simplifies preparing for tomorrow's review. Things aren't always so smooth, but the master data that we all work to now means that stacking model parts is much more predictable now than in the past.

Tonight I go to the gym and later out to a pub that has live music. Where I live a lot of this is just a walk away, as are three theatres. We get out to these fairly often; it's another creative world but quite unlike ours. I try to imagine how a career in the theatre would be. Lots of personalities to deal with, real time pressure, coming together to get to a result . . . maybe not so different after all!

Thursday

It's a rush this morning. The model needs to be dressed to be viewed. That means coating the surfaces in a painted foil called Dynoc, graphicing it up with tapes, before putting it on its wheels (the largest we can justify—they almost always look best) and rolling it out into the main part of the studio. People always gather round a model when it's being viewed. This can disturb a review if you're not careful, but models have a natural gravity for designers. Everyone has a view and everyone's is valid. But for today it is our director Gerry McGovern's view that is important. It's down to him to set the direction and guide the development of a design, along with his team. We need to get it right for him so he can stand beside the result and sell it through the business and ultimately at launch.

We view the model in our viewing garden. It's surprising how different a model looks outside. As it happens, we get a clean bill of health. Changes, but not a major carve-up. I'm happy, but probably not as happy as the modelling team who only have a very limited time now to get the model ready for the paint shop and subsequent finishing next week.

Early afternoon and we have a joint Jaguar Land Rover advanced design review. We do this occasionally to share our latest work and get feedback from our colleagues, a kind of peer review. This is a good discipline, as the critique is very open and can lead to genuine insights on a project. The fact that we are all one team, while being

geographically separated, both preserves the strong split in DNA as well as giving each team the role of expert outsider to the other.

Otherwise, there is administration to finish, before heading off to Birmingham airport for the flight to Germany tonight. I dislike flying and generally don't like being away for too long, so I'm not too concerned that constant travelling isn't part of our remit. The exceptions are when we support some high level research in a nice part of the world, like Santa Monica for instance. The research we did there a couple of years ago on LRX was not only illuminating and enjoyable, but the spark of the idea behind the car was ignited there. Seeing a Mini Cooper parked behind a Range Rover in the bright Californian sun got me really thinking. The rest flowed from there.

Smooth flight—thank goodness, and a Eurobland hotel. (But the beer's always good in Germany!)

Friday

A big breakfast, then travel to the supplier's offices. We talk over the issues and make a lot of progress, while triggering some new ideas for how we designers could work in the future. By mid-afternoon, we are finished and I meet some old friends from the automotive design business. It genuinely is a small community and most people know each other. People move around too, so they get to know the different brands. This can lead to some cross fertilisation at times, but actually the number of publications and websites devoted to auto design spread the ideas around anyway. Real innovation and novelty can be quite a rarity. Still it's great to see old friends and discuss the moves, intrigues, and rumours. There's always something going on somewhere, and without the personalities it would be much less interesting. Being here in Germany also reminds me of my time in Stuttgart working for Mercedes Advanced Design. We eat and drink well, and it is a harsh transition into the cold night and onto the train to the airport again for a late flight home.

Time in the air gives a chance to reflect on a productive week and to give a little thought to the next. Designers never stop thinking about what they are doing, designing in their minds, resolving 3D problems, wrestling products out of the future and into the present . . . and it all begins again next week!

THE DESIGN
process

**What is automotive design? Simply, it is the aesthetic cultivation
of every element of an automobile that is visible to a consumer.
Historically, the typical moniker for automotive design was "styling."**

Yet in the twenty-first century it seems archaic to suggest that
automotive design is the mere consideration of aesthetic form, the
visual styling of vehicles to entice and, ideally, delight consumers,
when the backdrop to which cars are created is so complex. Car
design—far from being insubstantial, which was one perception
of automotive styling in the past—is complicated, increasingly so.
Even with the introduction of digital and virtual design technologies,
which have the potential to ease and accelerate the design process,
the increasing demands of security, engineering, safety, and
environmental regulations, and the ever-changing demands of
legislation, mean that today's automotive designers have to consider
and accommodate a number of potential design constraints.

At the very least, design has to achieve increasingly high
standards in order to be successful. What's more, in order to do

so, designers have to be excellent communicators to convey their design intent to other internal disciplines, including marketing, engineering, and safety. Not least of these is the real-world requirement to convince the automaker's executive management of the potential commercial rewards of executing a specific design. This is particularly challenging when you consider that the very best car designs are often those that are the most difficult to appreciate, particularly by a non-designer. It is also the case that once the go-ahead is given, the design process may incorporate dozens of individuals all working together to create a single automotive product. Effective communication remains key throughout the design process in order to successfully steer the evolution of a vehicle product through a process that has to account for a range of influences, all impacting on the final design.

Factors that influence the design of a car include branding, function, and useful effectiveness (usability), safety for both occupants and pedestrians, vehicle security, and engineering, including cost, material, and manufacturing constraints—such as component and platform sharing—as well as, increasingly,

environmental considerations such as recyclability, emissions, and the cradle-to-grave life cycle impact of the automotive product itself. All of these factors have the potential to have a compromising or even negative influence on the final vehicle form.

Although differences may exist between individual organisations, the automotive design process is broadly similar across all of the world's automakers. Typically, the stages of the automotive design process are the ones we detail here:

Stage 1: Early specification
It is rare for a car design to originate solely in a design studio. In fact, vehicle development usually begins with a series of strategic meetings comprising a multidisciplinary team from departments including design, marketing, and engineering, all of whom establish parameters—real and conceptual—of how the design development process will advance and what the timeframe will be. During this period a design brief is created, allowing the design process to begin. Vehicle type, powertrain, materials, customer audience, production considerations, and final vehicle price may all be considered.

Stage 2: Generation of early concept sketches

Usually a design boss will encourage some or all of his designers to generate concept designs inspired by theme and mood boards that contextualise the lifestyle and product segment criteria of the vehicle. These mood and theme boards are usually generated in earlier planning meetings. Theme and mood boards may focus on elements like the emotions that the vehicle design should evoke, the lifestyle context for the vehicle, a theme that suggests evolution. They also may reference one or more existing or historic vehicles, benchmark a competitor vehicle in order to create a response to it, and may even look at an entirely futuristic context or ask "what would we do if we ignored everything we know in terms of brand heritage and instead just started over?"

Once themes are agreed, an intense period of early sketching begins. Sketching is a quick and effective way to visualise large numbers of ideas. Though this period is highly competitive, designers typically encourage and enhance one another's designs for the greater good. Often it is the case that designs that make the shortlist may have been worked on by a number of designers in concert.

Stage 3: Design shortlist

Once the design team has decided upon its favourite sketches, more sketches are then created from this shortlist of possible designs. Designers that haven't had their designs chosen will be redeployed on the shortlisted designs and will help to generate more sketches showing different exterior—and sometimes interior—viewpoints or details of a vehicle.

At this point there is often a further review by management, though this will depend how many designs were being worked on in the first shortlist. It may be that management will decide to shortlist further or it may be that management decides to generate computer-aided design (CAD) models using software such as Alias Autodesk.

Stage 4: Final shortlist and clay and digital modelling

Once the last few designs are chosen, three-dimensional virtual or clay model development can begin. Digital modelling using CAD offers the possibility to evaluate designs using different virtual environments and to explore changes quickly, and the possibilities for visualisation in different environments—albeit virtual ones—are numerous.

On the other hand, the more traditional clay model has a physical form that cannot be bettered in terms of appreciating actual real-world size and shape. In the case of a 1:1 scale model, it can be perceived and understood at actual size. Clays are often rolled outside into the daylight to better understand surfaces, lines, and creases in natural light. Clay models also offer the advantage of designers being able to physically walk around them to better appreciate different viewpoints and perspectives.

Design directors may prefer either method or, indeed, utilise both—which is often, though not exclusively, the case. It is very unusual for a full-size clay model not to be produced from CAD data at this point.

Stage 5: Interior design

The interior design of a vehicle begins as soon as possible after the exterior work has begun, usually around three months later. The interior design of a car is more complex, incorporating a far larger number of surfaces and material constraints and involves designers working in concert with colour and trim specialists.

The colour and trim team research and create mood boards and colour, material, and even textural palettes for the interior design in line with the lifestyle and perceived customer requirements, as well as taking into consideration cost, weight, and safety restrictions.

As with the exterior design, designers compete and then collaborate on the interior design of the vehicle. When the final interior design is chosen, 3D digital modelling can begin to generate mathematical data for the final model/prototype build.

Stage 6: Final model/prototype build

Once mathematical data is finalised, the prototype component parts can be produced ahead of the construction of a vehicle prototype. This can often even mean a working prototype, which may be assembled in the design studio or built elsewhere by a specialist supplier.

Stage 8: Feasibility

Once management approves of a final design, the full-size clay is scanned to create a new 3D digital model and generate final data to be used by engineering and manufacturing operations to create final components and tooling parts.

Stage 9: Final approval

Final approval for the design and the final green light is given by management for production of the vehicle design.

CHAPTER 8

WHAT IS GOOD
design?

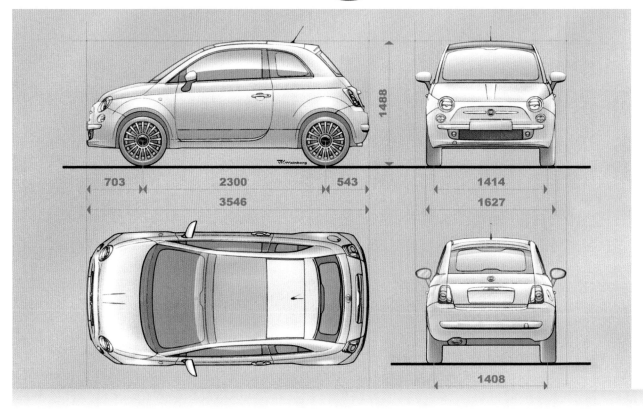

Professor Dale Harrow, head of vehicle design at the Royal College of Art in London—home to the world's leading transportation design course—looks at the nature of car design and considers how car designers have a responsibility to wider society.

When you consider the complexity of designing and constructing a modern motor car with all of the engineering, manufacturing, component-and platform-sharing demands, packaging component-legislation and safety regulations, not to mention the sheer number of people involved in the process, it is surprising that there is any room for creativity, innovation, and—that often-used term to describe cars—beauty. Car design is a complex subject, all too easily dismissed as "styling." However, beautiful and fascinating style does not come spontaneously; it is a result of combining a high degree of skill in understanding, interpreting and controlling a fluid three-dimensional shape with a knowledge of the historical, emotional, and cultural expressions involved.

The conception by many is that cars all look the same nowadays, yet nothing could be further from the truth. In any street we can see a wide range of cars—from simple sedans to super-luxury cars, off-road cars, sports cars, family MPVs, and, increasingly, new types of cars with new power sources, new structures and mechanical layouts, and new interpretations of what automotive design is.

The car has perhaps been the most ubiquitous and the most dominant visual form of the twentieth century. Cars are often described as art, design, or engineering—but how do design and designers work and what makes for good car design? There are some basic fantasies associated with the car: speed, freedom, comfort, and status. These have sustained people's love affair with the car and with brands like Ferrari, Volkswagen, and Rolls-Royce.

A process of refinement

Design is defined as a planning process, similar to the one an architect or engineer would carry out, but it can also be a form of communication or a method of problem solving. The aesthetics of vehicle design are most commonly described as resulting from the relationship and the successful management of the balance between form and function. Car design is also seen as pitting the intuitive against the cognitive, art against engineering. This definition assumes that the visual style of a car—such as the **original Mini**—is a functional design created as a direct result of architect Louis Sullivan's philosophy that form follows function, and that deliberately styled cars, such as the chrome fantasies created by Harley Earl and others in 1950s America, are solely based on an intuitive gut reaction to create a fashionable and desirable product. In reality, all car design exists in a space between the two extremes, and it's this tension between the logical and the intuitive, engineering versus art, that has characterised the history of car design.

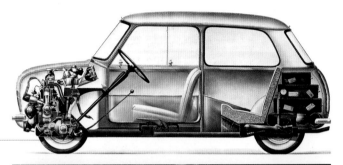

The engineering process has evolved to produce cars that have amazing ability and function. The processes and methods used by designers may have changed, but all car design starts with a sketch, a theme, or an idea that can be developed and refined to a conclusion. Car design features a high degree of experimentation through the development and reviewing of drawings and models,

where a three-dimensional object is refined and finessed through a series of stages to its final solution. The process is unique in that despite the many sophisticated technologies that allow designers to visualise and animate CAD data on screen, many designs are still signed off for production on a final review of a physical model.

Similar, yet individualized

But car design is not just about function. In some ways it is closer to fashion design, where trends come and go and certain styles are popular for a time and then disappear. The motor industry has a strong tradition of innovation, and there are concept cars at every motor show demonstrating new styles and innovations, including electric and hybrid power, suspensions systems that are ride-adjustable, aerodynamic styling, and new packages and layout. So why do so many new concepts fail to translate to mainstream manufacturing?

The high cost of putting a car into production has sometimes driven companies to produce safe design—cars that have little character, created to have mass market appeal. This was an accountant's dream—a single world car that could be produced and sold everywhere to the same consumer. Now we are in a different age. There are new companies and emerging markets, and many separate car makers have been merged to form super-companies where cost, technology, and expertise can be shared through common platforms and components and where design is at the centre, adding value and differentiation. If you buy an Audi TT, VW Golf, Skoda Octavia, or **SEAT Leon**, the car is basically the same, but the consumer is not. In the future, consumers will have a greater role in the design process. The Ford Mustang in the 1960s introduced the idea of the personal car. Up until that point everyone more or less drove a sedan. But with the Mustang you could choose your own car with an option list—convertible or fastback, your choice of engine, your own trim type and colour, body colour, wheels—that gave the consumer choice, as well as a role in the design process. It is a scenario that will have a big impact in the future as we move to flexible manufacturing techniques and the ability to customise for the individual.

Communication

Designers now talk about this being the age of emotions. Increasingly aware that the consumer is an emotional being, savvy designers know that today's consumer is more sophisticated and better informed and so will be very critical and want more control of the automotive products they buy.

J Mays, group vice president of design and chief creative officer at Ford Motor Company, says, "We are in the entertainment business," as he contends that all cars are well engineered, and that it is design that makes the difference and design that makes the emotional connection with the consumer.

We have many categories of style in the market at the moment—retro, technical, sculptural, product design, toy, and eco. All set out to satisfy many different consumers, and designers need to have an in-built radar to understand them. When Audi launched the first TT—which proved to be a pivotal design and very influential with its refined, pure logical shape—it immediately became the car of architects, designers, and media people. **The TT's design** communicated technology, refinement, inner confidence and the high-quality

engineering value that the consumer wanted to be associated with. It's no secret that the designers involved were searching to find ways to visually suggest such attributes to support and enhance the engineering and technical achievements, including turbocharging, four-wheel drive, excellent production, etc.—technologies that were being developed by Audi at the time and that had been increasingly associated with the Audi brand. The Audi TT is a good example of one of the fundamentals of good car design. It communicates the designer's intentions to the viewer in a clear and often subliminal way.

So, what tools does a designer have when creating new cars? There are form and shape, obviously, line and surface, contrast, texture, colour, and material finish. All can be used to bring out an overall design character.

But every designer wants to generate great design when they are faced with a new challenge and a blank piece of paper. There are many different approaches to this. Many car designers talk of wanting to achieve an emotional connection in their work, a passion for the object that makes you want to buy the car. This is often achieved by making the car dynamic—"looking as if is moving when standing still" is a common term—with the use of diving graphic lines and a sculptural body shape. Some say that the best design is one that can be easily understood, drawn with few lines, and is defined by its simplicity and an instantly recognisable profile. For others it's the evocation and retention of past values through the use of materials and historical reference. But for all cars to be successful, they have to exist as a piece of sculpture (using surface form and design), have good stance (the relation to the road surface and how it sits on the wheels), great proportions (the relationship between wheelbase and overhangs front and rear), have perfect volume (balance of mass of the sculpture in relationship to its proportions), use graphics well (window areas, light, and window shapes), and finally have surface lines and details that enhance the body shape (door shuts and other lines on surface) in order to achieve the perfect overall composition.

Consider, for example, how the car headlight has evolved in recent years—and the amount of time, energy, and effort that has been put into the detailing of that component. Marvel at the technology on even the average headlight and the sheer quality of it. Headlights have become a reflection of the amount of technology hidden inside the car and a reflection of the quality of the engineering. Good design will communicate this.

For tomorrow

As we move further into the brave new world of the twenty-first century, designers are creating our own futures as manufacturers look to designers to communicate their brands and differentiate their products. The world of car design is changing. There are new issues: climate change, urbanisation, an ageing population, and increasing numbers of drivers worldwide. All of these are going to have the greatest impact on car design in the future.

We are in a new age where traffic jams, congestion charging, parking spaces, safety, and environmental concerns are all determinants of the changing landscape for private and public transport. The motorcar, the defining machine of the twentieth century and the technological achievement that facilitated private transport for the masses, has to respond to the changing social, cultural, economic, and environmental agendas of the twenty-first century.

Looking forward to the next decade, we can be sure that the car will adapt and change. We will still crave personal mobility, but after what has been a period of evolution and incremental improvement we can expect a revolution.

Some key designers share these views. Chris Bangle, until recently design director of BMW Group, sees the car as an avatar—something far deeper than just a form or shape. He describes the car as a vessel for personal expression and emotion, for the person you become. He also suggests that if a car is an avatar then, by deduction, public transport is an elevator—something that goes from A to B that you personally have little connection with. There will also be a new category that Bangle calls swim fins—personal transportation, such as skateboards, bicycles and Segways, which are part of the overall mobility scheme.

The car industry is already changing radically, with new start-up companies producing cars for the first time. The motoring landscape, where major manufacturers develop and produce cars for a worldwide market, may change as the technology for electric vehicles is much simpler to acquire and more adaptable in its application. New lightweight materials used in the manufacturing of cars will result in greater efficiencies in car construction, resulting in environmental improvements in both the production process and, ultimately, the products they build.

Aerodynamics will again become a major preoccupation for car design, and this may also reduce the overall size of the car. Cars will be smoother and less aggressive in appearance as they won't need the big cooling apertures required for internal combustion engines. As a result, they will fit in better with the urban landscape and the changing social culture around the car in the city.

Cars will communicate with each other and to other road users so that they can find less congested routes and avoid the possibility of collisions. In the city, they may even have a function

when stationary, becoming a piece of street furniture or a display or information point—or even a store for energy.

New patterns of ownership, such as car sharing, will have an impact as traditionally cars have been designed as a personal space and status purchase. Imagine if the car interior self-cleaned or the exterior was finished in a material that aged well and got better with time.

Car designers will have to respond to these factors in order to realise truly successful designs. Good car design is the successful answer to the questions that society raises, ideally in the form of an automobile that entices and excites its customers and communicates its brand and even, perhaps, manages to be beautiful.

DESIGN AND
identity

What comes to your mind when you think of the Ferrari brand? What about Aston Martin, BMW, Citroën, Fiat, Mazda, or Volvo? Perhaps, more importantly, what do you feel? Interest, excitement, passion, indifference?

The emotion you feel for an individual automotive brand will almost certainly stem from your knowledge and understanding of it and any experience you may have had with its products. But what about those more visceral responses you may have, the subjective, more personal—even irrational—impressions of beauty or aesthetic form? Real passion for autos is most likely to be generated by a marque's car designs and its design heritage.

One's emotional responses to a brand are based on a myriad of factors that are unique to each one of us. When it comes to cars, it's not just a car's marketing and advertising that's designed to seduce; the styling of the cars is cleverly tailored to make us identify with the brand and ultimately desire the cars.

Today's automakers are looking to sign you up to become a loyal and committed follower of their badge. They want you to buy their cars, and if you can't buy them, they want you to aspire to.

For most of the world's design studios, the days when car design was solely focused on the creation of automotive form have passed. The simple business of creating attractive and desirable cars, if it ever was simple, has been surpassed by the role that design now plays in the broader theatre of brand image and communication. Today's automotive industry demands that car design contribute to the overall perception of the automaker.

Increasingly, vehicle styling is required to enhance a marque's image in what has become a very crowded automotive marketplace. These days design directors will be as concerned with the brand message their latest concept vehicles communicate as they are with the form resolution of their creations.

Distinguishing automotive brands used to be a lot easier in the days before cars shared components and platforms, when car marques were singularly owned rather than part of a global automaker's stable. Today, cars can share a high commonality of parts, often from the same component suppliers and even between rival car companies. The result, along with more than a hundred years' worth of technological advancement, safety regulations, and end-of-life regulations, means that technical and performance differences between competing cars are often slight—and to some car buyers, barely discernible or of little interest to them.

This is where car design comes into its own, to bring as much individuality and distinctiveness as possible to a product, to help it stand out and attract buyers, whilst enhancing and underlining the values of the carmaker's brand. The marque's identity and the message it relays need to be distinctive, clear, and consistent.

To achieve this, car designers generate a design language constructed from those historical and contemporary design elements that are considered of most value. These elements are then used in the design of a vehicle to introduce, enhance, or transition an automotive brand's image. These design elements can be explicit or implicit and are created to maximise the possibility of making an emotional connection with as many potential car buyers as possible.

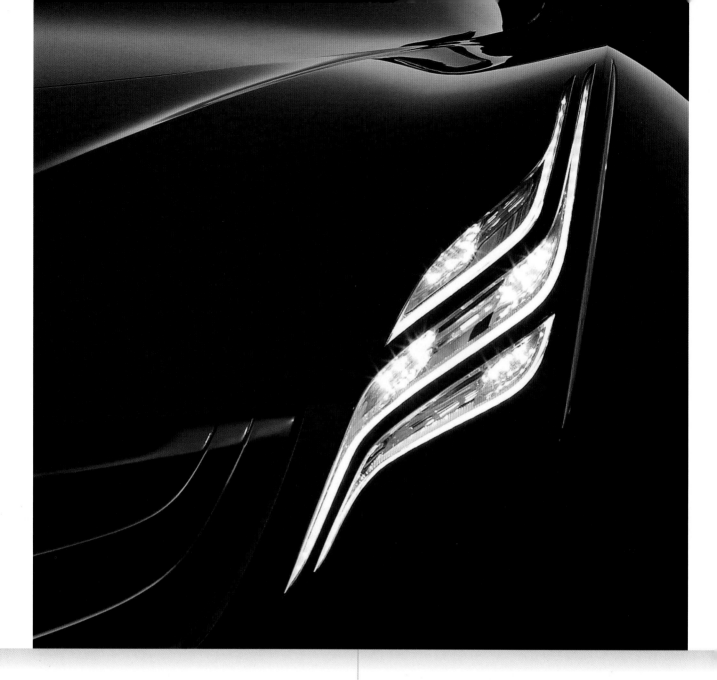

These elements are often part of a long evolution of an automotive brand. But sometimes, for a range of reasons, automakers may decide that a marque needs a revamp, to freshen its key brand values with the goal of achieving a whole new image within the marketplace, created then communicated through product design. It is at these times that change may be so dramatic that it seems more of a revolutionary step than an evolutionary one.

Car brands that have undertaken such an image rebirth in the past include Ford of Europe with its Kinetic Design initiative, Mazda with its **Nagare** (or Flow) design identity, and Renault with its successful Touch Design language. Other brands, including Audi, BMW, and Toyota, have all undergone significant changes design-wise in order to enhance or manipulate their overall image perception.

Designers begin this process by asking themselves what lies at the heart of their brand, what the marque means to consumers, and what is the brand's identity. They think about how consumers perceive the brand, whether it is being communicated effectively, and whether the image is as the company intended it. Only through such analysis can the difficult process of honestly evaluating where a brand is positioned and how it is perceived within the marketplace begin.

It is during this process that car designers work closely with marketing and brand strategists to target how and where they may want to position or reposition their brand. Once defining or, more commonly, redefining the brand has been achieved, they then evaluate which elements of a carmaker's design language successfully communicate these brand values to consumers and which detract from the desired message. In some circumstances, a whole new design language will be created to revamp a brand, taking the best of its heritage, in brand and design terms, and combining those elements with new ones that represent where the automaker wants to take the brand.

Case Studies
Volvo

One of the most successful examples of such a brand reinvention is Volvo, which began to create a new design identity in the early 1990s. Long marketed for safety, solidity, and reliability, over the years Volvo had become so associated with safety that it had become devoid of excitement in the eyes of consumers. For years, this had been all that had been communicated through its vehicle design. But when its competitors began to make serious inroads into its market by improving their own safety performance, the marque's design was left lacking. Volvo cars were considered clunky, **boxy, and brick-shaped**, and they were seen to be slow, heavy, and even dull.

The automaker needed to revamp its image with a cool, stylish Scandinavian design language to get away from the sturdy, boxy,

and, arguably, ugly aesthetic it had become associated with. Under an initiative started by British designer Peter Horbury in 1992, Volvo design began to change consumer perceptions of the brand by transforming its look. Horbury set out to replace the utilitarian designs of its earlier cars with a more stylish design language. Distinctive curved surfaces and an overall softer form became part of the marque's designs, while Horbury maintained key Volvo design cues, such as the V-shaped bonnet and upright grille. Through beautiful designs including the **C70** and S80, the carmaker was able to gradually change consumers' perception of its brand by suggesting that in addition to safety Volvo cars also stood for attractive design.

Audi

Perhaps the automotive world's most transitioned brand, Audi has successfully managed the visual design identity of its products and ensured it has a unified, coherent visual identity across its entire media.

In the early 1990s Audi set out to reposition its brand and move it upmarket by communicating its underlying brand values—which were summarised in the cue words human, leading, visionary, and passionate—and aimed to give Audi a greater emotional appeal.

Audi realised it needed to encourage an emotional connection between consumers and its brand. Its management knew that car buyers no longer purchased its cars for purely practical or rational reasons and reached a similar conclusion as Volvo did.

Audi began to set itself apart through a commitment to advanced technologies, including aluminium, which was displayed beautifully on the 1991 Audi **Avus Quattro** concept—penned by J Mays—and later seen on the A8 concept introduced at the Geneva Motor Show in 1994. Ultimately, this use of aluminium became so closely identified with the German automaker that it contributed

to the communication of its key brand value of being seen as technology leader.

Ultimately, the Avus concept's form led to the shape of the Audi TT coupé and roadster concepts, both launched in 1995. These cars took heritage Audi design elements and combined them with stylish design cues from the Avus concept to build a new design language for the brand. This new design language, in combination with the established brand slogan *Vorsprung durch Technik* ("progress through technology"), helped Audi successfully gain its desired place within the premium segment.

Today Audi design's goal remains the visual communication of *Vorsprung durch Technik* by blending form and function harmoniously. Audi designers communicate this technological leadership via a design language that has incorporated strict, well-defined guidelines to suggest premium, progressive and sporty elegance. In many respects, the carmaker has succeeded in taking the lead it set out to achieve in the 1990s, resulting in what is arguably the car world's strongest visual identity.

Mazda

In recent years, Mazda's products have undergone an equally substantial design evolution using its still emerging design language, Nagare. The Japanese carmaker unveiled the first of its new concept vehicles at the LA Auto Show in 2006. Called **Nagare**—the word for flow in Japanese—the car had a dramatic futuristic wedge-like shape and an unusual exterior body form with textured surface elements.

The Nagare concept was notable not just for its unusual form, but also because it was visually different to the three concept vehicles that had preceded it. Why, when these cars had been so successful, would the automaker make such a significant, and risky, transition in terms of its brand image?

Led by the then Global Design Director Laurens van den Acker, Mazda felt it needed to communicate its brand image better. At the time, the company's marketing identity was synonymous with its famous "zoom-zoom" tagline. Zoom-zoom communicated the promise of an exciting and emotional motoring experience for Mazda drivers. The design studio set out to capture the driving spirit embodied in zoom-zoom into a new, bolder design language and

to communicate such emotion even when the cars were stationary. Such dramatic and fundamental shifts in the re-imagining of automotive brands are relatively rare. They are risky because they can alienate existing customers and require true courage and vision on behalf of the automaker.

Designers began by evaluating the marque and summarised the brand into a series of adjectives—zoom-zoom, young, stylish, spirited, insightful, emotion in motion, innovative—all had become associated with Mazda over the years. Also, Mazda products were heralded for their exceptional functionality, responsive handling, and excellent driving performance. The design team concluded that such powerful brand characteristics were not being communicated as effectively as they could be and wanted to create a new and fresh aesthetic that would redefine the Japanese carmaker, one that visually communicated the brand, and that would become something

that it could "own" from a design perspective.

The most obvious element that the design team created was the exterior surface treatment itself, first seen on the Nagare concept, and used in the four subsequent concepts the **Taiki**, **Furai**, Ryuga and **Hakaze**. The unusual textured surfaces were designed to enhance Mazda's image by conveying fluid movement even when the car was stationary. Designers achieved this by suggesting airflow or water flowing over the vehicle's side surfaces. Such surface design, so unusual in terms of its texture, was created to play with light to suggest that the car was speeding through the air, thus communicating the brand's dynamic driving characteristics. This became a fundamental design cue for all of the Nagare concept vehicles and thus for the Mazda brand. Although the textural surface elements vary depending on vehicle type, it quickly became a recognisable Mazda design cue, as did the five-point grille and head and taillight treatments.

NEW FRONTIERS IN
car design

You won't find any powerful luxury cars, heavyweight SUVs, or 200-mile-per-hour supercars parked outside the offices of Gordon Murray Design—even though Murray is the father of one of the most sensational sports cars ever built, the three-seat McLaren F1, as well as the architect of many of the Formula One designs that dominated the racetracks from the 1970s to the 1990s. Instead, it's smaller and more modest cars that monopolise the GMD parking lot: Minis, Polos, the odd Toyota iQ, Mitsubishi i, and new Fiat 500. Murray himself is a fan of the old 500 and assorted smarts—and indeed there are two smart Roadster coupés parked in the directors' bays closest to the main entrance.

Such a swing towards smaller and more intelligent cars comes as no surprise. Gordon Murray Design is one of many engineering consultancies worldwide now turning their expertise toward conceiving cars that are more compact, lighter, and more economical, rather than ever faster and more powerful. Murray, famous in Formula One for his radical but invariably effective solutions, has been able to mobilise this free-thinking inventiveness to develop not just a new family of vehicles, but also a low

GORDON MURRAY DESIGN

environmental impact manufacturing process to go with them, insisting that a lightweight design is by far the best tool with which to chase low fuel consumption and low emissions.

One of Murray's new family of vehicles, codenamed T25, is a tiny city car, shorter and narrower than a smart Fortwo but which seats three and is able to swallow an impressive 750 litres of cargo with just the driver aboard; most impressively of all, however, is that it weighs under 600 kilogrammes—half the weight of a compact hatchback such as a Polo—and is capable of double the economy. By any standards this is a dramatic rewriting of the rules of the car business, and Murray is negotiating with potential production partners among leading auto-sector suppliers.

While Murray's T25 has a small gasoline engine mounted in the rear, the T27 battery model under parallel development offers designers even greater flexibility when it comes to the positioning of the major mechanical and electrical assemblies. No longer is there the large, immovable lump of the engine and transmission unit to force the proportions and the packaging of the vehicle. Batteries can be placed almost anywhere (though low down and in the centre

is clearly best for handling and stability), and the relatively compact motors can be located on either axle—or even in the wheels themselves.

Such freedoms provide engineers and designers with an unaccustomed opportunity to rethink not just the way vehicles are powered, but also how they are configured and packaged, where the hard points are, and where the passengers and luggage are accommodated. An unusually prescient concept was presented as early as 2002 by GM in the United States: the Autonomy, running exclusively on fuel cell electric power, contained all its engineering within its thin skateboard-like chassis, leaving designers free to choose different upper body superstructures to suit the vehicle's commercial role.

The primary structure of Murray's T25 is in effect the same thing: All the mechanical elements are contained within this chassis module, and it takes all the point loads of the suspension and seat belts so that it can be driven on its own, even minus the unstressed upper bodywork. The scope for multiple body variations at little extra cost is clear.

Developing a new mindset . . .

Sharing the same lightweighting philosophy but towards the opposite end of the market is Mindset, based in Switzerland. It, too, has thrown out the rulebook in terms of configurations and packaging. If you try to build an electric car off the basis of a conventional vehicle, it will never be fully effective, says designer David Wilkie, responsible for the interior: "This is what a lot of the major carmakers will be doing, because of the need to keep investment low by maximising carryover parts. But if you start from zero—a fresh design—there are a lot of possibilities."

Mindset's design is a tall **2+2-seater luxury coupé (see previous pages)** running on electric or hybrid power. Its design has a high-quality minimalist theme to echo its engineering philosophy of simplification and low weight. "We used the fact that the car had to be lightweight as an advantage in the design and the presentation," says Wilkie. "We don't want to overload the car with heavy things to make it luxurious—that's the opposite of what you need in an EV. It's a great thing for designers—it gives us new freedoms."

Internally, the Mindset shows its simplicity with a clean, elegant dashboard and a smooth bench seat front and rear. Its exterior is even more unusual. Designer Murat Günak, with extensive experience at Mercedes, Peugeot, and Volkswagen, was determined to advertise the Mindset's alternative drivetrain by making a highlight of its large, but very narrow, exposed wheels.

Mindset and Murray have a further factor in common: Neither has yet found the funding to progress to the stage of manufacture. Norway-based Think, on the other hand, is an electric car maker that has twice launched into series production. **Think's small City model**, now in its fifth generation, is being adopted by several European cities for zero-emission urban car schemes. Yet, to look at—and in contrast to the eye-grabbing Mindset—the City comes across as a smaller version of a conventional car. Chief designer Katinka von der Lippe explains that as Think is a pioneer, a small company and not yet such a known brand in the car segment, its initial models cannot afford to appear too far from the mainstream.

"Customers must be reassured that this is a real car, that you can trust it, that it will drive and handle well," she says. "So we have made it similar to [conventional] automobiles."

Yet the details, she says, are definitely not similar to those on conventional cars, and here Think does begin to advertise its

alternative status. The body panels are unpainted textured plastic with a matte finish, for instance, emblematic of the sustainability ethos that underpins every aspect of Think's business. "People want to show they have made a different choice," she explains.

Von der Lippe sees fresh approaches developing as customers become more familiar with electric vehicles. The **2008 Think 0x** concept, for instance, proposed a TFT screen-coated A-pillar that could convey messages, such as state of charge and availability for lift sharing. Yet even with these advantages, she does not see dramatic changes in format or shape for small electric vehicles: "Think will still be in the automotive realm and still clearly recognisable as a car. Yes, we will be more towards a consumer product than other manufacturers, and to some extent we will be the missing link between private and public transport. But the personal car will still be an important thing, and customers will still relate to the car—so cars need a stronger identity than consumer products."

Silicon Valley focus turns to electric cars

It's a measure of how far the pendulum has already swung toward low- and zero-emission solutions that manufacture and sale in the United States is an important element in Think's strategy. Though the staple US model, a five-seat SUV, will be slightly larger than the City that is sold in Europe, the move is a significant step and comes at a time when, with the Detroit Big Three automakers facing serious upheavals, the full force of California's Silicon Valley enterprise is being focused on hybrids and EVs. Already, Colorado-based energy visionary Amory Lovins had been investing heavily in developing the fuel-efficient Hypercar made from lightweight composite materials, but it was only during 2007 and 2008 that credible, viable products and companies began to emerge from the mass of highly motivated but often hopelessly optimistic Californian start-ups.

First out of the blocks was Tesla Motors with its Roadster, a pure electric sports car based on the British Lotus Elise. This model, despite its high price, has been enthusiastically reviewed, even though in aesthetic and packaging terms it breaks no new ground. In 2009 Tesla showed a concept version of its planned four-seat **luxury sedan (see pages 94-95)**. The styling, by Franz von Holzenhausen, is smooth and swish in the current four-door coupé idiom and appears to package generous passenger space within compact

overall proportions. Yet, as with Think, there does not appear to have been any desire to exploit the packaging opportunities of the electric powertrain to achieve a clean break from the familiar proportions or form language of standard luxury cars.

Furthest along the route to a general market breakthrough is the **Fisker Karma**, a plug-in hybrid four-door luxury sedan developed in California by ex–Aston Martin and BMW designer Henrik Fisker. The Karma and its associated coupé-convertible are voluptuously styled and low slung in a way that might have been difficult with a conventional gasoline powertrain. While the Karma is certainly distinctive, it again avoids any major shock-of-the-new shifts in its external design, the motive again being easy market acceptance. The Karma will begin production in 2010 at the Valmet plant in Finland— ironically where Think has also just placed its manufacturing—and Fisker is tooling up an ex-GM factory in Ohio to build its upcoming mainstream volume plug-in hybrid. The visual signature Fisker chooses for this key market breakthrough model will be an important indicator of the industry's preparedness to develop a distinct identity for its electric cars.

Mainstream programmes

However, not all those dipping their toes into the electric car business are high-minded start-ups or idealistic engineers with visions of a zero-emission future. The big firms are keen to get in on the action too. Anyone visiting any of the major international auto shows in 2009 would have been left in little doubt that the future is electric, or at least plug-in hybrid electric. For mainstream automakers, having a battery-powered car on display brought an immediate impression of future-mindedness, of a willingness to embrace the challenge of carbon—even if, as was the case with both Audi and Mercedes-Benz, the electric cars in question were prototype high-performance supercars derived from existing gasoline-powered designs. As the decade drew to a close, the only company to have shown a proper, production-ready electric car was Nissan. Its five-passenger **Leaf** small car is not radical in its styling themes, though it is easily distinguished from the Tiida small car on which it is based.

Rather more exciting to the show-goer have been the various concept cars developed by automakers such as Renault and intended to give future customers a clearer idea of what battery driving might look like. While the Renault Fluence ZE is a near production-ready electric version of the combustion-powered model, the **Zoe ZE (opposite)** proposes an unusual proportion and much interesting design detailing for a Golf-sized family car running on electricity. Emerging fast as a signifier of electric power is the use of cool blue LEDs and highlighting, in much the same way as automakers are now employing strings of LED running lights to provide brand-specific frontal signatures for their models.

Where designers are displaying more imagination in their application of electric power is in the wave of smaller concept proposals fusing influences from the motorcycle and scooter design worlds. Renault's **Twizy**, a narrow-track four-wheeler, appears to devote almost all its small size to carrying two people and their bags, testifying to the compactness of the batteries and electric motor. It also introduces the notion of wheel spats to reduce drag and mitigate the consequences of accidents with pedestrians, and its front panel

with hexagonal LED cells is able to spell out messages as well as carrying out the normal lighting and signalling functions.

Peugeot's BB1 proposal goes a step further, miraculously managing to seat four people in an overall length of 2.5 metres—significantly shorter than a smart. It achieves this through a layout that is effectively two scooters side by side. The four riders sit astride twin parallel motorbike-like dual seats, the batteries being housed under each seat; the driver has bike-style handlebar controls rather than the steering wheel of the Twizy. But where the BB1 signals potentially the most significant step forward in packaging is in its use of Michelin's patented wheel motors.

The so-called Active Wheel packages an electric motor, steering, brakes, and suspension within the enclosure of the wheel. All it needs is a mechanical fixing to the chassis and connections for electric current, cooling, and control systems. Its potential for car design is immense: At a stroke, the device replaces all the bulky components designers have spent so many years struggling to accommodate. Engine, clutch, gearbox, driveshafts, suspension,

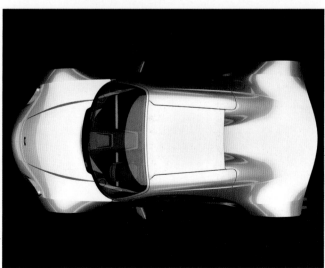

brakes, hubs, radiators, exhausts—all could plausibly be consigned to the museum of engineering history, leaving exterior and packaging designers with freedoms they have never before experienced.

Though the baby Peugeot is not fully engineered, PSA design director Jean-Pierre Ploué and his team are keen to explore production possibilities, making the BB1 one of several innovative car-motorcycle hybrids to be considered for volume manufacture. As for Michelin's Active Wheels, they were given a preview in 2008 on an electric sports car concept developed by Venturi, also from France. Outwardly, the **Volage** has the allure of something like a Lotus Exige —a compact mid-engined coupé—but closer inspection reveals that the rear compartment is almost completely empty. A motorised wheel is set at each corner, large aerodynamic tunnels now dominate the space normally occupied by an engine, and the chassis tub is immensely simple; all-up weight is 1,075 kilogrammes, including the batteries that are integrated into its structure. It is easy to imagine a similar platform being used for a variety of roles with minimum adaptation.

A new approach

Electric power in its various forms—pure battery, plug-in hybrid, and fuel cell hybrid— clearly offers the greatest potential for a Lego-set approach to car design, allowing the individual pieces to be dismantled and rearranged to form a new shape or package. The **Mercedes-Benz Blue Zero** concept (discussed in chapter 5) is another important pointer toward the future freeing up of design through the use of a shared sandwich chassis across many different versions.

As with Murray's T25 and the French electric car projects, the Blue Zero is able to exploit new technologies and engineering methods to help advance new packaging concepts and body-style formats. Yet automakers who seek to do this the other way round do so at their peril. In line with the industry consensus, engineers at Gordon Murray Design believe the original **smart**, though revolutionary in concept, would have been successful much sooner if it had not been built using the conventional method of welded-steel pressings. "The smart is as small as you can go by scaling down conventional technology," says design director Barry Lett, noting that

its manufacturing investment is similar to that of a larger vehicle. "We want to ensure [our T25] has a much lower start-up investment than the smart."

Yet what the smart has unquestionably done is open up consumers' minds to the idea of a microcar, and in consequence it has given other automakers the confidence to move into this area. Competitors to date have been largely conventional and generally seek to provide more flexibility and to seat more than two within a footprint that is little or no larger than the smart's. Good examples of what can be achieved by rethinking and redistributing conventional hardware are the **Mitsubishi i**—which mounts its engine centrally under the floor for more passenger space—and the Toyota iQ, which rearranges the gearbox and differential on a standard front-drive platform to allow an asymmetric 3+1 seating layout within a length of under three metres.

However clever these cars are, few would label them revolutionary or mould-breaking. Perhaps more dramatic in this respect is the step taken by India's Tata—in a very different corner of the market to the classy city car territory inhabited by the Mitsubishi and Toyota. The **Nano**, announced in 2008, is the result of Tata boss Ratan Tata's personal mission to bring an ultra low-cost car to help mobilise the many millions of Indian people who today travel in great danger, with whole families often crammed onto a single flimsy motorcycle. By providing a car at a price midway between a scooter and existing small cars, Tata believes he can tap a lucrative market at the same time as making family travel safer and more comfortable.

To achieve the targeted 1-Lakh price—that's around $1,500—Tata's design team had to come up with innovative engineering and clever solutions, many of which involved keeping the weight low and making sure as many components as possible perform multiple functions. The packaging concept—tall, narrow, and with the engine between the rear wheels—helped with the lightness, and the simplicity of assembly was aided by the one-piece dashboard moulding and the single instrument unit.

Indeed, lightness—both visually and in terms of kilogrammes—is emerging as the common theme across a whole raft of forward-looking design projects. It is especially important in electric vehicles, where the batteries themselves can account for a high proportion

of the all-up weight. Lightweighting is a virtuous circle. The lighter the basic structure, the lower the braking and suspension loads are, enabling lighter suspension and brakes; lower weight also means less consumption, allowing for a smaller fuel tank or battery for the same range, again permitting a further round of weight reduction.

For Gordon Murray—schooled in the science of racing cars, where every unnecessary gramme is a competitive handicap—strict discipline on the weight front is the key starting point for his new generation of city cars. "Light weight is *the* tool we have right now to help us with fuel consumption and emissions," he says. "No matter what powertrain you've got, light weight is working for you one hundred per cent of the time."

While light weight is at the heart of the T25/T27 concept (pictured, p. 101) and underpins his new low-energy iStream manufacturing process, Murray admits that most of the major companies visiting his operation have been more interested in the production systems than the T25 design itself; in fact, programmes T26 and T28—Murray's projects are always numbered chronologically—are studies for a Japanese and a European carmaker, respectively.

"All these projects use iStream," he says. "And they all have the advantage that iStream gives in low capital investment, low-energy manufacturing, low lifecycle damage—and flexibility of different bodies on different chassis."

Management inertia and huge amounts of investment tied up in conventional stamped-body manufacture have meant that automakers have habitually steered clear of new ways of making cars, says Murray. Recently, however, environmental pressures, the recession, and the need for rapid product flexibility have forced the automakers to sit up and realise that they do need to change. Most of the senior executives visiting Gordon Murray Design are coming from the perspective of possible parallel production and wanting to do a business study, he judges. "If the business case looks good enough, you'd just start it in parallel. It's nothing to do with losing stamped-steel cars overnight—it's to do with something more sustainable in terms of energy, and it's a lot more to do with having a platform that can deal with the volatile market. Even with platform sharing these days, once you've spent your hundreds of thousands on the dies, the stamping tools and the body-in-white shop, that's what you make. And if the public doesn't like it or someone else comes up with something better, you're stuck with it. Any change in a stamped-steel platform is expensive."

Revolutionary though Murray's iStream manufacturing process undoubtedly is, it will not be immediately obvious to the customer—apart, of course, from the advantages it promises in terms of price, performance, and fuel economy. Ironically, where Murray's initiative may have a much bigger impact is in a non-technical domain—that of branding and the new business models that might follow.

New technologies, such as fuel cell and battery power, are already drawing in suppliers from outside the traditional auto industry. These suppliers have no fixed assets committed to conventional manufacture (such as engine production or stamped-steel plants) and are thus open to new approaches; so too are the so-called Tier One suppliers—major producers of subsystems, such as electronics, suspensions, brakes, who are generally prepared to work for anyone who will buy their products. What

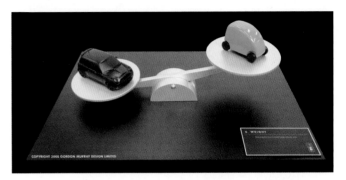

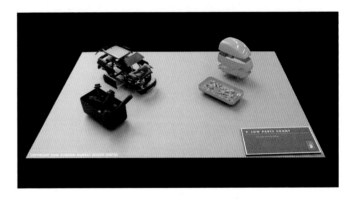

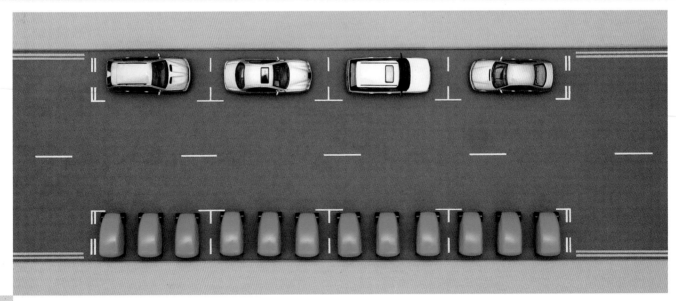

these potential groupings do not, however, have is any automotive brand name—and this is where the big jump may come. With both propulsion technology and manufacturing reaching important turning points, this could be the perfect opportunity for a non-automotive brand to pitch in and grab a slice of the market for mobility. Names such as Sony, Dell, Easy, Apple, or even Google spring to mind. These are global brands with high recognition across all age groups and would have a major head start over any other newcomers to the sector.

This is why Gordon Murray and his head of design, Andy Jones, have deliberately designed the T25 as an unbranded car. "Its style is a vanilla one," says Jones. "It's not masculine or feminine, young or old—the shape is very generic. There is nothing striking, no classic design cues, such as the VW front."

The thinking here is to pitch the design as a blank canvas, a fresh surface on which the chosen brand can apply its own identity. "We have been approached by some non-automotive companies, and it's very exciting," says Jones.

The model's wraparound dashboard design presents major opportunities for linkages to these new brands and to create exciting multifunctional and interactive interior environments never before seen in any car, let alone a small and affordable one. "An Apple version could have a bespoke centre console, for instance," says Jones, "and its membrane switch technology, as seen on the iPhone, could be used on the dash. Downloadable sat-nav, integrated MP3, fantastic sound—anything's possible."

And with Murray's new business model as just one of many initiatives to approach car design from completely fresh angles, it does indeed appear that anything is now possible. The sweeping under-the-surface changes taking place in the auto industry will of course take some time to filter through into radically new shapes on the road, and the scale of investment makes it unlikely that the car business will ever experience the four-wheeled equivalent of the iPod—an innovation that completely revolutionised the way people listen to music and media. But the sense right now is that we are closer than ever before to just such a new era—the exciting new world of car design, where old values are overturned and creative, forward-looking thinking can at last flourish.

GENESIS OF A
revolution

How Gordon Murray shaped the three-seater T25

"The idea began in 1993 when I was stuck in a traffic jam on the A3 motorway and, looking around me, realised that all the cars around me were large but with just one occupant. At that stage I was only thinking about congestion, not pollution.

"Conventional small cars use proportionally fewer materials than large ones, but the number of parts is about the same—so I began to think about the manufacturing process too. It had to be low energy and the platform would have to be flexible so it could be used for other vehicles, such as pickups, a van, an inner-city ambulance, and so on.

"I started off with the footprint. A natural length was 2.4 metres, which would allow it to park nose-in to the kerb; the width of 1.3 metres allows two to run in parallel on each lane of a dual carriageway.

"We really wanted to capture the urban market, so we looked at six functions, including dropping people at the train station, leaving the car at the station, dropping your kids at school, a week's shopping for a family of four or five people. It was pretty obvious that the car had to be a minivan to do that. The next big step forward was the seating layout, the occupancy—and, of course, the powertrain. We needed to select that at an early stage. It becomes pretty obvious that if you want to make a car substantially under three metres and still have some crash length, you've got to put the engine at the back. It's forced upon you, really.

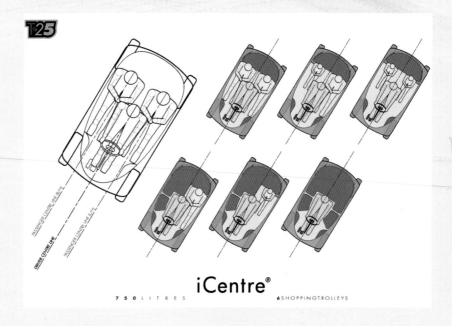

"In the UK, eighty-five per cent of all car trips are single occupancy. But you can't design a car for facts and figures—you've got to get out there and talk to people, and you've got to look at cases like the Smart. So many people would rather buy something slightly bigger with four seats, even though they probably never have more than two in the car.

"We had this dilemma: two-point-four metres is tiny. It's either going to be a single seater or have more than two seats; at one-point-three metres wide, side-by-side seating is going to be impossible when it comes to passing impact tests from the side. Comfort, too.

"So the McLaren layout that I dreamt up for the F1 seemed perfect. That gave us the flexibility on the market. Capturing the shopping market will give us the biggest gain in appeal. This will be a first-time buyer's car, a student's car, or a second car in a family. It will never be the only car in a family. If you have a smart in the family and you want to do the shopping, you'll probably take the big car so you can open the boot and chuck everything in. So six shopping trolleys was our target. You need about five hundred or six

hundred litres for the average number of bags for a family of four or five's weekly shop. We have that—in fact, if you pack the thing to the roof, you've got seven hundred and fifty.

"It's a completely flat floor at a good height for your back and with no lip to lift over. We've tried to think about absolutely everything to assist the market. We've also done a design for a van, and it's brilliant. It doesn't take much more design to get a cubic metre of load space.

"We'd been looking at various materials. What I didn't want was any steel pressings. The smart went a little way there, but they've still got a pressed-steel section—I think it's about one hundred and thirty parts—to make up the Tridion. My thinking was that if we are to make a break from an investment point of view and an energy point of view, we don't want any pressings at all. So apart from a few minor stampings for strut tower caps and brackets and things, which come from a jobbing shop, our factory doesn't need a press plant. It doesn't have a body in white plant; it doesn't have an E-coat or paint plant.

"The other thing I was keen to do was to open up the opportunity for the build-to-order car. If you stamp a car, you have this pristine, Class-A [visible exterior panel finish] body, which you have to E-coat. Then you have to go straight to paint, which has to be under clean conditions and a partial vacuum. You take it out of that and hope it hasn't got any grains of dust under the paint. Then you don't want to move it under any circumstances more than a few metres to your assembly plant.

"We don't have that issue. Our frame is very damage tolerant. It's a combination of quite coarse composites and steel tubes; there's no Class-A finish involved. You could have a central frame plant. The bodies are all injection-moulded and painted somewhere else. A Tier One could make the frames and ship them in on the back of a truck, because you can stack them with some very cheap stillaging. We've designed them so that compared with bodies in white you can get twelve times the number of frames in a shipping container. They stack like IKEA furniture—it's a flat-pack car."

CHANGE OR continuity?

Should carmakers launch fresh new styles at regular intervals in order to stimulate sales among potential buyers? Or should they fine-tune a familiar formula to breed brand recognition and rely on technical innovation to inspire interest? It's an age-old debate, and one which shows no sign of being settled.

Here we track the model policies of mainstream European carmakers over 35 years and six model generations of family hatchbacks to decide which formula works best. Our findings are clear: Radical looks and revolutionary changes of style may generate instant excitement, but the steady step-by-step evolution of a strong basic design is the best strategy for building up long-term brand values and customer loyalty. Of the five model series examined, the steadily evolving Volkswagen Golf is the only one to keep the same name between 1974 and 2010 and to pass on recognisable design DNA through all its generations.

VOLKSWAGEN **Golf Mk1 1974**

Crisp, fresh, pure, and above all modern, the original Giugiaro-designed Golf was just what was needed to fire up a Volkswagen organisation that had become stuffy and unadventurous. Buyers were fired up too, flocking to the new VW in droves as the Golf came to be seen as the successor to the legendary Beetle as the true people's car—or Volkswagen. The Golf's hatchback format and its taut and precise (but still friendly) design language inspired a

generation of imitators, while its powerful C-pillar, forward-kinked at its leading edge, became a key Golf identifier and something that would be retained to provide an instant identity for five further generations of Golfs.

A single facelift midway through its long nine-year life brought broader rear lights and bigger bumpers to add substance to the Mk 1's design, but the sheet metal remained unaltered and the sporty GTI and groundbreaking Cabriolet remain icons to this day.

OPEL-VAUXHALL **Kadett D/Astra 1 1979**

Replacing the simple rear-drive Kadett C (Chevette in the UK), the '79 Kadett D (Astra in the UK) was Opel-Vauxhall's first front-drive car. Designed to compete with the Golf, it had a simple boxy style but with a strong, rear-raked grille and large rectangular lights. Good looking and well accepted by buyers, it put GM back on the map as a maker of competitive small cars.

FORD **Escort Mk 2 1975**

It is scarcely believable that this smartened-up revamp of the ancient rear-drive Mk 1 Escort was launched a year after the Mk 1 Golf. Yet Ford did a reasonable job, adding a tauter, more grown-up look to its mainstay model, the tidy lines, planar surfaces, and angled bonnet and boot-lid panels being contemporary touches. Underneath, however, it was hopelessly out of date.

FIAT **Ritmo/Strada 1978**

Styled by Bertone with smart surfaces and a wealth of unusual features, the Ritmo/Strada was big news in 1978 as an aspiring Golf challenger. It was unusual for its era not only for being assembled by robots, but also for its radical take on details. Quality and reliability were poor, however, and despite facelifts in 1982 and 1985 aimed at making the design more mainstream, the Ritmo never sold well outside its home market.

RENAULT **9 (1981) & 11 (1983)**

Taking over from the characterful but troublesome Renault 14 hatchback in 1981, the 9 and, two years later, the 11, were the French company's attempt to build a family car with Japanese levels of efficiency. Unfortunately, both the 9 sedan and the 11 hatchback proved to be desperately dull designs, and reliability was still patchy—ensuring former Renault buyers shopped elsewhere for their next car.

VOLKSWAGEN Golf Mk 2 1983

A Volkswagen in-house design that nevertheless retained the key visual cues of the Giugiaro original, the Mk 2 of 1983 signalled a move away from the lightweight clarity and big-window feel of the Mk 1 towards the weightier and more substantial look that would come to define the Golf brand for the next three decades. Still evident on the Mk 2 are the angled flat bonnet drawn by Giugiaro

for the Mk 1, as well as the thick, parallel-sided C-pillar and the full-width rectangular grille, red-rimmed on the iconic GTI version. Yet the surfaces are less crisply defined and there is less energy in the design language.

Compared with the Mk 1, there is more mass to the body and less emphasis on the glasshouse—especially evident at the rear where the horizontal graphic of the rear window contrasts with the near-square proportions of the original tailgate glass. Nevertheless, despite these many changes, the Golf identity is clearly carried over.

OPEL-VAUXHALL
Kadett E/Astra 2 1984
A complete change of theme came in 1984 as the Kadett/Astra embraced the aerodynamic era with a smooth, rounded design with a high, Alfasud-like tail. The shape worked best as a hatchback, especially in its characteristic white, but none of the versions showed any continuity with the previous model.

FORD Escort Mk 3 1980
This was the big culture shift at Ford as its mainstream model moved over to front-wheel drive. The styling was crisp, fresh, and innovative—in particular the much-discussed "bustle back," which sought to combine hatchback practicality with an element of the look of a sedan to appease conservative customers. This was a passable shot at a Golf competitor, especially as the Mk 1 version of the VW had by now been in production for six years.

FIAT Tipo 1988
Fuelled by the success of the progressively styled Uno, Fiat hoped a radical approach to the replacement for the fading Ritmo would bring parallel success to its larger hatchback range. The Tipo enlarged the Uno look and had a distinctive rear glasshouse with twin parallel C- and D-pillars, yet even with a lot more interior space than its rivals and the reassurance of a rustproof all-galvanised body, it lacked the charm of the Uno and did not sell as well as had been hoped.

RENAULT Renault 19 1988
Styled by the master, Giugiaro—who had shaped the original Golf—the Renault 19 had clean and simple, if unexciting, good looks and sold steadily for almost a decade as a hatchback, a sedan and, for the first time, a convertible. There was little visual continuity with the unloved and insignificant-looking 9 and 11, but the facelifted versions introduced in 1992 paved the way for the frontal identity of the 1995 Mégane, a critical family in Renault's revival.

VOLKSWAGEN Golf Mk 3 1991

The 1991 Mk 3 Golf, designed to meet tightening safety requirements and increasing commercial pressures, was ironically the closest the model has come to a near-death experience. Its blob-like looks and bug-eyed lights were greeted with horror by commentators, who deplored its general shapelessness and the loss of the taut, fresh feel they had become used to with the two preceding generations. The ponderous, heavyweight look of the Mk 3 seemed to symbolise the onset of middle-age spread and a more conservative outlook for the VW line, a trait especially evident on the lower-grade models with their small, narrow wheels and absence of features to relieve the amorphous mass of the body. Only the now-characteristic strong C-pillars truly identified it as a Golf—a remarkable achievement considering how far away from the original ideal the rest of the style had strayed.

Though the Mk 3 stayed in production, as planned, for six years, it represented a serious lapse of form for VW and is the only generation of Golf not regarded with affection by enthusiasts.

OPEL-VAUXHALL Astra F 1991

The rounded theme continued in 1991, by which time Opel had adopted the Astra name too. This harmonious and neatly detailed design gave the appearance of space and comfort and was again best as a hatchback; critically, it avoided the dull amorphousness of many of the smoothed-out designs of the era, including the Mk 3 Golf launched at the same time.

FORD Escort Mk 4 1986

Buyers quickly saw the 1986 Mk 4 Escort for what it was—a superficial makeover of the 1980 version. The facelift consisted of little more than detailed tweaks and a general rounding off of styling features such as the lights and grille; the effect might have been in tune with contemporary tastes, but it diluted the fresh feel of the original design.

FORD Escort Mk 5 1990

This was a relaunch that backfired badly as the press rounded on the dull style of the new Escort's body and the inadequacy of its engines and its chassis. The more rounded theme reflected the mood of the moment, but personality was desperately lacking. The model, once a massive seller, steadily lost ground over the following years, with Ford facelifting it twice in order to stem its steady decline.

VOLKSWAGEN Golf Mk 4 1997

Coming after the unloved Mk 3, 1997's Mk 4 Golf had a lot of damage to repair. It needed to freshen up an image that had become bloated and stodgy; it needed to look younger and more modern, and it needed to elevate the VW brand above that of its mainstream competitors by offering a classy, premium feel.

It did this with remarkable success, and over a decade later it is still regarded—along with the Mk 1—as perhaps the most accomplished of all Golf executions. VW resisted the temptation to make the Golf bigger and fatter, instead choosing to invest in an interior that stunned the industry with its genuine premium quality

and feel and that left competitors struggling to catch up.

Externally, the Mk 4 referenced the strongest points of the Mk 1—its deep glass areas; its clean, sheer sides; and its simple clarity—to provide much-needed freshness, even though an echo of the Mk 3's roundness remained in the front fender area and the dumbbell arrangement of the narrow grille flanked by almond-shaped headlights.

Still, however, the key broad C-pillar remained, flowing smoothly down into the rear fender without an intervening shoulder line; this, as with all Golfs, puts the visual emphasis on the pillar structure and, cleverly, suggests integrity and lightness at the same time.

OPEL-VAUXHALL Astra G 1998

Appearing a crucial 12 months later than its direct competitor, the Mk 4 Golf, the 1998 Astra G marked the point where Opel-Vauxhall ceded the initiative to VW. The new design was an unremarkable corporate committee affair, with lots of detailing but little overall impact. The lack of visual carryover from the previous model was a weakness in terms of brand equity, further weakening Opel's perceived presence in the segment.

FORD Focus I 1998

The 1998 Focus showed Ford at its radical best, bouncing back from the dark Escort years with a creative and imaginatively styled replacement that won praise not only for its dramatically different looks but also for its roomy accommodation and good driving characteristics. The peak of Ford's New Edge design phase, the Focus cleverly disguised its high build with its amalgam of curved surfaces, angled cuts, and sharp points. Its interior, echoing the same radical theme, was less well received, and the sedan and station wagon versions were more conservative.

FIAT Bravo/Brava 1995

This duo took over from the Tipo in 1995, the first time an automaker had introduced different names and substantial body differences for the three- and five-door versions of the same basic car. Both were smooth and rounded in style and owed little to the Tipo—the Bravo being the sportier three-door design while the five-door Brava had a distinctive arrangement with three individual lozenge-shaped tail lights on each side. Ultimately, however, Fiat's originality in design was undermined by poor quality and reliability, and the range never fulfilled its potential.

RENAULT Mégane 1995

It is impossible to overstate the importance of the Mégane to Renault. The five-door hatchback and two-door coupé launched in 1995 expanded into a family the following year with launch of the Scénic, which, as the world's first compact minivan, went on to become a major success. Externally, the hatchback models were contemporary rather than innovative, making extensive use of gentle curves and smooth radii rather than straight lines and flat surfaces.

VOLKSWAGEN Golf Mk 5 2003

The Golf had been at the top of its game for six years by the time the Mk 5 appeared, slightly delayed, in dealers' showrooms at the end of 2003. In terms of external style, it once again fine-tuned details of the generic Golf look to project a greater sense of substance and status. Bigger headlight units brought a stronger identity to the front, with the narrower grille moving to a less horizontal graphic—especially on the GTI, where a chromed or blacked-out frame linked it vertically to the lower air intake.

This was the first Golf where the bonnet was dished between the front fenders, adding to its visual presence. The body sides, too,

showed a weightier look, with a higher waistline and the beginnings of a shoulder line to break the continuity between the now more upright C-pillar and the rear fender for the first time. Nevertheless, this could not be anything but a Golf.

Notable, too was the greater depth of body side above the wheel arches, again strengthening the impression of quality and gravitas. Here, Volkswagen could clearly be seen to be capitalising on the premium status earned for the Golf nameplate by the Mk 4. This was reflected in VW's initial strategy to charge premium prices for the model, something resisted by consumers until the company upped the equipment content to a suitable level.

OPEL-VAUXHALL Astra H 2003

A much less timid design than its predecessor, the 2003 Astra merged a more sharp-edged form language with a bold grille and headlight and glasshouse graphics to produce a crisply contemporary shape that sold well and stood out among its competitors. The GTC coupé, with its steeply raked rear window line, became emblematic of a revival in Opel design values.

FORD Focus 2 2004

A more conventional car that had been given a handful of design cues to make it look like the original Focus, the second-generation model marked a retreat by Ford from the radical stance of the original. Only the shape of the headlights and the angled rear lights set high up into the C-pillars identified it as a Focus, and the cautious executive-style dashboard signalled the abandonment of innovation in the interior, too. A facelift in late 2007 strengthened the frontal appearance with a more prominent grille, successfully bringing the Focus identity up to date despite the fact that the design links to the original are tenuous.

FIAT Stilo 2001

Often referred to as the forgotten Fiat, the Stilo was developed in record time with the aid of outside contractors tasked with dramatically improving the brand's quality and reliability. The calm, well-measured design again had a different rear-end look for three- and five-door versions, and interior finish was a quantum step up from earlier Fiat offerings. Perversely, this led commentators to complain that character was in short supply, and this well-conceived model never recovered from its poor start amid the market hiatus following the events of September 11.

RENAULT Mégane 2 2002

A mixture of shock, admiration, and disbelief greeted the unveiling of the second-generation Mégane hatchbacks in 2002. Gone were all the visual cues of the original, to be replaced by a much more adventurous design with a vertical wraparound rear window and projecting rump-like hatchback tailgate that stirred up huge arguments at the time. The whole shape was neatly sculpted and attractive, and buyers soon took to it even though it did not look as large or as imposing as some competitors.

VOLKSWAGEN Golf Mk 6 2008

Not so much a full model change as a comprehensive facelift, the Mk 6 Golf sharpened up the design language of the Mk 5 and upgraded the interior quality and refinement features such as soundproofing. Externally, the shape has been given greater definition by the inclusion of VW's latest corporate grille, the shallow full-width band running into the large, swept-back headlights forming the front corners of the fenders. For the first time, the central VW badge breaks into the front edge of the bonnet. All these small changes have helped to give the Mk 6 a strong horizontal graphic, emphasising its width—though it retains similar overall dimensions to its predecessor.

The same technique is employed at the rear, too, where a horizontal colour split in the taillights makes for a wider, sportier look. Viewed from the rear, a new feature becomes evident: a strengthening shoulder line, running forward from the top of the rear light; under certain light conditions, this can have the effect of visually separating the substantial sheetmetal area of the lower bodywork from the C-pillar, which still retains the thickness and forward-leaning angle so characteristic of the Golf.

The overall effect, once again, is to make the car look more solid and more substantial. The gently curved bodyside surfaces give a feeling of weight, albeit at the expense of the precision and sharpness that characterised Giugiaro's original Mk 1 and, to a lesser extent, the Mk 4 of 1997. This, more than anything, shows how the Golf's design language has evolved over the years—yet, thanks largely to the clever manipulation of key visual clues such as the broad C-pillar, the brand's identity remains as clear as ever.

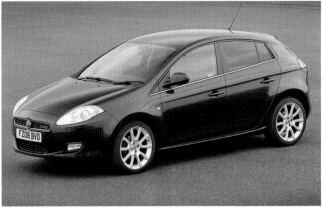

OPEL-VAUXHALL

New Astra 2009

All change again in 2009 as the Astra takes on the curvier, more organic form of the larger (and well received) Insignia. Strong design cues are the arched cantrail, the strong shoulder running forwards from the rear lights, and the kick-up from the sill in front of the rear wheel aperture. It's an attractive design, but lost in the mix is any sense of continuity with the previous generations.

FIAT Bravo 2 2007

Fiat's occasional practice of enlarging a successful small-car design to create a new medium model at last struck lucky in 2007 when the Bravo 2 appeared as a grown-up version of the fast-selling Grande Punto, the model that revived Fiat's fortunes in the supermini segment. With its sportscar-like front, diving waistline, and high tail, the Bravo 2 has brought some originality into the family hatchback sector and may in the future serve as a useful template on which to build a much-needed design identity for Fiat models.

FORD Focus 3, 2010

A strong return to form for Ford for the third-generation Focus under the design direction of Martin Smith. Gone is the cautious look of the 2004 edition, to be replaced by a confident design building on the edgy themes of the smaller Fiesta but with a greater sense of substance to suit the buyer profile of a family hatchback.

Like the Fiesta, the 2010 Focus has a beltline that rises sharply from the low front to the raised rear, communicating dynamism; the dynamic impression is heightened by a glasshouse that tapers towards the rear, and by the arrowhead rear lights that mark a complete break from the C-pillar mounted lights that were such a hallmark of the first two generations.

This less clinical, more sculptural approach also works well as a sedan and a sporty station wagon, versions that in previous Focus generations have been awkward in their proportions.

A further mark of confidence is the simple grille composed of a single bar and a centrally-mounted Ford oval emblem, breaking into the front edge of the hood for added prominence.

RENAULT Mégane 3 2008

Sensing that the radical shape of Patrick le Quément's second-generation Mégane had peaked quickly but faded relatively soon in a competitive market, Renault opted for a more cautious—though more complicated—design for the replacement model in the hope that it would sustain its sales performance for longer. No visual continuity is evident between the generations, though the new one again differentiates strongly between the three- and five-door hatchbacks. The design is larger, heavier, and with much less visual clarity than the previous car, again emphasising the disconnect between the two. Renault appeared to succeed in transferring the substantial brand equity earned with the first Mégane generation to the second; however, keeping the momentum into this very different third iteration may be a tougher task.

CHAPTER 12

STUDENT work

The designers of tomorrow share their views and their designs

We have seen iconic designs, both contemporary and historical; we have heard what today's designers prefer, what they work on, how they think, and how they organise their working lives; we have even gained an insight into how they expect to tackle the challenges to come. But what about the aspiring designers of tomorrow, the rising generation of fresh talent that will shape the cars of the 2020s and 2030s? Who do they admire, what are their favourite designs, and what fires their passions? And, most importantly of all, what kinds of cars will they be designing for us in the decades to come? We contacted tomorrow's decision makers—students working on automotive design in colleges around the world—to hear their preferences, their priorities, and their passions and to glimpse some of the designs that they have in store.

Name:	**Paul Nichols**
Nationality:	**American**
Age:	**21**
College/university:	**Coventry University**
Course:	**Automotive Design**
Year:	**4**

What is your favourite car? Ferrari 250 GTO, the definition of a great Ferrari—race-bred, road-driven, limited production. Probably the most beautiful car ever.

What is your favourite design icon? The Transamerica Pyramid. The simplicity helps shield it from ageing, and I think it's iconic because it was a new take on a classic shape.

Which designer do you admire most? Without sounding cliché, I admire Chris Bangle most because he affected almost all automotive studios while directing and working at only one. `

What type of car or product do you most want to design? I'd most like to help on the design of a halo car—a concept car that embodies the future of a brand. I think designing a car such as this is always a great opportunity to move design on to something more interesting.

Which will have the biggest influence on car design in the future: fashion, environment, or cost? I think it will vary with each car; with some types of cars, fashion is more important, with others cost. It's usually a combination of all three with an emphasis on one. I don't think one will ever clearly override the rest.

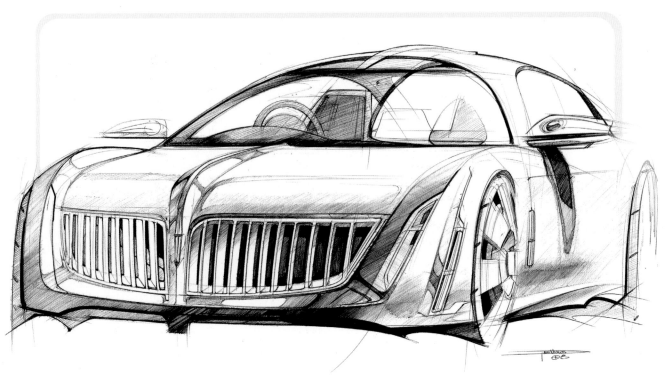

Name:	**Douglas Hogg**
Nationality:	**British**
Age:	**21**
College/university:	**Coventry University**
Course:	**Automotive Design**
Year:	**4**

What is your favourite car? Scimitar GTE SE5A. Proves that a car doesn't have to be pretty to be cool. Classless Tom Karen design still influences design today.

What is your favourite design icon? Lamborghini Miura SV. The original mid-engined supercar and still one of the most beautiful and influential designs of the last 50 years.

Which designer do you admire most? Choosing just one is very difficult. I admire a graphic designer named Mike Okuda. He invented the *Star Trek* LCARS operating system in the mid-1980s. It is a totally unique-looking and distinct touch-screen interface design that has been in use in every *Star Trek* show and film for over 25 years and still looks cool today.

What type of car or product do you most want to design? Something that makes the user feel good.

Which will have the biggest influence on car design in the future: fashion, environment, or cost? I think the biggest emerging influence in car design will be the environment, and in turn, fashion. It is increasingly popular to be viewed as environmentally friendly, both among consumers and manufacturers, and car design will reflect this trend.

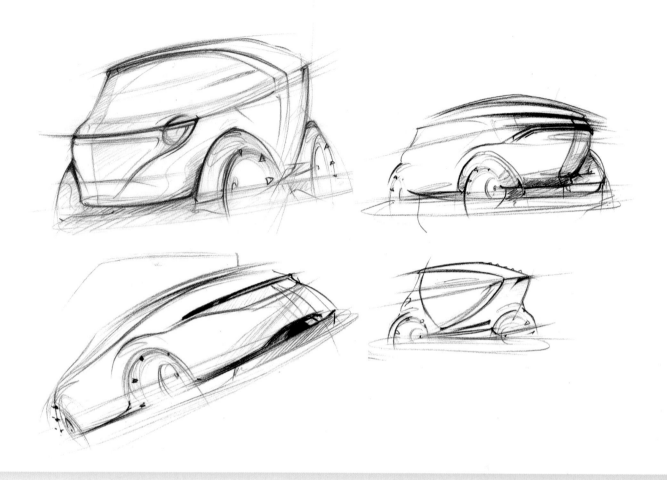

Name: **Louise McCallum**
Nationality: **British**
Age: **21**
College/university: **Coventry University**
Course: **Automotive Design**
Year: **4**

What is your favourite car ? Land Rover LRX—in white

What is your favourite design icon? Arne Jacobsen's egg chair—a truly timeless piece of product design. I aspire to have one in my home one day!

Which designer do you admire most? Frank Gehry—the architectural equivalent of Chris Bangle: dramatic, influential, and brave designs.

What type of car or product do you most want to design? I would like to create dynamic yet accessible design for the mainstream consumer market, vehicles like the new Ford Fiesta. Also, some opportunities to break some boundaries with concept car design would be great.

Which will have the biggest influence on car design in the future: fashion, environment, or cost? I would hope that all three will be combined in future car designs, and I feel like they will have to be. Environmental influence will not take a step back until radical changes are made to combat climate change. More environmental designs will always have to be desirable and accessible in cost.

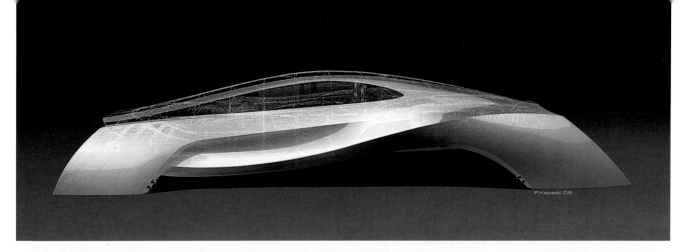

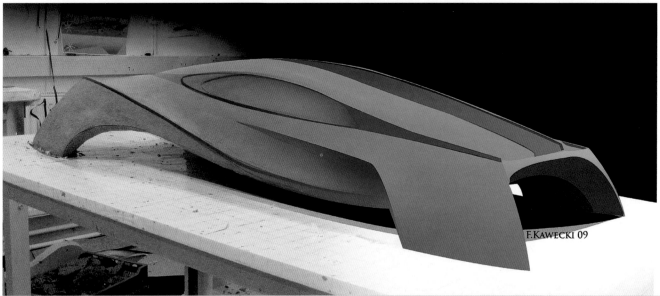

Name:	**Frank Kawecki**
Nationality:	**Polish**
Age:	**22**
College/university:	**Coventry University**
Course:	**Automotive Design**
Year:	**4**

What is your favourite car? BMW 507 coupé

What is your favourite design icon? Leonardo Da Vinci is my favourite design icon, as he was diversely talented in variety of fields—not only design, but also art, sculpture, architecture, math, and engineering—which all interest me.

Which designer do you admire most? Daniel Simon is the designer that I admire most in the field of 3D-design, modelling, and visuallisation.

What type of car or product do you most want to design? I would love to design an entire range—car, motorbike, boat, architecture, and lifestyle. I was always fascinated by the things surrounding me and questioned how were they made and how could I design and manufacture my own since a very young age.

Which will have the biggest influence on car design in the future: fashion, environment, or cost? I believe that environment will become more influential over the other factors. However, customers' personal perception of the world at the given time will determine which factor is more important for them.

Name: **Ian Barnes**
Nationality: **British**
Age: **22**
College/university: **Coventry University**
Course: **Automotive Design**
Year: **4**

What is your favourite car? It's constantly changing. At the moment, I'd probably have to say something like the Lamborghini Murcielago roadster. For all its exaggeration and flamboyance, it's a refreshingly honest car in that it's not trying to be anything except a true Lamborghini!

What is your favourite design icon? I think it would be the Wally 118-foot superyacht. It's an object that in a lot of ways encapsulates what I love about design. It's about the detail and the exotic proportions but with that defining, precise, industrial aesthetic.

Which designer do you admire most? I honestly don't know. For a car design student I know embarrassingly little about famous designers. I have forever focused on visual images, the pictures of the cars themselves and not who designed them. If I had to pick I would probably say Ken Okuyama for all the cars he has designed and overseen.

What type of car or product do you most want to design? I'd love to design real concept cars, those that may inspire other vehicles, ideas, and fashions and are otherwise free of some of the constraints of production-ready vehicles. I've always wanted to be at the very

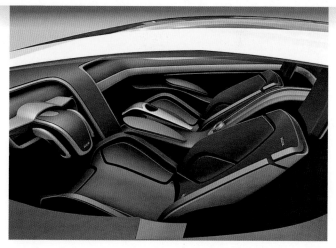

beginning of any creative process, to come up with the initial idea or to create that first inspirational sketch.

Which will have the biggest influence on car design in the future: fashion, environment, or cost? I think the three are most definitely linked. However, the difficult part for manufacturers will be how to ensure that their new environmental policies will still persuade people to buy their cars and if they can afford the development costs required to make them not just as good as current vehicles, but better in every way.

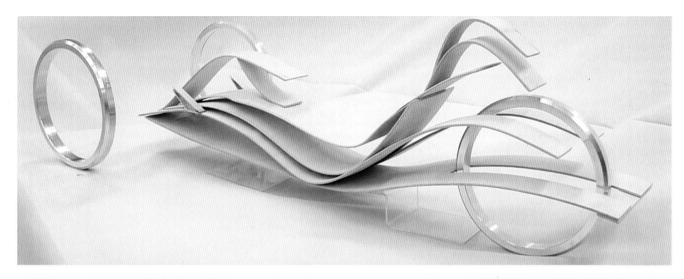

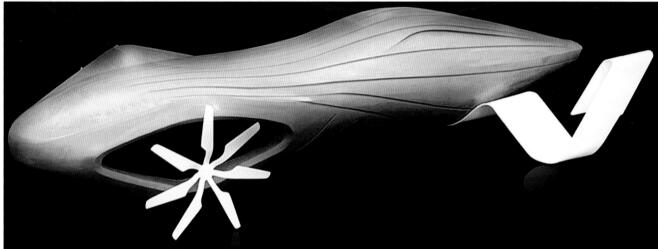

Name:	**Graham Hetherington**
Nationality:	**British**
Age:	**25**
College/university:	**Coventry University**
Course:	**Automotive Design**
Year:	**4**

What is your favourite car? Two choices: One made me investigate car design as a career when I was 15 and that car is the TVR Tuscan. At that time, it was very influential to me and is the reason I am here at Coventry. My other favourite is the Ferrari 599 GTB.

What is your favourite design icon? The Eames chair— a timeless piece of design that is still desirable today.

Which designer do you admire most? Chris Bangle. He took a lot of criticism from the media and public but under pressure never changed his vision, keeping strong to his own beliefs.

What type of car or product do you most want to design? Architecture has always fascinated me, and therefore I would like to be involved with the design and growth of a modern and contemporary house set against a country background. Preferably my own in years to come.

Which will have the biggest influence on car design in the future: fashion, environment, or cost? The influence of fashion will always have a strong relationship with car design as car design itself is very fashion conscious. However, it will be the environment that has the biggest influence as public perceptions change to demand cleaner, more environmentally friendly vehicles.

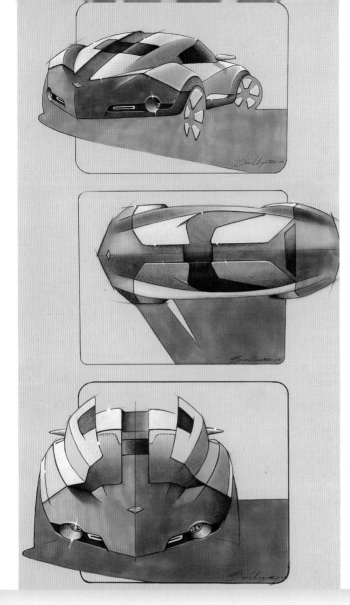

Name: **Sam Holgate**
Nationality: **English**
Age: **22**
College/university: **Coventry University**
Course: **Automotive Design**
Year: **4**

What is your favourite car? 1954 Mercedes 300SL Gullwing

What is your favourite design icon? The robot from Bjork music video "All Is Full of Love"

Which designer do you admire most? Patrick le Quément, for the design innovations introduced to small production vehicles in the 1990s and creating Renault's distinct design language.

What type of car or product do you most want to design? A vehicle for a brand with a great sporting heritage, e.g: Mercedes or Alfa Romeo, where there is a vast range of inspiration from previous vehicles.

Which will have the biggest influence on car design in the future: fashion, environment, or cost? Environment: The need to reduce the impact of vehicles in order to be more sustainable will have a dramatic effect not only on a car's appearance, but also how we treat personal transport.

Name: **Florian Sieve**
Nationality: **German**
Age: **28**
College/university: **Hochschule Pforzheim**
Course: **Transportation Design**
Year: **4**

What is your favourite car? Aston Martin Vantage, Porsche 356 Speedster

What is your favourite design icon? Porsche Design Carrera sunglasses, Artemide Tolomeo lamp

Which designer do you admire most? Maison Martin Margiella, fashion designer

What type of car or product do you most want to design? I would like to design a Porsche 911

Which will have the biggest influence on car design in the future: fashion, environment, or cost? In this order: environment, architecture+nature, fashion

Name: **Klaud Wasiak**
Nationality: **Canadian**
Age: **27**
College/university: **Umeå Institute of Design, Sweden**
Course: **MA Transportation Design**
Year: **2**

What is your favourite car? Audi R8

What is your favourite design icon? The Barcelona Chair, by Ludwig Mies van der Rohe. It's a blend of modern and classic styles with an amazing stance.

Which designer do you admire most? Chris Bangle

What type of car or product do you most want to design? I like to design objects that tell a story, that have a strong visual impact and depth, which keep the viewers/users captivated throughout that object interaction.

Which will have the biggest influence on car design in the future: fashion, environment, or cost? Materials and production methods have become so progressive that even the most economical cars can feel expensive. Environmental considerations have already become standard in the design process, and sustainable products shouldn't be so conspicuous. Since cars are such emotional products, I believe fashion will influence design the most in the future. That visceral reaction is needed to stimulate an emotional bond between the users and their vehicle.

Name:	**Andrew Webber**
Nationality:	**British**
Age:	**21**
College/university:	**Coventry University**
Course:	**Automotive Design**
Year:	**4**

What is your favourite car? Citroën SM

What is your favourite design icon? The Panton Chair

Which designer do you admire most? Marc Newson. I've always admired the way he uses materials, particularly in his chairs, and the 021c concept vehicle, which was created with Ford, is a good example of a product design–inspired vehicle.

What type of car or product do you most want to design? Luxury vehicles: It's a segment that gives you the most freedom to explore new materials and technology and also to create something that has to survive the test of time due to vehicle owners' much higher expectations.

Which will have the biggest influence on car design in the future: fashion, environment, or cost? Fashion. I believe the environment is no longer a factor when designing; it should be assumed that a vehicle or product will not have a negative impact. As people become more demanding of vehicles, it is likely that fashion and trends will become an important factor in car design.

J.BATTERSBY 09

Name: **Jason Battersby**
Nationality: **Canadian**
Age: **24**
College/university: **Umeå Institute of Design, Sweden**
Course: **MA Transportation Design**
Year: **2**

What is your favourite car? 1963 Aston Martin DB5

What is your favourite design icon? Coke bottle

Which designer do you admire most? Chip Foose

What type of car or product do you most want to design? Anything that will excite people. Part of what drives me to create beautiful and interesting shapes is seeing people's reactions to my work.

Which will have the biggest influence on car design in the future: fashion, environment, or cost? I believe part of our job as designers is to find interesting ways to create beauty. There is no doubt we have to consider both the environment and cost, but these influences will only be second to the fact that people still want to be fashionable and stand out. Fashion allows us to make a statement, which is always an underlying message in design.

Name: **Derek Chik Kin Ng**
Nationality: **from Hong Kong**
Age: **31**
College/university: **Umeå Institute of Design, Sweden**
Course: **MA Transportation Design**
What is your favourite car? Saab Aero X
What is your favourite design icon? Evangelion
Which designer do you admire most? GAINAX
What type of car or product do you most want to design? Aircraft and ASIMO
Which will have the biggest influence on car design in the future: fashion, environment, or cost? Fashion

Name: **Luis Camino**
Nationality: **Spain**
Age: **27**
College/university: **Umeå Institute of Design, Sweden**
Course: **Masters in Transportation Design**
Year: **2**

What is your favourite car? Any convertible. But I look forward to having a family just so I can justify a Skoda Roomster.

What is your favourite design icon? Underground maps

Which designer do you admire most? Tom Matano

What type of car or product do you most want to design? Production cars. I crave moving lines up and down 2 millimeters on a boring sedan. We always want what we don't have!

Which will have the biggest influence on car design in the future: fashion, environment, or cost? Cost is the mother of all influences. The environment is just another parameter that happens to be a popular challenge nowadays in the same way that safety was hot in the 1990s.

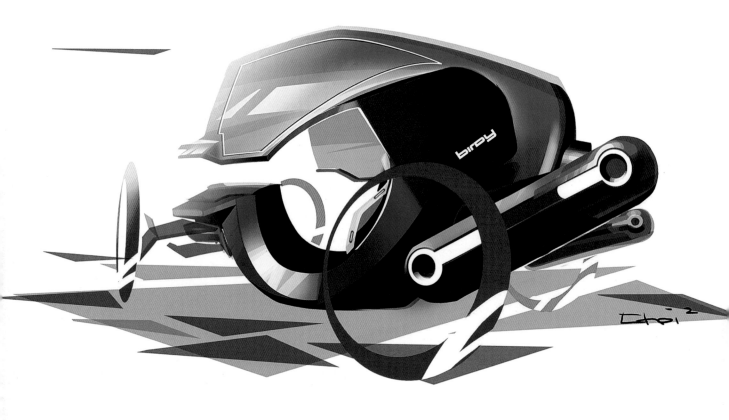

Name: **Jea-woon Cho-choi**
Nationality: **South Korean**
Age: **28**
College/university: **Umeå Institute of Design, Sweden**
Course: **Masters in Transportation Design**
Year: **2**

What is your favourite car? BMW M1 concept car, Ferrari 250 GT, Ford Mustang GT 500, Aston Martin DBS

What is your favourite design icon? Golf Mk 1, old Casio watches, Arco lamp from Castiglioni, Barcelona chair

Which designer do you admire most? Daniel Simon, Zaha Hadid, Chris Bangle

What type of car or product do you most want to design? A car that you never forget after you watched it once.

Which will have the biggest influence on car design in the future: fashion, environment, or cost? Environment is going to be the most important issue. Not only the way of using alternative energy sources, but the way of the production as well. The other question will be: If the car changes, how would the driving experience change? We should always have fun driving cars.

Name: **Michal Plata**
Nationality: **German**
Age: **24**
College/university: **Hochschule Pforzheim**
Course: **Transportation Design (BATD)**
Year: **3**

What is your favourite car? Citroën DS

What is your favourite design icon? The paperclip and the Bic pen. Simple, functional, and timeless.

Which designer do you admire most? Ludwig Wittgenstein, an Austrian philosopher who designed a house according to his philosophy. I remember this being an important influence for me before my studies.

What type of car or product do you most want to design? The paperclip and Bic pen car, obviously.

Which will have the biggest influence on car design in the future: fashion, environment, or cost? The society and its consciousness have always been and will be the biggest influence. Aspects such as fashion, architecture, environment, and cost are only symptoms of society's consciousness. Aiming at influencing it by design, we should look at the bigger picture. Furthermore, I think that developments in medicine could have an influence on car design. Talking especially about prosthetics and orthosis.

Name: **Ingo Scheinhütte**
Nationality: **Austrian**
Age: **25**
College/university: **Hochschule Pforzheim**
Course: **Transportation Design**
Year of study: **2004–2008**

What is your favourite car? Aston Martin V-8 Vantage
What is your favourite design icon? Porsche 911
Which designer do you admire most? Erwin Komenda
What type of car or product do you most want to design? Sportscars
Which will have the biggest influence on car design in the future: fashion, environment, or cost? Cost will influence the segments, fashion the styling

Name: **Tsanko Petrov**
Nationality: **Bulgarian**
Age: **25**
College/university: **Hochschule Pforzheim**
Course: **Transportation Design**
Year: **4**

What is your favourite car? De Tomaso Pantera
What is your favourite design icon ?
Citroën DS 19 (1956)
Which designer do you admire most? I don't have a favorite. Everyone
has the possibility to be a good designer. Everyone is a great designer.
What type of car or product do you most want to design? Something
that doesn't exist yet!
**Which will have the biggest influence on car design in the future:
fashion, environment, or cost?** Environment.

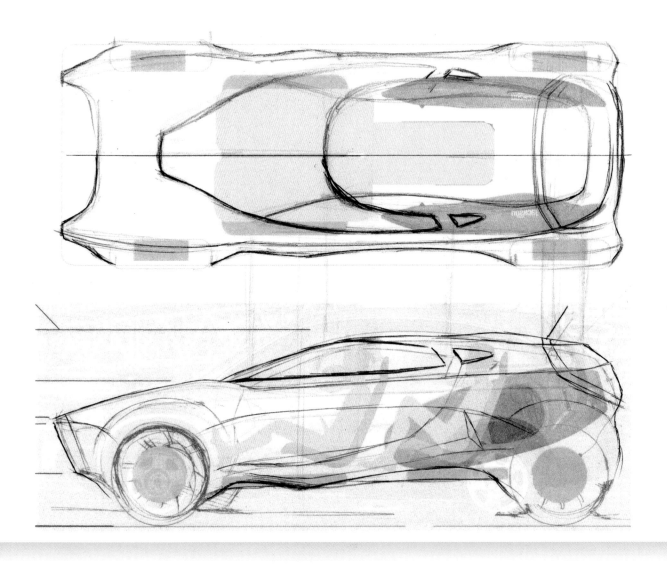

Name: **Dean Bakker**
Nationality: **Dutch/Canadian**
Age: **20**
College/university: **College for Creative Studies, Detroit**
Course: **Car Design**
What is your favourite car? None specific
What is your favourite design icon? None specific
Which designer do you admire most? None specific
What type of car or product do you most want to design? Body
**Which will have the biggest influence on car design in the future:
fashion, environment, or cost?** All of these. Better yet: the power
source (electricity, gas, etc.)

Name: **Frank Wu**
Nationality: **American**
Age: **21**
College/university: **College for Creative Studies, Detroit**
Course: **Automotive Design**
What is your favourite car? Spyker C8
What is your favourite design icon?
Coca-Cola bottle
Which designer do you admire most?
Frank Stephenson
What type of car or product do you most want to design? Luxury sports car
Which will have the biggest influence on car design in the future: fashion, environment, or cost? All have a great effect on car design, but environment will definitely be the greatest influence towards future car design.

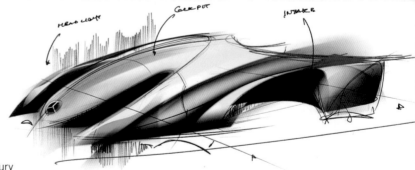

tutorials

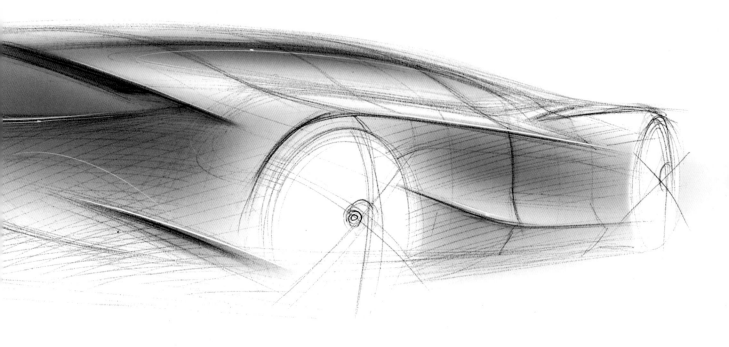

A good sketching technique is the foundation on which a designer's professional skills are built. Professional automotive designer Allan Macdonald takes us through three tutorials that will show you how to produce drawings with speed, effectiveness, and impact. Mr. Macdonald is a graduate of Coventry University's MDes Transportation Design Course, and has worked for Arup Design Research, MG-Rover, and Volvo Trucks.

Although we all like to see and admire well-crafted illustrations, as a professional designer you will find that these constitute only a small percentage of the work you will produce. As a designer your job is to create many and varied ideas in a short space of time and to do so in a way that others can see and understand your thinking. A good sketching technique is important for both of these. When practising sketching, it can be very hard at first to know when to stop. This can lead to every drawing becoming a time-consuming rendering. It is important to learn not to be overly precious when sketching. By doing so you will produce more and improve much faster. Over the next few pages, we aim to show a good technique for working out ideas in both a fast and a readable manner.

Tutorial: Perspectives

When drawing, a basic understanding of the rules of perspective is essential if you are to achieve a realistic effect. Only once you have learned these rules can you begin to distort or exaggerate them in order to accentuate elements of your design. There are three basic forms of perspective (one, two, and three point). There are also three main elements present in each of these (the vanishing point, convergence lines, and horizon line). This tutorial shows the basics behind one- and two-point perspective only; three-point perspective is not required in automotive sketching.

Horizon line
This line, as its name suggests, describes the horizon, which is always considered to be at eye level. For instance, an object sited above the horizon line is above the viewer's eye level and will therefore show its underside.

Vanishing points
Sited on the horizon line, these are the points where all convergence lines meet. Although always on the horizon, their position depends on the viewer's angle.

Convergence lines
All parallel lines in a scene will always appear to converge to a single point (the vanishing point). The exception to this rule is that lines viewed in parallel or perpendicular to the viewer will not converge. For instance, the lines running lengthways through the vehicle in picture A. In one- and two-point perspective, you can also consider all vertical lines as nonconverging lines.

One-point perspective
One-point perspective is evident when the object being viewed lies parallel or perpendicular to the viewer. This means that only lines travelling toward or away from the viewer appear to converge to a single vanishing point on the horizon. Picture one shows how this makes for a very simple version of perspective, which is especially useful for sketching quick side views of a vehicle.

Ellipses
Getting correct ellipses when drawing a car is probably the hardest part of perspective. If you look at a circle straight on at an angle of 90 degrees, what you see is indeed a circle. But once you start to reduce the angle you view the circle from, it starts to appear to be an ellipse. An ellipse consists of a major axis and a minor axis. In picture C, you can see where these are situated on an ellipse. The major axis divides the ellipse into two equal halves along the longest dimension, whilst the minor axis divides the ellipse into two equal halves along its shortest dimension. A good rule of thumb is that you should always align the minor axis with the axle of your vehicle. The major axis, and therefore the longest dimension of the ellipses, should therefore run perpendicular to your axle line. Finally, how do you ensure that the angle of your ellipse is correct?

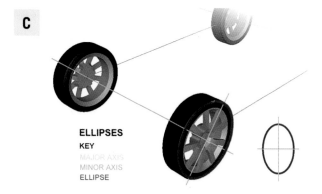

C

ELLIPSES
KEY
MAJOR AXIS
MINOR AXIS
ELLIPSE

Two-point perspective
When the object being viewed lies at an angle to the viewer, as in picture B, all the horizontal lines appear to converge. This, therefore, introduces a second vanishing point on the horizon. Where the vanishing points fall on the horizon line depends on the angle of the object to the viewer. Looking at picture two, you can see that if the vehicle were turned so that more of the side was visible, then the right vanishing point would move to the right and out of the image.

Courtesy Car Design News

1 POINT PERSPECTIVE

A

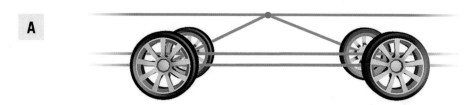

2 POINT PERSPECTIVE

B

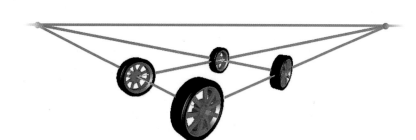

KEY
VANISHING POINTS
CONVERGENCE LINES
HORIZON LINE

One-point perspective

When I begin a sketching programme, I almost always start by
drawing only in side views. The point of early sketch work is for the
designer to find many ideas in a short space of time. By sketching in
side view (and usually reasonably small), I can generate many pages
of ideas very quickly. This is mostly down to the fact that you need
to think about perspective very little and can therefore concentrate
on thinking about ideas. Almost the only element of perspective
visible in these drawings is the way that you can see the far side
wheels. This is due to the fact that in one-point perspective the only
convergence lines that converge are those moving toward or away
from the viewer.

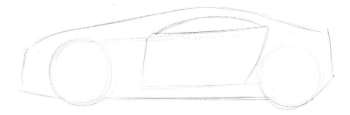

01 You can see here that I have started by gently roughing in a
ground line and two wheel positions. I have also lined in a shoulder
height for the vehicle. The important thing to remember here is to
keep your line work fast and light. This way you can change and
move things around as the sketch progresses. A common mistake
when learning to sketch is starting a new drawing when you realise
something is out of place. Don't! Continue with the drawing, using the
mistake as a guide to sorting out the problem.

02 Here I have lightly marked in the rough proportions of the vehicle,
using a centre line and the window opening. When putting in the
centre line, try to avoid the temptation to shorten the overhangs too
much by bringing the front and the rear very close to the wheels.
Look at a photograph of a car in side view and you will see that the
corner of the vehicle falls somewhere in the space you are leaving. If
your vehicle has a lot of plan shape at the front or the rear, then you
will have to leave even more space.

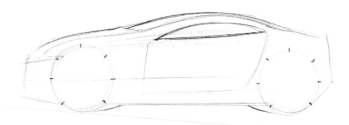

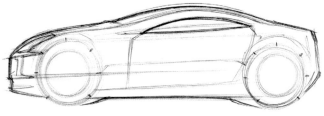

03 I have now defined the top edge of the bodywork from the rear
window, over the roof, and down to the front bumper. Remember
when drawing this line that it denotes the curvature over the roof
and through the two screens (when looking directly from in front or
behind the vehicle). For instance, you can see that the rear screen
has a little curvature, which flattens out into the roof (although not
completely flat), and then as the corner surface travels into the
windscreen, the curvature increases. You can see that the closer the
edge line is to the centre line, the less curvature is implied for the
surface between.

04 Once you are happy with the general shape and proportion, you
can begin to firm up some of the details (remembering, of course,
that it is only a sketch). I have added some light reflection lines in the
side window and down the body side. I have also defined the front
corner. Again the same rule applies here as when drawing the roof.
The further the corner is from the centre line of the front end, the
more curvature you are giving the front bumper in plan view (viewing
from above).

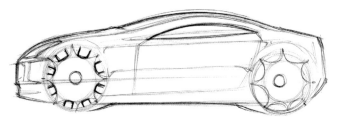

05 This is the final stage before applying colour. Here you can see I have firmed up all the details I am happy with and added some detail to the wheels. It is always worth putting a little bit of effort into getting the spacing reasonably correct on the wheel details since it will lift the look of your sketch a lot. Also important to note is that the sketch is still very loose and fast in its line work. This will only come through perseverance and practice.

06 When you are happy with the general design and proportions, you can begin to add colour. Here I have simply shaded the windows and wheels using a dark grey marker five or six. Note that this does not have to be super accurate. I have then further darkened the lower area of the windows and the front wheels, by letting the marker dry and going over the area again. The reason I have only darkened the front wheels further, and not the rears, is to help give the drawing a sense of movement. If you give all areas of your sketch the same weight and level of work, the final result can look very flat on the page.

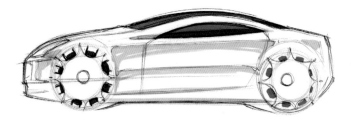

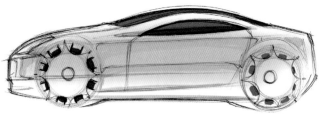

07 This is the stage where you will have to force yourself to not become precious about your sketch. Hopefully, you will now have a nice drawing on the paper, and to attack it in a loose and fast manner with a marker pen is not easy. These lines represent the scenery reflecting in the body side. You can see that I have continued the reflection in the window onto the bodywork and darkened down just beneath the shoulder. The area I have lightly marked halfway up the body side represents the horizon line, which is reflecting from behind the viewer. The important thing here is to be very loose and to keep your choice of marker very light.

08 This is probably the simplest part of the drawing, yet the one where you really see your sketch coming to life. Just choose a colour of pastel similar in colour to the previous marker work and apply it along the length of the bodywork, centring just beneath the shoulder line. Do not worry about going over the edges of the drawing.

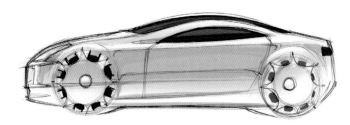

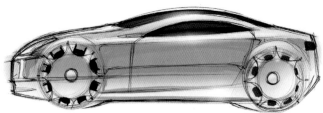

09 You are now in the final stage of the sketch and really just finishing off. Using an eraser and gently rubbing out all the areas where pastel has fallen on upwards-facing surfaces, you can really bring out the 3D form of your vehicle. This is the point you could stop. The drawing is now complete enough that anybody can look at it and get a good idea of the 3D form you are trying to describe. For a little bit of extra sparkle to the drawing, however, you will probably want to add the smallest hint of highlights.

10 By using an airbrush (this is easiest to do in Photoshop), you can brush a very quick faint line down through the bodywork. Then, on all the upward-facing surfaces it falls on, you can spray a light halo of white. Remember to be subtle here since you don't want to lose the definition of your surfaces—you only want to add that final bit of sparkle.

Courtesy Car Design News

Flat two-point perspective

While you are producing the side views we've just been describing, you will want to work out what is happening at the front and rear of the vehicle. To do this without resorting to a simple front or rear view, you will now have to begin sketching in two-point perspective. For these early sketches, however, you will not want to get too lost in trying to draw good perspective. Because of this, I like to sketch in a view I call flat perspective. Essentially, this is a car viewed at an angle but from down low so that all the convergence lines fall on the horizon line and through the centre of the vehicle.

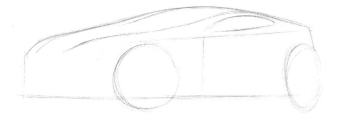

01 You start this drawing in a similar fashion to the side view, by sketching in a ground line and two wheels. You can see, however, that this time the rear wheel is at an angle. The more you want to see the front of the vehicle, the thinner this ellipse will be. Remember to sketch lightly, since you are now more likely to want to adjust things than when drawing a simple side view.

02 I have now added the profile of the vehicle. During this stage, I am lightly working out the rough proportions and theme of the vehicle. If at this point I want to adjust something, such as the position of the wheels, in order to fine-tune the proportion of the vehicle, then I can. By sketching lightly at this stage, you can make these adjustments without fear of spoiling your sketch. Take note of the way the centre line is most visible on the more vertical surfaces.

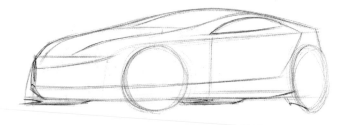

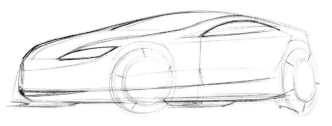

03 Here you can see that I have added the wheels from the far side of the car. A trick usually employed by designers is to exaggerate the position of the front wheel, putting it out in front of the car. This gives a dark background against which to emphasise the body shape of the bumper. At this stage I am still working things out and sketching lightly, making changes where necessary.

04 Once you are happy with your design and its proportions, you can begin to firm up the lines you want to emphasise. These are usually the lines that represent a strong graphic element of your design. Other lines, which represent changes in the body surface, should be left lighter, since you can emphasise these better with the use of colour and shading.

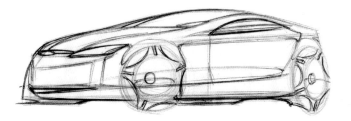

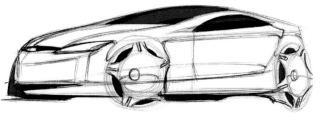

05 In this final stage before adding colour, you can see that I have drawn the final details and added some more light line work defining my surfaces a little better. Take note of things like how the shoulder highlight runs through the front wheel and down, becoming the corner of the bumper.

06 Now that you can begin to add colour to the design, the process is very similar to a side view sketch. You can see that I have used a dark grey marker, in a similar manner as with the side views, to colour all of the windows. The reason for using such a dark colour on these elements and a light colour on the bodywork is that it makes the sketch easier to read. At a glance, you can get a feel for the shape and graphic of the vehicle because of the strong contrast.

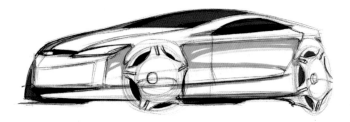

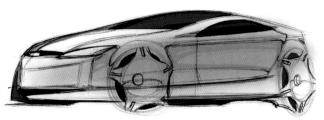

07 Following the same rules as in the side view sketch, you can now add a little light marker work representing reflections in the body side. Keep these simple and loose without adding too much marker. You can see that I have also shaded everything on the far side of the centre line (with the exception of the upward-facing surface on the bumper). This helps to emphasise the curvature of these surfaces and the general 3D feeling of the sketch.

08 This, as in the previous example, is the easiest part of the sketch. Just apply a quick brush of pastel along the body side of the vehicle.

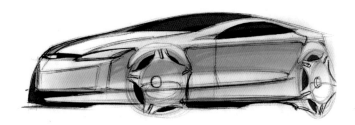

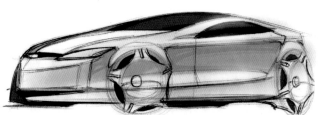

09 Using an eraser, I have now picked out all the upward-facing surfaces on the vehicle. This includes the surfaces of the spokes on the wheels. Try to be gentle when erasing against a line that represents a soft change in the body surface, since a sharply erased edge will obviously signify a sharp angle in the body.

10 Finally, you can if you wish add some gentle highlighting.

Courtesy Car Design News

Full two-point perspective

Proper two-point perspective is the hardest of the three examples here to get correct. For this reason I usually wait until I have a rough idea of my design before moving to this kind of view. It is, however, essential that you do learn to sketch using full two-point perspective, since sketching with simplified viewpoints does not allow you to fully resolve all the surfaces in a design. You can see in my initial sketch below that using this kind of perspective means that all parallel lines running both down the body side and across the front or the rear of

the vehicle will converge. This can make it hard to figure out how to draw things such as sloping shoulder lines. A good way to practise is to begin by sketching a simple cube or rectangle in perspective and then adding wheels at each corner. Once you are confident at this, you can begin to add simple forms to this box, building the drawing into a more car-like image. From there you can begin to disregard the box and only use the guidelines you feel will help you sketch your design.

01 I have started this sketch by drawing some simple guidelines, all showing the convergence of the parallel lines. Onto this I have sketched the wheels. You can see that, as explained earlier, the major axes of the ellipses are at right angles to the axle lines on the vehicle. Remember to sketch lightly here, as it is almost certain you will want to adjust your ellipses as the sketch progresses.

02 In the second step, I have built up a simple side surface for the vehicle. You can see how the shoulder line of the vehicle also creates the rear corner, creating a single surface down the side of the vehicle. It is usually easier to work in this way, working out the major surfaces before adding the smaller surface details, such as wheel arches. You can see I have also added the front shut line from the door to help me define this side surface.

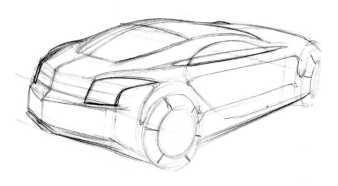

03 This stage is the hardest part of drawing in perspective. You must now work out how the surfaces you have drawn on the near side of the vehicle will appear on the far side. The important thing is that you understand the general rules and principles of perspective. From there you should practise sketching using only simple guidelines, which will ensure that the sketches remain fast, fluid, and spontaneous. It is usually helpful at this point to have some pictures of similar vehicles at the same angle of view on your desk that you can look at. As in the previous step, you can see that I have worked out all the major surfaces first. Also of note is the way the tumblehome (leaning inwards) of the side windows flattens out the far edge of the vehicle.

04 Once you are happy with the rough proportions and are confident you have got the major elements of the perspective correct, you can add the rest of the detail surfaces. Note how the centre line of the vehicle can be used to emphasise the treatment of the surfaces. You can also see that I have exaggerated the plan curve of the rear by putting the far side light almost out of sight around the corner of the body.

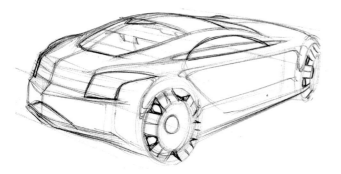

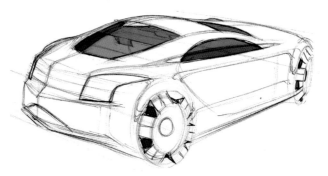

05 The final ballpoint stage is to add some interior and alloy wheel details to the drawing. When adding the interior details, you don't have to spend a lot of time, since all you want to do is give a suggestion of the shapes inside.

06 To shade the inside of the vehicle, I have used two grades of marker. With these two markers, you can achieve four tones of colour. By using only two grades of dark grey, you can help keep the change in shades very subtle. If you half shut your eyes and look at the sketch, you should read the whole window and not each separate shade. The same should be true after you have applied the colour to the bodywork, which is why you should choose a reasonably dark colour for your windows and a light one for the bodywork (or vice versa).

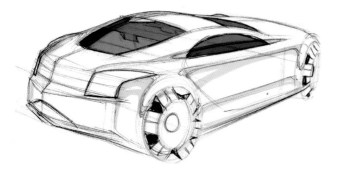

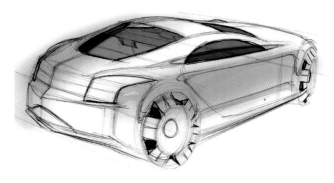

07 Remembering to keep things simple, you can now add a light-coloured marker to the bodywork. You can see that I have also added a little marker at the furthest edge of the vehicle. You could also try blocking in every surface on the far side of the centre line except the upwards-facing ones, as shown in the flat two-point perspective sketch.

08 It can be easy to overcomplicate the pastel work when shading a two-point perspective sketch, since you try to correctly shade every surface. I always try to resist this temptation and try to use only two dominant areas of colour. The first one passes down the body side of your vehicle just as in the side view sketch, whilst the second goes on the far surfaces. This leaves a core of brightness running through the surfaces closest to the viewer, which helps give the sketch a strong 3D feel.

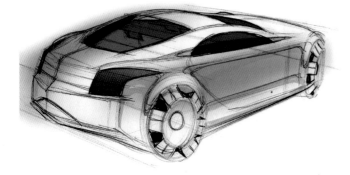

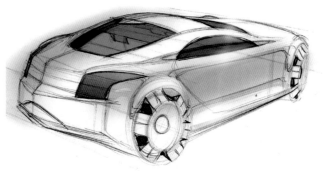

09 The last two stages are quick and simple. Add a quick bit of red marker or pencil to the rear lights and erase the pastel from the up-facing surfaces just as in both previous examples . . .

10 . . . and finally add the little bit of airbrush shine.

Courtesy Car Design News

Tutorial: Rendering in Photoshop By Cor Steenstra
Introduction

During sketch development I find that I understand what I would like to 'sculpture' in my design from the section lines I draw as a base, as well as from 'leaving out' areas. However, if you want this to come across to the people making the decisions, you need something that stands out and jumps off the wall in a presentation.

Traditionally I would create presentation sketches by using the base sketch as an underlay, over which I would then draw the clean lines, and would put some marker and pastel on it to to express the 3D form. However, if you did this quickly, it would look too sketchy,

and if you did it properly it would actually become an elaborate rendering and be quite time consuming. Another risk would be that in 'cleaning up' the linework, some of the character of the original concept sketch would be lost.

Without trying to take any importance away from traditional art methodologies, these days it is possible to use the original sketch to make quick and eye-catching artwork that not only represents the original raw design ideas to the max, but also does the job of jumping off the wall during a presentation. A good sell.

The following pages show a step-by-step process for quickly creating a presentation rendering...

Start by scanning in a sketch that you want to use. The scanner should generally be set to give an image size in pixels of 1024x768 to 1600x1200 (or larger) depending on your working screen size, and planned print size.

It doesn't matter if the car was sketched on excellent marker paper or on a napkin at 'In-n-Out Burger.' It only needs to be just the thing you like and you want to present. Import the scan into Photoshop, duplicate the layer, clear the background layer, and set the transparency of the copied layer to 35 percent. This way you can see the sketch, still have a white background, and make the underlay sketch invisible once you're finished.

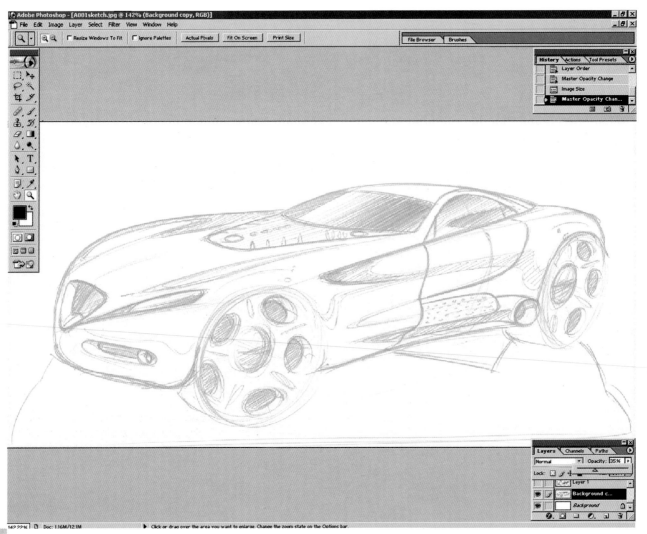

Block in the basic colours with 200-300 size airbrushes. In this case the car was going to be red, and I like using the warm and cold sides of the real world in my sketches to enhance the sculpture. Apply broad strokes of airbrush, and then simply erase the areas that form the hard reflections manually. This gives a more spontaneous effect and is quick.

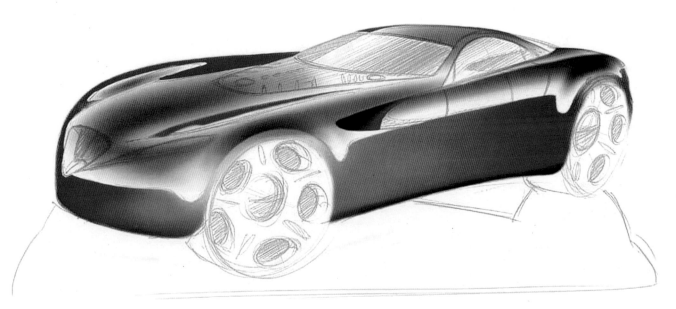

On a new layer again quickly airbrush the soft sky reflections, also here using the warm and cold colours. And again manually erase the overflow of airbrush. Set the eraser to Airbrush and use at 65-100 opacity. Working on a separate layer enables you to erase these areas with a large soft eraser brush, while leaving the hard reflection areas undisturbed, and all without any masking.

Similarly build up the warm and cool glass reflections on their own
layers, using a large airbrush, followed by a hard-edged eraser brush
to redefine the edges. Initially use the colours lightly, then duplicate
that layer and erase the highlight parts of the interior off of the first
glass layer. This way it seems you can look through the car, which
enhances the realism.

This is the time to put the car on the ground. Make a quick path in
the path tools menu, and adjust it to fit the area of shadow marked
off in the sketch. In the path menu save this path, go to 'Make
Selection' with a zero Feather, and go to the layer menu to make a
new layer. On this layer you fill the selection with the background
color you want, and here I have added a few brush strokes in
different colors to add warmth.

Subsequently put in the wheels, so the car sits properly. You can usually colour the wheels you had sketched, but for enhanced realism you can quickly take some wheels/tires rendered in Alias and use these. Also you can use images of wheels/tires from existing cars, but if these are very recognizable or don't suit your overall design it may not help you.

In the lower segments of the body sides and the front you may want to add some soft sculpture to enhance the expression of the vehicle. Simply make a new layer, and play with black and white soft airbrush, then alter the transparency of this new layer to get the desired effect. Again, using separate layers for each of these elements drastically reduces your workload, as no masking is required, and you can experiment safely without affecting underlying layers.

Again use the path tool to draw some clean cut lines on a separate layer.

For this project we wanted to use existing headlights to reduce costs, so you can make several variations with different headlights. On this example they obviously stem from a Mercedes-Benz.

And add the corporate graphics to create the final result.

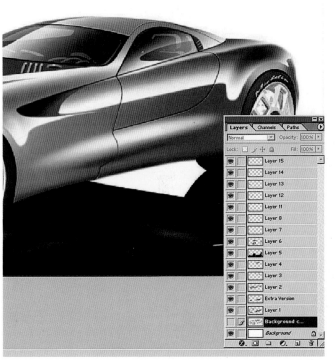

As you can see at left, it took quite a few layers, but that makes it easy to make corrections afterwards, and eliminates the need for masking. This color sketch took about 45 minutes, but this can vary of course depending on the level of detail.

Though I have clearly used the new digital technologies, the technique is built upon experiences I gained earlier in using vellum paper, marker and pastel. I think you have to go through this stage of traditional techniques before you can successfully optimize your digital workflow and not end up with generic-looking impersonal artwork. In that same respect, I use all of my clay modeling experience in making my Alias models. Again, being familiar with both traditional workflows and the new digital methods is something you *have* to do to be most effective in your design work.

Cor Steenstra is a graduate of the Royal College of Art, and is Director of Design for Foresee Car Design, located in California and Gibraltar. http://4c-foresee.com/

Computer Aided Design

While good sketching techniques remain the foundation of any car design, these days the successful transformation of initial sketches into the digital domain has become critical to the modern car design process.

The use of digital design techniques has revolutionised the car industry because it enables designers to create digital prototypes of future concept and production vehicles, visualise them in different environments, and even interact with them without ever having to undertake a costly and time-consuming model-building process. What's more, these digital prototypes can also be utilised to generate engineering data to be used, ultimately, in the creation of production tools for manufacturing. This means car manufacturers can explore a complete product in a virtual world before it is built for real.

Computer Aided Design software (CAD) can be used at a number of key stages in the design development process—creation, validation, optimisation and design management—from the conceptual phase through to the manufacturing process. By using a digital prototype, manufacturers can visualise and simulate the real-world performance of the design with less reliance on costly and vulnerable physical prototypes.

Before such technology existed, modellers would build models from 3D sketches. This process is still used in the car industry today but digital prototyping techniques have reduced the need to make as many models as before. Models often require time-consuming reworking to incorporate subsequent design changes and, thanks to digital modelling, some of this reworking of designs has been reduced.

The use of digital techniques blends the creative artistry of design with the cold, hard efficiencies of mathematical computer engineering data. This offers a number of advantages: the process is quicker, allowing vehicles to be brought to market with shorter lead times, thus saving man-hours and expense. Second, changes to the design—and the resulting data—can be undertaken quickly and "tweaks" can be carried out as often as a design director decides. Similarly, a larger number of potential designs can be explored "virtually" before "sign off" of a successful design, allowing a much greater freedom for creative exploration while also increasing design productivity.

These tools are also highly useful in terms of workflow. Today's car design process is complex and multifaceted. For example, it is not unusual for an exterior design to be done in California while an interior for the same vehicle is done in Frankfurt. Digital design allows teams to share designs for review as they develop.

The most popular CAD software packages are Adobe Photoshop and Autodesk's Alias Automotive, which are used by the majority of

automotive manufacturers worldwide. They can be used to design and visualise full-scale automotive projects from initial concept sketches to Class-A (visible to the customer) surfacing. Autodesk also produces a range of products including sketching tools and rendering and visualisation software for use at different stages of the design development process.

Hand-drawn sketches can be imported to Autodesk Alias Automotive, where the design and form can be defined from the initial concept sketches through to Class-A surfacing. Alternatively, sketches can be created digitally on a computer using software such as Autodesk Sketchbook Pro with a digitised pen tablet such as a Wacom tablet. Using software such as this, designers can sketch entirely digitally if they so wish, without having to switch between pen and PC. Virtual modellers can take a design and model it using Alias Surface software which allows the 3D modelling of concept models using scanned data—such as from a full-size clay—to create high-quality Class-A surfaces.

At the end of this process, the models can be visualised for review in different virtual environments. Designers can take the 3D CAD data that has been created from their initial sketches and transform them into visually realistic images. Software such as Autodesk Maya allows advanced rendering (adding colour, texture and light and shade), modelling and animation to create hyper-realistic virtual environments. Autodesk Showcase or Bunkspeed Drive allow visualisation so that images can be projected and animated on very large screens—known as powerwalls—and are realistic enough to show "real" reflections and other physical properties.

Although this process is linear, designers can drop in and out to rework a design at any stage using such software. This is something that can happen countless times in a real world working automotive design studio.

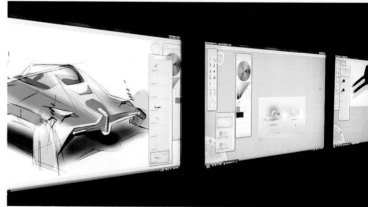

Common Software: A Brief Overview

Adobe Photoshop

Surprisingly, the most common software used to digitally create automotive designs is Adobe Photoshop, an application which was never developed specifically for vehicle design use. Photoshop has been adopted by car designers due to the ease with which 2D sketches can be scanned and then manipulated within the digital space. Once the original sketch has been scanned into the computer, the artwork can then be modified.

From there, individual designers may then work in different ways. Most build layers and use different path tools and filters within Photoshop so they can manipulate and explore different forms and textures—using shading and colouring techniques—as well as creating key vehicle elements such as wheel designs. They can also generate backgrounds and add the finishing touches of soft highlights and reflections to ensure their design looks realistic. In the hands of an experienced designer this process is quick and efficient.

Autodesk SketchBook Pro

This painting and drawing application is in essence a digital replacement for the traditional pen and pencil sketching techniques. Rather than creating designs on paper and scanning into the computer, vehicle designs can be created using digitized pen tablets and tablet PCs—versions even exist for Apple's iPhone and iPad.

The advantage is that automotive designers can generate designs without having to switch from pen to keyboard and back again and without the need to scan their work. Some designers are beginning to favour this method over pen-based sketching, although the more traditional method is considered the purist approach.

Autodesk Alias Automotive

Autodesk Alias Automotive software provides a more comprehensive range of visualisation tools for vehicle design. Using Autodesk Alias Automotive, designers can control their designs further into the car development process. Vehicle designs can be refined to generate production-quality and reusable NURBS surfaces for engineering: real mathematical data that can be utilised for the actual production development or prototyping.

Autodesk Alias Surface

Autodesk Alias Surface software offers a full set of dynamic 3D modelling capabilities that enable virtual modellers to evolve concept models and scan data into high-quality Class-A surfaces for automotive design and styling.

Autodesk Maya

Originally developed for the movie and entertainment industries—recent computer-animated films made with Maya software include Avatar, Ice Age, Pan's Labyrinth and Spider-Man 3—Maya is increasingly used for the animation and simulation of car designs. By using advanced visual effects designs can be rendered inside simulated environments for review or for use in marketing and promotional media, such as putting a concept car into a 'life like' urban driving environment, when (of course) the car has never been there, and in fact doesn't even have an engine to power it.

Autodesk Showcase

Created for design managers who need to show design work to executive management, Autodesk's Showcase software allows designers to take their 3D CAD data and transform it into visually realistic images for management review. Car companies are making more and more decisions digitally where in the past such major decisions would be dependent on viewing full size clay models. On a powerwall a design can be shown in extremely high definition. It also allows for different background environments to be generated; to see how paint may affect the look of a vehicle under different lighting conditions; to see how reflections may affect a vehicle's lines and even how changing a vehicle's colour may affect the perception of its form. All these changes can be made quickly so that management can review them quickly, too, enhancing the decision-making process.

Bunkspeed Drive

Bunkspeed Drive is used for automotive and transportation design visualisation, whether for design review or for marketing communication. Designs can be manipulated for realistic presentation in create driving animations with near photographic 'realism', so that reflections and other physical properties can be better understood using a powerwall or other full screen presentation method.

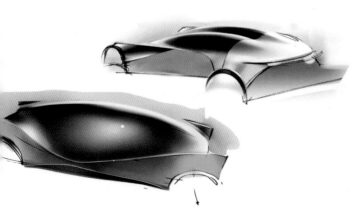

CHAPTER 14

DESIGN AND THE GREAT
designers

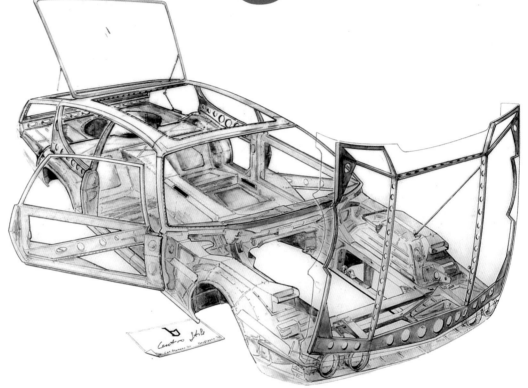

Automotive design, as a distinct and recognised discipline separate from engineering, is considered to have truly begun with Harley Earl at General Motors in 1927.

Before Earl, the process of automotive production followed similar lines in both Europe and North America. Carmakers placed no particular value on the way their vehicles looked and instead focused on volume manufacturing, usually producing either of two types of vehicle. First was the mass produced car for the everyman, with Henry Ford's Model T the most famous example. These vehicles offered simple functionality, affordability, and reliability; they were certainly not styled in any meaningful way. The second type were bespoke luxury cars for the wealthy. For these carmakers built only the mechanical elements of the car—such as the chassis and drivetrain—before handing it over to an independent coachbuilder for "dressing"; in most cases the buyer chose the form or style of

bodywork. It wasn't until the arrival of Alfred P. Sloan as president of General Motors in 1923 that these two worlds began to fuse.

The late 1920s saw the beginnings of the transformation of the motor car from an object of democratising utility to an aspirational, desirable and emotional status symbol. By the beginning of the 1920s, the Model T had begun to look outmoded. Its democratic and uniform utility was becoming increasingly less attractive in the face of a more diverse product offering from GM. American car buyers no longer wanted a car that everyone else could own; instead they wanted an automobile that allowed them to differentiate themselves from their peers. Under Sloan's leadership, GM set out to provide a "car for every purse and purpose," selling a wide range of products instead of a single cheap and standardised model. Sloan invented planned obsolescence, a strategy to encourage car owners to buy new models by having GM designers undertake annual model

restylings that effectively rendered their predecessors out of date. The business of car design had begun. In essence GM's planned obsolescence is the model by which the automotive industry has created automobiles ever since.

Here we list who we consider to be the most influential designers of the last 100 years. Their work is some of the best the world has seen, but more than that they all share one common trait: Their influence has been wide-ranging and has moved automotive design, and often automotive manufacturing, forwards in fundamental, often unexpected, ways.

Harley Earl (1893–1969)

It is largely thanks to **Harley Earl (inset)** that the discipline of automotive styling exists as we know it today. Earl cut his teeth styling cars for Hollywood movie stars at his father's coachbuilding company, Earl Automotive Works. His designs—and his use of modelling clay to create them—so impressed GM that the automaker brought him on board to add some drama and glamour to the company's designs. The result was the 1927 **Cadillac LaSalle**, which was visually innovative thanks to its elegant long and low shape and quite different from any production car that preceded it. Harley Earl's LaSalle was essentially the first production car to be styled rather than just engineered and manufactured.

The car's success led GM to create an Art and Color Division— later renamed the Styling Division—with Earl as its first director. During his three-decade career at GM, Earl made the company a world leader in car design and styling while defining the car design process and its use of the 2D sketch, modelling clay, the full-size clay model, and the concept car. It is ironic, considering that he was the son of coachbuilder, that Earl's revolutionary work would ultimately signal the beginning of the end for coachbuilding as automakers began to take more and more creative responsibility in house.

Battista Pininfarina (Born Farina, 1893–1966)

Founder of Carrozzeria Pininfarina, **Battista "Pinin" Farina** (inset) will be forever linked with postwar European sports car design, especially for Ferrari.

His work streamlining cars for Alfa Romeo (6C 2300 B Berlinetta Aerodinamica, 1935) and Lancia (Aprilla, 1937) set Pininfarina on a path to evolve aerodynamic simplicity, producing designs that were devoid of clutter and free flowing in form. The lack of chrome and any other elaborate decorative elements in his designs gave his cars clarity and purity. His 1947 **Cisitalia 202 sports Berlinetta** design, is for many, Battista's crowning glory.

By the 1950s Pininfarina was penning what would become the most classic of Ferrari's designs, combining aerodynamic form with simple aesthetics. Over the course of the 1950s and 1960s, designs including the 250 GT Spyder (1957), 250 GT Berlinetta (1961), **250 GT** (1963), and the Dino 206 GT would establish Pininfarina as Ferrari's premier designer and forever link the names of the two companies.

Raymond Loewy (1893–1986)

He may have come up with the Shell logo, the Lucky Strike cigarette packet, and a number of streamlined locomotives, but it is for his automotive design that industrial designer **Raymond Loewy** is most celebrated.

Loewy's car design career began in 1934 working for the Hupp Motor Company, designing the Hupmobile. Loewy introduced streamlining by integrating the headlights and spare wheel housing in order to give the vehicle a sleek and attractive form, eliminating any protruding elements. Though interrupted by World War II, Loewy's automotive design continued with Studebaker. In 1947, Studebaker launched the **Champion**, which featured a far more exotic and European (Italian) look compared to most other American cars. The Champion had sculpted, clean lines; flush fenders and doors; and a tapering rear end. Overall, it was a very restrained look, with a notable lack of chrome used on the exterior. This was to be Loewy's legacy: the creation of smooth, simplified, sculptural body forms, with few seams and a minimum of fuss.

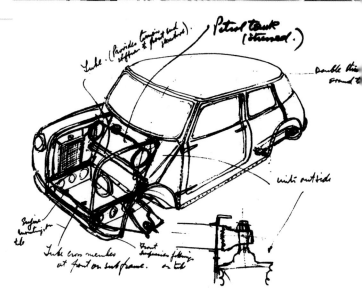

Alec Issigonis (1906–1988)

Though employed as a car designer, **Alec Issigonis** was actually a trained draftsman and engineer; his background imbued him with a practical understanding of the complete car and gave him a pragmatic and problem-solving approach to designing them. Creator of the Morris Minor and the **BMC Mini**, Issigonis' work wasn't driven by the desire to create beautiful cars. Instead, his BMC Mini design was created to develop a fuel-efficient vehicle in light of harsh fuel rationing after the Suez Crisis and partly to create a more practical rival to the increasing popularity of bubble cars in the UK. Issigonis was briefed to come up with the smallest car that four people could travel in with luggage, using minimal fuel. He mounted the Mini's engine sideways (transversely), pushed the car's four unusually small wheels into the corners as far as possible, and located the gearbox under the engine in the sump. By rearranging these key elements, Issigonis was able to maximise interior space. Despite the utilitarian approach—the Mini essentially wasn't styled but was a practically engineered solution to a very specific problem—it went on to become a sixties style icon. Its timeless design meant that the car stayed in production until 2000, and it remains the best-selling British car in history. Issigonis' solution was so innovative it has influenced car design ever since. The box-like design has become the basis for almost all small front-wheel drive cars designed in the past half century.

Streamlining

Raymond Loewy wasn't the first to explore ideas in streamlining or streamforming—far from it. As early as 1913, Giuseppe Merosi at Castagna created a streamlined, teardrop-shaped body on an Alfa chassis. Streamlining started with a series of one-off vehicles, but it wasn't until the 1930s that the streamlining movement could be considered to have truly begun. In the United States, consumers were fascinated by it, perceiving it as being at the forefront of modernity, human progress, and speed, despite the fact that in car design aerodynamics were essentially symbolic. During this time, designers, including Norman Bel Geddes, William Bushnell Stout and Paul Jaray, penned cars including the Motor Car Number 1 (1928), Stout Scarab (1935), and **Tatra 77** (1934), but it was Carl Breer's Chrysler Airflow (1934) that is, arguably, the most attractive. By World War II the movement was pretty much over, but the legacy of streamlining remains in the form of the unified body shell with a minimum of protuberances—a characteristic that has become the norm on all modern cars.

Nuccio Bertone (1914–1997)

One of history's greatest designers was in fact not a car designer but an extremely clever businessman. **Nuccio Bertone** was a design genius not because of the cars he designed, but for the way in which he managed his father's coachbuilding business when he took over the running of Carrozzeria Bertone in 1952. Realising that the future of Bertone did not lie in coachbuilding for individual clients or in small production runs, he committed himself to the styling of cars for automotive customers. Some of the most memorable car designs of the second half of the twentieth century originated at Bertone, cars like the BAT (Berlina Aerodinamica Technica) cars of **1953**, 1954, and 1955; **Lamborghini Miura**, Espada, and Countach; as well as other icons of design, the Lancia Stratos and Fiat Dino coupé. But, along with the BAT cars, it is the Alfa Romeo Giulietta Sprint that is most closely associated with Nuccio Bertone. The car went on to become the Italian GT car—it was fabulous and affordable—and although Alfa had only expected to build a few hundred cars, the design was so successful Bertone went on to build almost 40,000 of their bodies for Alfa. The Giulietta Sprint marked the transformation of Carrozzeria Bertone from a craft-scale producer to an industrial manufacturer of vehicles.

Nuccio Bertone was also an insightful developer of design talent. He understood what great design was and had a gut feeling for what made a great designer, encouraging those qualities in his stable. Two of the greatest car designers in history—Giorgetto Giugiaro and Marcello Gandini—began their careers under his watchful and influential eye. According to the Automotive News Automotive Hall of Fame, Nuccio Bertone once declared, "A car is the product of a feeling, or rather, a series of feelings. The most important of these is the sense of wonder and surprise generated by the form of the vehicle. If a car fails to fill me with this sense of wonder at first sight, I am almost certain that it will not be a success."

Bill Mitchell (1912–1988)

In many ways, **Bill Mitchell's** designs represent the very best of classic American car design. It was Mitchell who penned the 1959 Chevrolet Corvair, the 1963 Chevrolet Corvette **Sting Ray**, and the 1967 Pontiac Firebird. Mitchell's work, unlike much US car design of the period, was not inspired by aircraft or space-age fantasy. Instead Mitchell, who was hired by Harley Earl, believed that design belonged to the car alone and took American car design beyond elaborate chrome and fantastic fins, a period that many believe was America's weakest.

It was under Mitchell that cars evolved to a cleaner and more minimal styling. Perhaps the car that best defines his approach and that was his greatest achievement is the Corvette Sting Ray. Rather than endow the car with chrome and jewellery to add interest, Mitchell took the inspirational form of the mako shark. The result was a clean, low, flat, and streamlined appearance that quite literally resembled the creature it was inspired by. It is also undoubtedly one of the finest, most exciting, and best-loved car designs of all time. At a time when American cars had become ostentatious and garish, Bill Mitchell ensured US car design was beautiful again. He proved that automotive sculpture, when executed exactly, can provide all of the drama and excitement a vehicle needs.

Coachbuilding in France

It is perhaps unsurprising that the link between automobiles and fashion first occurred in Paris. Between the world wars, the work of the French *carrossiers* led the world in automotive high fashion. Coachbuilders including Saoutchik, Facel, Figoni & Falaschi, and Chapron created elegant bodies for Bugatti, Cadillac, Daimler, **Mercedes-Benz**, and Rolls-Royce. The cars were extravagant, making use of materials that would ultimately come to define automotive luxury: chrome, leather, and highly exotic woods. But by the end of World War II, the growing influence of mass car ownership and changing practices in construction meant that the French coachbuilding industry was all but dead. The automakers turned to the Italians as they adapted their methods to meet the demands of volume production.

Bruno Sacco (born 1933)

After unsuccessful attempts to join the Italian *carrozzerie*, **Bruno Sacco** joined Daimler-Benz as a stylist in 1958. By 1975 he was head of the Daimler-Benz styling centre and from then on influenced every Mercedes product until his retirement in 1999. Today he is considered one of the car industry's greatest designers.

At Mercedes, Sacco created a culture of continuity in design. He developed visual relationships using common styling cues to create a family resemblance across all Mercedes vehicles, a resemblance that still defines Mercedes design today. At the same time, he created a process by which no succeeding car would render its predecessors stylistically obsolete. The result was timeless design, most seminally seen in his **Mercedes-Benz 190 (1982)**, considered to be his best. What's more, he was able to do this even during the vast expansion that Mercedes lineup underwent in the 1990s. Today such an approach is common, particular amongst German manufacturers.

Marcello Gandini (born 1938)

One of Stile Bertone's most famous chief designers, **Marcello Gandini (top, with Nuccio Bertone)** succeeded Giorgetto Giugiaro in 1965. He went on to create a number of exotic cars, both concept and production, including Lamborghini's Miura and **Countach**; these are considered to be two of the most influential supercars in history. Gandini famously introduced the idea of scissor doors on the Alfa Romeo 33 Carabo prototype, which was fantastically space age when it was introduced in 1968. The scissor doors would inspire his Countach design, which at its launch in 1974 was quite unlike any car yet produced. It was highly unusual due to its great width, short length and low height, as well as its wedge shape of sharp, trapezoidal panels that are almost entirely devoid of curves. The Countach remains a design icon, despite the fact that ergonomically it was problematic, dynamically performed less well than it should have, and was almost impossible to reverse due to the scissor doors and poor visibility. It was quite simply outrageous, and for many people it remains the definitive Lamborghini. Gandini did design far more practical family cars as well, including the Citroën BX and the first-generation BMW 5 Series, but it is for his Lamborghini designs that he will always be remembered, along with the magnificent **Lancia Stratos**. Gandini gave the world the wedge-shaped and cab-forward design seen in so many sports cars since.

Giorgetto Giugiaro (born 1938)

Giorgetto Giugiaro is quite simply the greatest and most auspicious vehicle designer the automobile business has so far produced. He has designed more cars than any other designer in history, and his work is not only prolific but also commercially successful. His creations stem from his exemplarily understanding of engineering and sculptural form, having had a background in both. More than any other designer, Giugiaro has the ability to create beautiful cars based on his practical understanding of the requirements of engineering. The result is a long and distinguished career that has seen him create some of the most significant designs of all time, including the Audi 80; Alfa Romeo Alfasud; **BMW M1**; Fiat Panda, Uno, and Punto; **Lotus Esprit**; Lamborghini Gallardo; Lancia Delta; and Volkswagen Golf/Rabbit and Scirocco. Each of these has moved the automotive form forward significantly at different points in motoring history.

Giugiaro was the first to develop a highly successful problem-solving approach to car design—his so-called Giugiaro method—which called for evolving a car design without detriment to practical requirements, resulting in cars being simultaneously practical, comfortable, and attractive. Credited with initiating the folded paper era of the 1970s, when cars like his Lotus Esprit, VW Golf and Lancia Delta were created with sharp edges, Giugiaro also began the trend toward taller cars to increase interior space, seen in his Panda and Uno designs for Fiat. He also created the forerunner to the modern minivan segment with his minivan concept Megagamma in 1978. Without Giugiaro, the modern automobile would not be as inventive and imaginative as it now is.

J Mays (born 1954)

Whether he likes it or not, if one man can be associated with the retro or heritage design movement of the 1990s, it must be J Mays. His most famous designs are the Audi Avus concept (1991) and the Volkswagen Beetle Concept 1, but his influence can also be seen in the 2002 Ford Thunderbird, 2003 **Ford GT**, and 2005 **Ford Mustang**. Mays' Audi Avus harkened back to the excitement of the German Grand Prix race cars of the 1930s, and its form led directly to the development of the Audi TT, which is already considered a twentieth century design classic. Mays' reinterpretation of the classic Beetle—created to reboot interest in a flagging VW brand in the United States—was so well received it entered production in 1998.

Mays' designs looked back to the heritage of each brand, selecting the elements that resonated emotionally with car buyers and creating contemporary designs that exploited those emotions. His later work for Ford—specifically his Thunderbird, the Forty-Nine concept car and, most significantly, the Mustang (2005)—again successfully looked to the past to influence forward-looking designs. The results are still controversial. Many question how successful these vehicles remain over the passage of time. Regardless of one's viewpoint, there is no doubt that the way in which Mays approached his work has had a lasting effect on contemporary car design.

Chris Bangle (born 1956)

American designer Chris Bangle's career in car design has seen him become one of the most celebrated—and also reviled—designers in recent automotive history. After starting his career at Opel, he moved on to Fiat where he served as chief designer for the **Fiat Coupé**. Most famously known for leading BMW Group design through one of its most controversial periods, Bangle introduced flame surfacing to the Bavarian manufacturer, and the entire BMW lineup currently bears signatures of his work. Bangle's most controversial design was the **E65 7 Series**, introduced in 2001. A dramatic contrast to its more conservatively styled predecessor, it was named one of the 50 worst cars of all time by *Time* magazine. And yet it was also the best-selling 7 Series in BMW history. The design language that Bangle created for BMW was so individualistic that some of his peers suggested he had thrown the baby out with the bath water, in design terms. In an interview with *Business Week* magazine, Bangle was quoted as saying, "We aren't copying anyone else's design language, not even our own, and I think that makes some people uncomfortable." This type of deconstruction in automotive design had never been attempted on such a scale before.

Regardless of the relative merits of his designs, Bangle's work at BMW made him the most talked-about car designer in modern history, and there is absolutely no doubt that his work had a fundamental influence on automotive design. Ford's design director Martin Smith called Bangle's flame surfacing style "surface entertainment," and the American's lasting influence can be seen in the fact that surface entertainment can now be seen across the vehicle ranges of a number of automakers.

CONCEPT CARS THAT TRANSFORMED
car design

Many major advances in car design can be traced back to visionary concept models penned by imaginative designers. Few of these forward-looking show cars were fully understood when first unveiled; some were even greeted with shock or puzzlement, but all would go on to have a profound influence on the cars we buy and drive.

Briggs/Ford V-8, 1933

When Ford took this car along to a 1934 Chicago exhibition entitled "A Century of Progress," it was instigating a research method entirely new to the automotive industry. Engineers, company founders, entrepreneurs and crackpots had long been happy to demonstrate their spluttering prototypes at any public forum where an ogling crowd might be drawn. This time, though, Ford was carefully showcasing a design it might, or might not, proceed with; the decision would depend on the reaction from bystanders. This makes the Briggs the first concept car in the form we know it today—a non-functioning but, in all other ways, realistic representation of a car for the near (or distant) future.

Its origins, however, were from outside Ford. It was the work of the chief production design engineer of its Detroit supplier Briggs Body Company, John Tjaarda. Briggs had two important clients, Chrysler and Ford, and in 1932 Ford had complained it was being treated as a second-class customer at a time when Briggs was deep in collaboration with Chrysler on the upcoming Chrysler Airflow. Tjaarda's task was to claw back Ford's goodwill with presentations that showed how its own products could evolve. Since the late 1920s, he had studied a rear/mid-engined, aerodynamically proficient sedan called the Sterkenburg (after his town of birth, in Holland), and as Edsel Ford declared himself impressed by them, Tjaarda and Briggs turned these designs into running prototypes, using custom-made aluminium Ford V-8 engines.

The car shown in Chicago was an all-metal mockup intended to gauge reaction to its radical styling. Ford employed pollsters to mingle with showgoers and, on their clipboards, to record audience response to this startling exhibit. The feedback reflected the attitude of the wider American public to aerodynamic cars like the Chrysler Airflow: They were not keen on a low-set sloping nose without a radiator grille. And, in this case, they *definitely* didn't like the idea of an engine positioned behind the rear seats.

However, the character line of Tjaarda's design survived to form the basis of the 1936 Lincoln Zephyr, with the faired-in headlamps and much of the streamlined side profile remaining intact. It's a genesis that has become routine throughout the car design world.

Rover Jet 1, 1950

The crowds thronging the Festival of Britain exhibition on London's South Bank in 1951 probably sensed that, despite the bleak aftermath of World War II, Britain's motor industry was on top of its game. For here, on display, was a car demonstrating Britain had the technology and ingenuity to out-do both America and Europe.

It was Rover's Jet 1, a name echoed by its JET 1 number plate—the world's first gas turbine car. It's an interesting early example of adapting the lightly modified silhouette of a familiar production car as a showcase for groundbreaking alternative power technology; the open two-seater body used panels recognisable from the Rover 75 sedan. But as a jet-propelled car, it really did work, and it offered seamless power delivery.

Harold Hastings, of *The Motor* magazine, was among the few outsiders to drive it. "With a peculiar and rather eerie high-pitched whistle just behind my left ear, I cautiously pressed the accelerator," he wrote in 1955. "I was just about to ask what was wrong when I realised that, almost imperceptibly, we had begun to move."

In 1952, the car established a new record at 151.96 miles per hour for the flying kilometre; although other companies would build turbine cars too, none would pursue the technology as doggedly as Rover, with its experimental programme stretching into the mid-1960s.

For the tight-knit Jet 1 project team, led by Spencer King and Frank Bell, there were numerous engineering obstacles: The engine turned at 26,000 rpm, five times higher than most normal car engines in the early 1950s; it was air-cooled; and turbines have no internal engine braking. These were overcome, but two problems proved insurmountable: greedy fuel consumption (typically 5 miles per gallon) and the huge costs of making such an engine. These inherent drawbacks have never been solved by carmakers, and there's no imperative so to do.

Yet Jet 1 was such a useful publicity tool for Rover that its bodywork was updated to bring it into line with the evolving detail styling of the well-liked P4 sedan range—a real example of making a concept car earn its keep. Jet 1 is, today, a prized exhibit in London's Science Museum.

General Motors LeSabre, 1951

The 1951 LeSabre, the first significant postwar concept car from General Motors, would exert a huge influence on mainstream products from the company for the remainder of the decade.

Described pithily by one commentator as "a full-blown aero-military fantasy," it reflected the fascination with fighter aircraft that gripped GM's legendary design head Harley J. Earl. The Lockheed P-38 was a firm favourite of his, so was the Douglas Skyray.

The wraparound panoramic windscreen, later a GM production car signature, was a personal triumph for Earl, as he insisted that glazing engineers come up with what they said was impossible; even then, the handmade screen gave enough distortion as to make driving the LeSabre positively dangerous.

The car certainly did drive. Earl worked closely with Buick chief engineer Charles Chayne to make the LeSabre a "laboratory on wheels." It boasted a supercharged V-8 engine, air brakes, a rain sensor that automatically raised the roof when the driver was absent, and dual fuel tanks so that petrol supplied from one could be boosted with methanol from the other under hard acceleration. Earl no doubt was proud to show off these features at the country clubs he frequented because he used the LeSabre as his personal transport for several years. As the car cost some $1 million to create, that might have been regarded as an enormous abuse of

privilege, but it could be easily justified by the amount of attention the LeSabre garnered.

However, the entire credit for LeSabre cannot be accorded to Earl alone. The leader of GM's special automobile design studio, Edward Glowacke, was the visionary behind the stacked bullet taillights, the pointed "warheads" of the front bumpers, the puckered oval grille, and much of the fancy detail of the cockpit. The LeSabre began the countdown to 1954 and the Firebird series of concepts, where Earl's fighter jet obsession really took off.

Bertone/Chevrolet Testudo, 1963

In the United States in 1963, the Chevrolet Corvair was making a name for itself . . . for all the wrong reasons. This mainstream compact car with its flat-six engine in the back like a Volkswagen Beetle's would shortly be vilified for its poor crashworthiness and handling, to the immense embarrassment of General Motors.

But the Corvair proved alluring to those in awe of race car technology, a discipline that had benefited from the migration of the engine to a position behind the driver. Chevrolet's own Corvair Monza

GT was a 1962 show car intended to capitalise on this, packaging the Corvair's rear-biased drivetrain in a two-seater GT notable for a cockpit accessed through a single canopy that hinged forwards, taking the windscreen with it.

This obviously fired the imagination of management at Italy's Bertone, as the signature feature of the 1963 Testudo was the very same. The windscreen, glass roof, and doors all hinged forward as a giant, one-piece canopy to admit driver and passenger. The lack of windscreen pillars was matched by an extremely slender instrument panel set into the dashboard, where the main feature was a prominent grab handle for the passenger.

Impressively, the Testudo was conceived and constructed in a mere two months, from January to March 1963, at which point it was exhibited at the Geneva Motor Show. There, it caused a wave of excitement. Its smooth and aerodynamic form was the work of a promising young designer named Giorgio Giugiaro, an as-yet unknown who was, nonetheless, the force behind Bertone's influential output since the departure of Franco Scaglione.

The Testudo's very low frontal area, eliminating the radiator grille and with headlights that swivelled up from their lie-flat position (later copied for Porsche's 928) on the bonnet when switched on, was made possible because of the rear engine; cooling air was drawn in through intakes just aft of the canopy.

On a hot day, the Testudo would no doubt have been unbearable, with the sun blazing down through the glass top. But in spring 1963, conditions were almost perfect for driving the car, which Nuccio Bertone himself did from his Turin headquarters to the Geneva show hall—quite an achievement for a hastily completed concept car.

Pininfarina/BMC 1800 Berlina Aerodinamica, 1967

The consensus about this shining example of intelligent, scientific, and exuberant car design is that it was, by quite some distance, a vehicle ahead of its time. The Berlina Aerodinamica came about at the tail end of a long and, in general, productive relationship between the British Motor Corporation and Italian design consultant Pininfarina; the fact that its all-round excellence was never harnessed by BMC is, in retrospect, a tragedy, for BMC's usual 1800 was an ugly car. Pininfarina had tried its best to infuse some style into Alec Issigonis' undeniably spacious package envelope, but his stubborn insistence on proportion meant there was little to redeem it.

As an independent venture, Pininfarina decided it could do better; specifically, its designer Leonardo Fioravanti *knew* he had the design solution in his thesis for "the study of the engine and bodywork of an aerodynamic six-seater saloon," with which he had dazzled his tutors when graduating from Milan Polytechnic in 1964. The work reflected his admiration for the sharply truncated tail treatment advocated by aerodynamicist Dr. Wunibald Kamm, which cut slipstream drag and boosted road-holding. It also featured a two-box, four-door-coupé profile, unadorned body panels and a considerable front overhang to allow a sleek and graceful nose cone.

It was an amazing car for its time, yet one destined—despite admiration from Issigonis and the design community in general—to be overlooked as corporate turmoil at BMC and its successor British Leyland unfolded. Pininfarina's services were no longer wanted, and the Aerodinamica was sacrificed.

Citroën has always denied any formal link between itself and Pininfarina at the time, but this car is widely thought to have heavily influenced the Citroën CX of 1975. Even more uncanny was the similarity between a similar Fioravanti exercise on the BMC 1300 base and the Citroën GS. However, it should be added that, outstanding as both Pininfarina concepts were, car design was moving ahead in parallel at several unconnected organisations. In their own ways, the Alfa Romeo Alfasud, VW Passat, and even the Rover SD1 could be said to have drawn inspiration from them.

Bertone/Alfa Romeo Carabo, 1968

The Carabo sits at the very pinnacle of the wedge car design frenzy of the late 1960s and early 1970s. "A landmark," according to *Autocar* magazine in 1977. "For many years, nobody went beyond it." Along with a battalion of other concept cars—notably the Pininfarina Ferrari 512S, Italdesign's Maserati Boomerang, and the Vauxhall SRV—this fantasy machine took ground-hugging to extremes. They all used mid-engined layouts to turn what would normally have been a bonnet into an acute-angled shovel front from which the enormous windscreen was a continuation in one unbroken styling line. Abruptly truncated tails hinted at scientific aerodynamics, but the main intention of these cars was to shock and impress in just about equal measures.

There seems to be no evidence that the stated 160-mile-per-hour maximum speed of the Carabo was ever attained in reality, but its stunning lines—the work of Bertone designer Marcello Gandini—certainly cloaked a proper car. In this case, the chassis was from the Alfa Romeo Tipo 33 race car powered by a 1,995cc, 230 horsepower V-8 engine.

Bertone's deft public relations made the Carabo a headline-getter around the world upon its unveiling at the 1968 Paris Motor Show on its looks alone, its multiple slats and ribs, and hydropneumatically opening scissor doors resembling the scaly green scarab (what *carabo* means in Italian) beetle after which it was named. Toymakers rushed to produce miniature versions of it for eager schoolboys. Yet it was also a technology showcase, boasting lightweight copper-tinted glass from Belgian specialists VHR-Glaverbel and a diverting metallic green paint job with fluorescent orange highlights for safety.

No one, least of all Bertone, was claiming the Carabo would be on sale any time soon. But three short years later, it became obvious it had provided the inspiration for Lamborghini to proceed with the Countach. And that only added to the iconic status of the Carabo in the pantheon of car design.

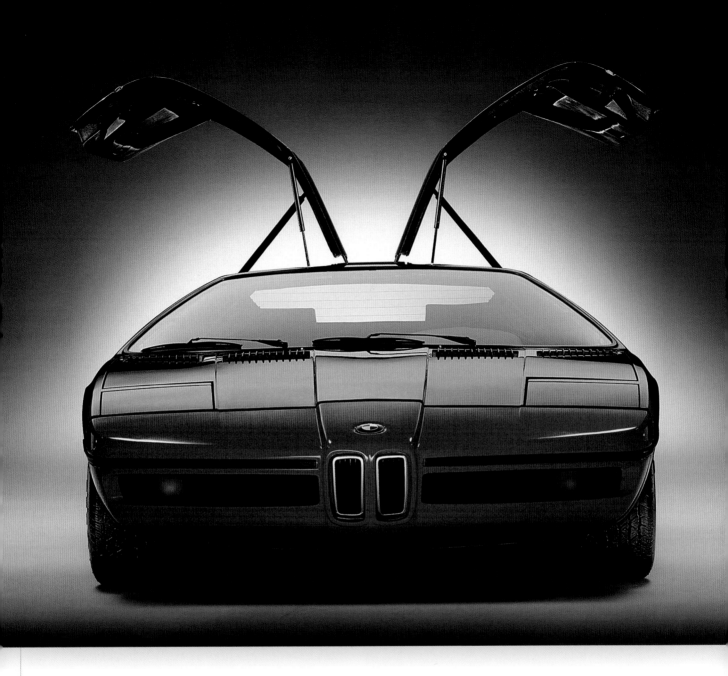

BMW Turbo, 1972

A major event like the 1972 Olympics could hardly go unmarked by BMW. The sporting arena for the summer games was centred on Munich, the marque's home city, and BMW was persuaded by its chief designer Paul Bracq that a concept car celebrating both speed and safety would be an appropriate way to salute the athletes. Officially, it was the E25, but the simple Turbo tag was enough to make it sound irresistible.

Bracq was very much the man of the design moment, glowing in the adulation heaped upon him for his work on designing the exterior of the French TGV high-speed train. Now, wearing his new BMW hat, he set about creating a unique supercar that was at once wedge-shaped, like its contemporaries, but also loaded with features to show that BMW cared about minimising the impact of collisions through passive safety. The core of this philosophy was the deformable front and rear ends of the Turbo—foam-filled plastic sections mounted on telescopic steel beams. The cockpit was, in effect, one giant roll cage, with a steering column jointed in three

places so it would collapse if struck. BMW's claim that the car, because of its low-to-the-ground stance, offered a safety advantage was a somewhat specious boon, but the inclusion of anti-lock brakes and a radar-activated proximity sensor were wise and proper active safety benefits.

While other potential supercars tapered to aggressively infinitesimal tips, the Turbo made a visual virtue of its soft and rounded ends with a striking paint job: bright, safety-style orange graduating to a deep claret red. The gullwing doors, meanwhile, provided some theatre to push back the worthiness.

Power came from a turbocharged, 200–brake horsepower 1,990cc BMW straight-four, an engine that found a production life in the 1973 2002 Turbo. The Turbo was constructed by Italian design studio Michelotti and, although a second, non-running car was commissioned for display purposes there was never any question of the Turbo going on sale. Or so it seemed—because plenty of the car's design features would indeed find a production car home when BMW marketed its mid-engined M1 in 1978.

Toyota MP-1, 1975

Chrysler's minivan range of 1983, initially sold as a Plymouth Voyager or a Dodge Caravan, is widely—and rightly—considered to be the first multipurpose vehicle (MPV) as we know it today. By that, it's generally expected to be a tall, roomy car, the interior of which can be altered in several different ways for various passenger/cargo configurations. Chrysler defined that in the minivan, even managing to incorporate sliding side doors without it seeming like a former delivery van. Yet a full seven years earlier, Toyota was right on the money, able to put a big tick against everything on the tentative MPV checklist with its MP-1. It offered a lofty passenger compartment with excellent all-round visibility; a compact, steeply sloped bonnet for a quasi-one-box profile; a modular interior; sliding rear aside doors; and a huge tailgate. With the ageing demographic of the population in mind, wheelchair access was a key feature, with a lifting platform built in to the step of one of the rear passenger doors.

It was such a thoroughly logical and sensible car that it seemed production-ready. The MP-1, though, was a concept, exhibited at the 1975 Tokyo Motor Show, and that's all it would remain. Eight years later, Toyota would be in early on the MPV party with its Model F Space Cruiser. But that was not in the Chrysler league because it was derived from the Liteace van, and its below-par driving dynamics immediately betrayed that fact.

Had Toyota been brave enough to push its MP-1 down the production line, things would have been very different; being based on the floorpan and running gear of the Crown saloon, it would certainly have been acceptably car-like to own and drive. The MP-1 proved what an on-the-ball organisation Toyota had become and set a template that the entire automotive industry would come to be grateful for. The only way to get your hands on an MP-1—literally—was to buy it in miniature, courtesy of Japan's Tomica toy brand.

Lancia Megagamma, 1978

Giugiaro the GT wizard; Giugiaro the family car mastermind; and now, Giugiaro the compactness and interior space visionary. The Megagamma saw the young Italian well into his third phase of car design. Here was the middle of three concepts in which Giorgetto Giugiaro redefined the importance of cabin spaciousness and anthropomorphic proportions. At the same time, his consultancy Italdesign would take a side-swipe at one of the auto industry's most long-held—and baseless—tenets: that sheer length equates to prestige.

The Megagamma, as its name suggests, took the Lancia Gamma chassis as its basis, complete with a compact, flat-four, 2.5-litre engine and the front-wheel drive that set it apart from many mainstream executive cars. Giugiaro then squeezed the proportions of the donor car to eradicate its long front and rear overhangs (length dropped from 458 to 431 centimetres) and greatly increase its height, which turned the doors from long to tall (height grew from 141 to 162 centimetres). This formed a cabin where drivers and passenger sat upright, with a commanding view out through deep glass.

It was, in essence, the abrupt antithesis to the trend, begun in Detroit in the 1950s and then embraced universally, for increasingly low-slung cars where the occupants sat close to the ground and often peered out through fairly narrow windows and screens. Customers seemed prepared to trade the relative discomfort this afforded in headroom and access for a sporty image.

The Megagamma, revealed at the 1978 Turin show, confounded this norm espoused by top-selling cars like, for instance, the Ford Cortina/Taunus. Giugiaro began his research in 1976 with an Alfa Romeo–based study for a compact, passenger-friendly New York taxi, and the Megagamma was followed in 1982 by the Capsula, with its engine and luggage concealed beneath a high-set floor.

Lancia, hidebound by its traditional luxury car values, declined to manufacture the five-door Megagamma. But Giugiaro's tall theme was enthusiastically espoused by Fiat for its 1983 Uno supermini and by Nissan for its Micra small car and Prairie minivan.

Fiat VSS, 1981

Renzo Piano is a world-renowned architect with a deep knowledge of materials and processes. In 1978, Fiat asked him, along with leading structural engineer Peter Rice, to take a long hard look at how it designed and built its cars and to summarise his findings in a way that would help it plan the cars of the 1990s. It was a $3.25-million project, and the I.DE.A Institute was founded in Turin to undertake it.

The team came to the eventual conclusion that what could transform both the engineering and the manufacturing processes would be a car manufactured in a series of subsystems. It was accepted that welded steel was still unbeatable for construction frames, with its excellent ability to absorb energy in an accident, although constructing it in a modular way as a space frame could slash weight by a fifth and boost crashworthiness. But instead of relying on a structural steel outer skin, various types of separate, non load-bearing plastic panels could be attached. This, said Piano, could by clever design also cut noise and vibration but, most important, allow a range of models to be built all using the same frame.

On the one hand, it was an ancient concept—that of a separate chassis supporting different body styles—but seen another way it was the birth of the platform-sharing configuration that would come to dominate mainstream car industry strategy. The findings were made real in the fully functioning Fiat VSS, standing for Vettura Sperimentale a Sottosistemi (or experimental subsystems car). It incorporated Fiat Ritmo/Strada parts in a structure that—angular looks aside—amply demonstrated Piano's vision.

There is a little of the VSS's style obvious in the Fiat Tipo of 1988, whose Piano-inspired platform was indeed used for a raft of other models, including the Lancia Dedra and Alfa Romeo 145. However, Piano's pure demonstration of technical flexibility was not fully embraced, principally because the retooling costs required for the factories were prohibitive but also partly because Fiat's sales departments protested against a visually detectable modularity. Piano himself lamented the car's appearance, saying it looked like a standard car "so people would not be frightened. It is not the way it should have been done. If you follow the process, you end up with a car that is drastically different." But the VSS would still prove a fundamentally influential design.

Renault Scénic, 1991

By the early 1990s the corporate glibness surrounding concept cars had become tedious. So when Renault exhorted visitors to accept an "invitation to travel" in "a car for life and living" at the 1991 Frankfurt motor show, it did seem rather like the usual moonshine.

However, the execution of this Scénic design study offered something different: a compact iteration of a large multipurpose vehicle (MPV) with a versatile interior and the interesting novelty of sliding doors on one side for both front- and rear-seat passengers, gliding apart from a centre point with no B-pillar; a single sliding driver's door meant solid metalwork aft of it allowed the Scénic to maintain excellent structural rigidity.

The cocoon-like five-seater cabin, in warm and inviting colours and materials, concealed a wealth of family friendly features, including underfloor storage lockers, seat-mounted belts, built-in child restraints, and both an airbag and a drowsiness sensor for the driver. It was 1991, remember, so the inclusion of satellite navigation and rear-vision micro cameras was also noteworthy.

A compact MPV was not an entirely new format, having been pioneered by the Nissan Prairie of 1982 and the Honda Civic Shuttle a year later (some would also point to the Fiat 600 Multipla of the mid-1950s). But with the Scénic, Renault was focusing not just on passenger accommodation, but also passenger convenience, well-being, and enjoyment. The concept became a dummy run for the Mégane Scénic of 1996. The adventurous door structure wasn't pursued, but a renewed emphasis on interior versatility and family friendliness most definitely was, and the production Scénic would go on to rip-roaring success, with rivals scrambling desperately to offer compact MPVs of their own.

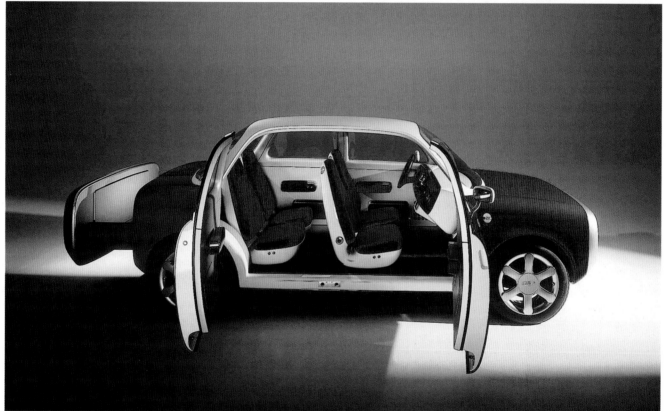

Ford 021C, 1999

It's a fair bet that design chief J Mays and the product bosses in Ford's Detroit headquarters had little idea what to expect when, early in 1999, they hired celebrity product designer Marc Newson to pen a concept car to be exhibited at that autumn's Tokyo motor show. For until that moment Newson, for all his pre-eminence as a designer of shapely furniture, fancy watches and Alessi kitchen gadgets, had not turned his hand to anything on wheels, let alone a car for a leading global automaker.

Newson was delighted to take up the task and immediately set to work, determined to figure out better ways of approaching design than those he had been studying in car magazines and books. Yet when the fruits of his labours were unveiled in Tokyo, the automotive world caught its breath: finished in bright orange and named after both the Pantone colour of that hue and the upcoming new millennium, the 021C emerged as a tiny, naive and toy-like box, devoid of external detail or ornamentation. The interior was simpler still: just four orange and white seats, a flat orange dashboard and

zero décor. Many commentators dismissed it as an expensive joke, the kind of car caricature a child would draw.

Behind the minimalist style, however, lay several technologies such as LED lighting, fibre optics and a height-adjustable dashboard that would later emerge on other production models. Yet the real significance of the 021C was the way it divided the critics on sharp, sector-dependent lines. The product design community applauded it for its purity and harmony and the way that it presented a fully integrated design conceived as a whole by a single individual: Newson is said to have designed every detail, right down to the carpets and tyre treads. Car critics, on the other hand, had difficulty grasping its significance, focusing on its naiveté rather than innovative features such as the swivelling front seats and pull-out trunk compartment. And though the 021C has not materially influenced the cars we see on the roads today, it has had a lasting influence on how today's designers approach their work and seek to shape their designs as an integrated whole.

Audi Steppenwolf, 2000

The art of the perfect crossover car is an inexact one, but in general it means that the vehicle in question adheres to conventional road car length and width parameters while adopting the stance, height, and image of an off-roader. Perhaps surprisingly, such a cocktail was rarely seen throughout the 1980s and 1990s. But then in 2000, Audi's Steppenwolf suddenly made the elements gel in the most convincing way yet seen, putting it among the *belles* of that year's Paris Motor Show.

The enormous, gleaming wheels were enough to hint at the car's off-road capability—vast 19-inch items shod with chunky tyres and set off by a dark grey protective perimeter finish to give the visual illusion of abnormal ground clearance for a car of around Audi A3 size. For the Steppenwolf had plenty in common with the A3 and even the Audi TT, being based on the same platform as these and other VW group cars like the new Beetle and Golf. A 3.2-litre V-6 was the power unit, allied to Quattro all-wheel drive and a Haldex clutch to equalise torque between front and rear axles.

The project was led by Romulus Rost, who aimed for a "four-wheeled mountain bike"; he had also been intimately involved with perfecting the Audi TT for market. The Steppenwolf was a masterly blend of compact coupé and capable off-roader. Inside, a prominent transmission tunnel defined it as a strict four-seater, resplendent with aluminium details and with rubber and leather trim even running to a leather-covered floor.

The Steppenwolf's adventurous off-road potential extended from spotlights in its door mirrors to a prominent sump guard and air suspension to vary the ride height by 60 millimetres to best cope with either motorways or mud baths. With even such once-mundane brands as Kia adopting a look like the Steppenwolf's, not to mention the perception-changing impact of the Nissan Qashqai, Ford Kuga, and BMW X6, it's clear Audi was well ahead of the curve. Still, its own entrant in this burgeoning sector, the Q5, proved a touch predictable alongside the still attention-grabbing Steppenwolf.

CHAPTER 16

RIGHT IDEA,
wrong time

Launching a 220-mile-per-hour supercar in the midst of a financial crisis or introducing a revolutionary super-economy lightweight family car just as incomes went up and fuel prices went down: Automotive history is peppered with instances of brilliant ideas that backfired because they were too far ahead of their time or circumstances conspired against them. Here we chronicle a dozen car programmes that didn't deserve to fail.

Chrysler Airflow, 1934

The Airflow appears to be a seminal example of motorised Art Deco design. In fact, it was America's first mainstream car with aerodynamics as its guiding principle—adventurous, certainly, but a sales disaster.

Chrysler consultant engineer Carl Breer's personal fascination with aerodynamics led to the Airflow programme, and by 1930 over 50 experimental models had been wind-tunnel tested. To cut weight, Chrysler devised a one-piece body with a lightweight metal frame, while further innovations included, on the Airflow limousine, the first curved, single-piece windscreen.

Early Airflows were fraught with quality problems, many arising from new welding techniques. But the main drag on sales was public resistance. Although the car was in tune stylistically with that other great Chrysler icon of the 1930s, New York's Chrysler Building, buyers preferred more traditional-looking cars without the Airflow's amorphous visage and faired-in wheels.

In an attempt to boost sales, the car was made *less* aerodynamic in 1936 when a prominent trunk was added to its tapering tail. But, by then, Chrysler's more traditional cars were outselling it massively. It was axed after 1937.

Stout Scarab, 1935

William Bushnell Stout called his nascent multipurpose vehicle (MPV) a "travelling machine." The Detroit entrepreneur and inventor decided to adapt an all-metal aircraft fuselage he'd designed into an office-on-wheels pitched at business tycoons.

He placed the Ford V-8 engine at the very back and moved the driving position forward so the steering wheel was almost directly above the front wheels. With no proper bonnet and wheels positioned at each

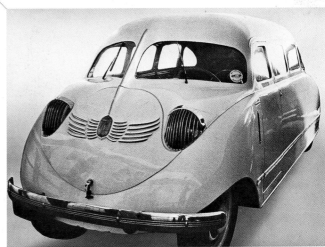

corner, the streamlined profile represented an extreme one-box shape.

The driver's seat was fixed, but the four other seats in the spacious passenger compartment were a paragon of versatility. The cushions on the rear bench seat could be rearranged into a full-length bed; the front passenger seat swivelled around and slid to face the rear, and a fold-down table was hinged on the left side of the interior for meetings. There were only two doors, one for the driver on the left and another to the rear compartment, usually at the back on the right. No two Scarabs were absolutely identical, and with a then-astronomical $5,000 price tag just nine were sold.

Tucker 49 Torpedo, 1947

Preston Tucker had been an office boy at Cadillac, a car salesman, and a partner in an Indianapolis racing car business before deciding to create a car that was strong on safety features. Early ideas were for a streamlined, rear-engined coupé with front and rear seat belts, a padded dashboard, and a windscreen that popped out in a crash. When that proved unfeasible, in late 1946 his team rethought the car as a four-door saloon, with a Franklin air-cooled (switched to water-cooled for production) flat-six helicopter engine in the back. The seat belts were dropped, as some felt they implied the car was unsafe, and so were swivelling headlights, disc brakes, and a central driving position. But an all-round independent suspension and a padded dashboard remained.

Public goodwill towards Tucker evaporated when US regulators alleged fraud for raising money from dealers and customers, while fundamentally changing the design of the car they had committed to. He protested an industry conspiracy against him, and his name was cleared, but the Tucker Corporation was finished after delivering just 51 cars.

Studebaker Avanti, 1962

The glass-fibre Avanti was a striking GT car conceived by Studebaker president Sherwood Egbert. But it was styled by Raymond Loewy, the legendary American industrial design genius most closely identified with the voluptuous Coca-Cola bottle. "Both Egbert and Loewy had pretty definite ideas about what the car should be," reported *Road & Track* magazine in 1962. "Their ideas boil down to fourteen mutually agreed upon requirements, the foremost of which were the disc brakes, built-in rollover bar, no useless ornamentation, no grille work, and no straight lines on the body." The interior was modelled on a typical Italian sports car, with clear instruments and leather-clad bucket seats. The standard Studebaker V-8 could be ordered with supercharging.

Showered with acclaim, the Avanti was destined for a short life luring buyers into Studebaker showrooms because the company went bust in 1964. However, two former Studebaker dealers bought the rights to the car and the Avanti II was relaunched. They continued hand-building about 100 a year until 1982, and other entrepreneurs kept this distinctive car alive way beyond that.

NSU Ro80, 1967

New models today rarely flare the imagination like the NSU Ro80. It was, in 1967, the most daringly modern car on the road. Designed by Dr. Felix Wankel, the Ro80 had an amazing twin-rotor power unit that gave the car extraordinary smoothness. Equally impressive was the car's stunning, wedge-shaped styling crafted by designer Claus Luthe.

For a large five-seater saloon, NSU Ro80 had unusual elegance. But there was science to its form too: The car was supremely aerodynamic, its co-efficient of drag, at 0.35, unparalleled for such a car. It still looked sleek and modern in 1987 next to such wind tunnel–shaped cars as the Audi 100.

Luthe did more than most to hone the modern German saloon with its visual solidity and confidence, but he would shortly become notable in Germany for entirely different reasons: During a violent row, Luthe fatally stabbed his drug-addict adult son. His quick release from a 33-month jail term reflected the sympathy Germans felt for the father in this tragedy. Sadly, NSU was brought to its knees by warranty claims against fragile Ro80 engines. Luthe subsequently worked as a designer for both Audi-NSU and BMW.

British Leyland Princess, 1975

This replacement for the old BMC 1800/2200 series bucked the trend once again with its distinctive styling. The work of designer Harris Mann, it followed his Allegro and TR7 in employing a wedge-shaped profile, elongated nose and prominent wheel arches. It looked dynamic but flattered to deceive. The car's profile suggested a versatile hatchback; instead, it had a conventional boot. A new suspension system was featured, employing Hydragas units for an absorbent ride, while the interior, typical of cars from the BMC/BL stable, was vastly roomy if, also as usual, unappealing.

At launch in 1975, it was offered in Austin, Morris, or Wolseley guises with either a 1.8-litre four-cylinder engine or a 2.2-litre straight-six. Within a year, however, British Leyland determined these venerable brands were the cause of weak sales, so they were all ditched and henceforth the cars were sold under the newly created Princess marque. It was an extraordinary about-turn. In 1978, the Princess 2 ushered in new engines and several improvements to boost indifferent quality. Still, the briefly trendy Princess exerted little influence on its peers.

AMC Pacer, 1975

Surprised by the fuel crisis of the mid-1970s, American manufacturers simply did not offer the right products. They could only look on aghast as economical Japanese imports piled in and snatched their sales. The Pacer was American Motors Corporation's bizarre fightback.

"Project Amigo," begun in 1971, sought to create "the first wide small car," keeping the roomy passenger compartment Americans liked but within a typical European length and using a refined and compact Wankel rotary engine. It was planned to exceed anticipated safety requirements; hence, the goldfish-bowl-like glasshouse (37 per cent of body surface) for optimum visibility, reinforced barrel-shaped flanks, and rollover bar incorporated into the roof.

The plan began to unravel in 1974, when General Motors, scheduled to supply the power unit, abandoned its rotary engine programme. American Motors was forced to install its own straight-six, a heavy, bulky, inefficient motor, saddling the Pacer with terrible performance and fuel economy. Novel touches like a driver's door four inches longer than the passenger's for easy access to the rear seats, plus a hatchback, did help sales in 1976 to top 117,000, but thereafter orders collapsed.

Ford Sierra, 1982

The Sierra caused a storm in 1982 with its curvaceous, wind-cheating shape; large plastic bumpers; and ergonomic interior. Horrified traditionalists declared it a "jelly mould." Under the skin, though, the car was based wholesale on the dated Ford Cortina it replaced. Although there was a new independent rear suspension system, the driveline was recognisably Cortina. This caused just as much controversy as the bold styling itself.

And yet the Sierra did innovate, as did the self-leveling suspension featured on the 2.3-litre Ghia estate and the XR4x4 helped popularise all-wheel drive for conventional road cars. As for sporty versions, the initial XR4i, despite its 150 brake horsepower and stiffer suspension, received a lukewarm reception, but the turbocharged Cosworths made sensational competition (and getaway) cars. On both, biplane rear aerofoils stood out.

With almost 3.5 million sold, the Sierra cannot be judged a failure. But it might have done so much better with a less scientific style and more technical substance. Many buyers felt they were being fooled and instead turned in their droves to modern, front-drive cars like the Opel Ascona/Vauxhall Cavalier and even the genuinely innovative Citroën BX.

Jaguar XJ220, 1991

When the XJ220 prototype was unveiled in 1988, it had Jaguar's classic V-12 engine and four-wheel drive. When it finally went on sale in 1991, its number of cylinders and driven wheels had halved. And the recession was in full force. People who'd eagerly placed orders for the £403,000 car—then the fastest road machine ever built—cancelled them in their droves. What should have been a story of triumph and celebration for Jaguar became a financial and public relations debacle as buyers said they would forego their deposits as long as they didn't have to pay the balance.

The V-12 of the show car gave way to a twin-turbo V-6, but still with as astonishing 542 horsepower. The wonderful looks, however, were unadulterated, and the civilised cabin offered an excellent driving position. In hindsight, the wisdom of producing a car so vast and utterly impractical was questionable. But with a top speed of at least 213 miles per hour, and possibly as much as 220 miles per hour if conditions allowed, it was every bit as fast as its name suggested.

Rover 75, 1998

BMW tried hard to redefine Rover, the British marque it acquired in 1994. It planned the Rover 75 with its typical rigour, creating an all-new front-drive platform for it. There was little deliberation about what kind of car the new big Rover would be: an executive saloon that dodged overt sportiness in favour of comfort, refinement, discreet style and something almost entirely absent from the sector—old-fashioned charm.

Rover stylist Richard Woolley, who had worked wonders turning the anodyne Honda Accord into the Rover 600, was responsible for the 75. His elegant four-door architecture, with its gentle curves and tasteful chrome highlights, hit the spot. It would have been the toast of the 1998 British motor show, had not BMW used this forum to lambast the British government and the indolence of its own Rover workforce. Two years later, the Rover 75 became the main intellectual asset of MG Rover, now uneasily liberated from German ownership. Good car that it was, the 75 could never buoy the fortunes of the surviving British motor industry alone. Until 2005, though, it did its level best.

Renault Avantime, 2001

The Avantime was a lemon. It was beloved of style critics, who loved to postulate about the way the car defied industry norms. But the public were no fools. The whole project was born out of consolation. French niche manufacturer Matra had, since 1984, derived its lifeblood from building the Espace for Renault—the groundbreaking, plastic-bodied MPV that Matra had also helped design. When Renault decided it wanted to make this in-house (and from steel), Matra was offered the sop of creating a top-end Renault luxury car. It chose to fashion a large, two-door, four-seater coupé on an MPV scale so Matra could build it like the old Espace—that is, with a galvanised steel structure and composite body panels.

The adventurous, high-riding Avantime caused great interest when shown as a concept in 1999. It featured clever, two-stage doors, simultaneously allowing superb rear access and cheek-by-jowl city parking. But by the time the plastic Avantime made its showroom debut three long years later, buyers' antennae detected issues (those doors were, allegedly, hard to perfect), and just 8,000 or so had been sold when Renault pulled the plug in 2003.

Audi A2, 2000

The A2 was the first mass-made small car with a space-frame chassis and body panels made from recyclable aluminium—said to be 40 per cent lighter than equivalent rivals. With a drag factor of 0.25, the 94-mile-per-gallon 1.2-litre diesel 3L version was the world's most aerodynamic production car of its day.

Audi elected to do away with an opening bonnet altogether on the A2. All the customer needed was water, oil, and screen-wash fillers and a dipstick handle, behind a neat folding flap. The user-friendly interface extended to the A2's interior, where the two rear seats (a three-abreast bench was optional) could fold singly, separately, or be removed altogether. Audi's Space Floor Concept gave rear passengers footwells sunken under the floor beneath the front seats, providing excellent seating posture. An optional full-length glass roof panel was available. So the A2 was ahead of the curve in terms of technology and thrift, but its strangely clinical, smoothly contoured futurism lost out to the new Mini's warmly retro character. The slow-selling baby Audi was axed in 2005 before it had the chance to truly shine in the global economic downturn.

LANDMARK
designs

Car design has progressed from the 1899 Benz to today's sophisticated models through a long series of steps, some larger and more revolutionary than others, some registering great leaps in technology, others triggering social change or altering the way we use our vehicles. Here we present our submissions in the challenge to select the most significant designs in 120 years of automotive history

Mercedes 35 horsepower, 1901

Gottlieb Daimler built the world's first four-wheeled car by adapting a horse-drawn coach; subsequent efforts were similarly short, tall, and unstable. So, driven by entrepreneur Emile Jellinek's marketing plans for his nascent Mercedes brand, Daimler's engineers rethought the automobile. Their Mercedes 35-horsepower sports-tourer was revolutionary, setting a packaging pattern followed by most mainstream carmakers for decades. Cradled by a pressed-steel chassis frame, occupants sat behind—rather than above—a four-cylinder engine under a bonnet and behind a honeycomb radiator. It had a gate gear change, a foot throttle, a raked steering column, and vastly better road-holding thanks to a lower centre of gravity.

Ford Model T, 1908

Henry Ford's Model T was cleverly planned as a light, simple, rugged car of a standard design that could be built in ever higher numbers at ever lower prices. There were, at first, five factory-built body styles on offer, but all Model Ts offered 10.5 inches of ground clearance to cope with America's rough, undeveloped rural roads. With the hood raised, the Model T was 7 feet tall. As moving-line mass production was introduced, "Japan black" paintwork was standardised because it was cheap, durable, and, on some components, faster-drying to speed up manufacturing; colour choice returned in 1926 with the advent of quick-drying cellulose paint.

Lancia Lambda, 1922

Lancia's sporty, fine-handling Lambda broke new ground in its V-4 engine, its independent front suspension, and especially in its construction concept because it was the first car to eliminate a separate chassis frame. Its rigid monocoque unit was a pressed-steel skeleton-forming chassis, scuttle, lower body, and rear end; even the seat squabs were part of the structure, while the engine was carried in an attached, lightweight cradle. This wholly integral construction meant buyers had to accept the factory's own style of open coachwork, rather than specifying their own designs from outside coachbuilders—unusual then for a premium car.

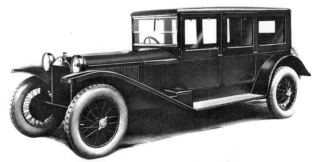

Bugatti Type 55, 1932

To the profound joy of company founder Ettore Bugatti, his son Jean developed a great perception for engineering and an artist's eye for line and form. At age just 22, Jean already influenced Bugatti engine design, with an American-inspired twin-camshaft motor, but it was as a coachwork designer he truly excelled. The Type 55 roadster was a mobile icon, with its uncompromising doorless cockpit, dramatic two-tone paint finish, and voluptuous mudguards; the cast aluminium wheels were the first standard alloys fitted to a road car. Under this exotic form was the detuned eight-cylinder specification of the twin-cam Type 51 GP car. Only 38 were sold.

Citroën Traction Avant, 1934

When first seen as the Citroën 7A, this four-door saloon's aura was immediately rakish and modern. Its low-slung appearance came from having the entire drivetrain mounted ahead of the cabin, engine power feeding through a three-speed manual gearbox to the front wheels. The car's construction also broke new ground, being a welded monocoque saloon that did away with a separate chassis frame altogether. Later in 1934, it was joined by the Light 15 with a 1,911cc motor. This became the signature model. The Traction Avant became synonymous with egalitarian Parisian style, and the final examples were built as late as 1957.

Citroën 2CV, 1938

Bauhaus architectural language transferred to cars in the Deux Chevaux. It was planned around the most utilitarian of principles: to be able to carry two countryfolk and 50 kilogrammes of produce across a ploughed field at 30 miles per hour while keeping both people and cargo intact. With Michelin backing, engineer-designer Pierre Boulanger came up with the minimal goods, and the little car, looking for all the world like a metal snail on wheels, provided motoring for echelons of French society who had never known it before the time when it was, finally, put on sale in 1948. It was then available for an incredible 40 years.

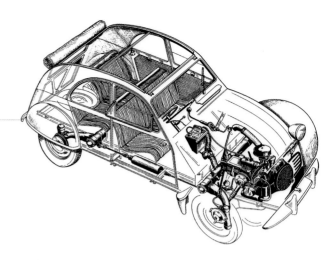

Volkswagen Beetle, 1938

Of course, it was never meant to be called Beetle; Adolf Hitler's personal vision for a German "people's car" was originally the Kraft durch Freude—the "strength through joy" car. The basic shape for a rear-engined, four-seater family car was arrived at by designer Ferdinand Porsche in 1938 after many prototypes. Its form very much followed its function. Shifting the drivetrain to the back of the car permitted a small frontal area and integrated body parts, allowing a streamlined overall shape with a tapered tail. Its packaging, if not exactly its profile, influenced Renault and Fiat, and 21 million were made until it ceased production in 2003.

Willys Jeep, 1942

Truly designed by soldiers, the Jeep became a rolling symbol of American ruggedness. More than 600,000 examples were made during the World War II and General George Marshall once called the Jeep "America's greatest contribution to modern warfare." In 1938, the US Army put out a tender for a light military all-purpose vehicle, and Willys-Overland's concept was selected. It boasted selectable two- or four-wheel drive, an 80-inch wheelbase, and a 660-pound payload. Jeep soon became a household word, a slurring of the acronym GP, for General Purpose. After the war, Willys registered the distinguished Jeep name as a trademark.

Cisitalia 202, 1947

The work of Pininfarina's Giovanni Sovunuzzi, this is the first Gran Turismo coupé of all and exquisitely pure of line. It was among the exhibits chosen for a 1950 exhibition at New York's Museum of Modern Art entitled "Eight Automobiles." The curator, Arthur Drexler, hailed the Cisitalia as "rolling sculpture," and it was the only one of the cars to remain in MOMA's permanent collection. Sovunuzzi was at Fiat when he drew the first ideas, finally seeing them come to fruition when he moved to Pininfarina. Details of the 202 were taken up in cars as diverse as the Bentley Continental and Porsche 356.

Jaguar XK120, 1949

The XK120 was a beautifully, classically proportioned two-seater roadster, although not really a groundbreaker. It was vaguely similar to late 1930s roadsters from BMW, Talbot, and Delahaye, yet none were so masterfully resolved as the Jaguar. The car confirmed company founder, and one-man styling arbiter, William Lyons as a design genius, but it also forced Jaguar to change its strategy. Lyons saw his marque as primarily a maker of profitable sports saloons, with the XK120 intended as just a sideshow for the 1948 Earl's Court motor show. But the unanticipated clamour for the car turned Jaguar into a sports and racing car powerhouse.

Lancia Aurelia B20, 1953

Lancia has a long history of distinguished design, but this example by Pininfarina is the most handsome of them all: It represents the origins of the sporting fastback. With a powerful (and pioneering) V-6 engine and a gearbox in the back axle, the car had perfect weight distribution, making it a favourite for rallying in the hands of wealthy sportsmen, but the sleek, elegant, and sophisticated shape was what endeared it to onlookers. Almost 4,000 were built, and today they're highly prized. The later Spider version, also designed at Pininfarina, was, if anything, even more glamorous yet in a much flashier way.

Chevrolet Corvette, 1953

When Motorama, a dazzling road show for General Motors' latest models, opened at the Waldorf Hotel in New York in January 1953, no one expected a new sports car to take centre stage. But for the first time chief stylist Harley Earl had created a dream car that looked production-ready, and the public reaction to this bold glass-fibre roadster was so enthusiastic that GM gave it the immediate green light. Amazingly, the Corvette went from clay model to showroom in just 15 months, but such expediency entailed using an ancient six-cylinder engine. A later V-8 conversion turned the car's patchy sales fortunes around.

Mercedes-Benz 300SL, 1954

Much more than just a racing car dressed up for the road, the 300SL was an awesome machine both to look at and to drive—a high-tech, 150-mile-per-hour sports car built expressly for crossing continents. With its gullwing doors, blistered wheel arches, and elegantly curved tail, the 300SL was one of the most instantly recognisable shapes on the road, and it was also one of the fastest: Only a handful of hand-built Ferraris and Maseratis could catch it. "SL" stood for Super Light because the body—built in steel with aluminium panels—was supported by a complex space frame of lightweight tubes.

Citroën DS19, 1955

Today, it's almost impossible to imagine the impact the DS made at its launch; every other car, whether European or American, was rendered old-fashioned overnight by its space-age lines. It was packed with new technology, including a hydro-pneumatic suspension, powered gearshift, and indicator lamps mounted in the plastic roof panel, but the public at the 1955 Paris show craned their necks to see its shark-like form. Created by Flaminio Bertoni, a former sculptor working as a Citroën designer, it inspired French cultural critic Roland Barthes to compare cars to cathedrals, noting it was "the supreme creation of an era, conceived with passion by unknown artists."

Chrysler 300, 1955

As well as being a closet supercar in its performance capability, Chrysler design chief Virgil Exner's clean, lean but barrel-sided two-door sports saloon—the company's top-of-the-range model of the day—boasted an exceptionally stylish shape, especially when compared to the chrome-strewn excesses of contemporary Cadillac and Lincoln rivals. As the years rolled by, though, the subsequent series of the 300 put on weight and decorative flab, and the original 300— the inspiration for such elegant cars as the Volvo Amazon, Rover 3-litre, and Peugeot 403— became a forgotten yardstick for elegance and solidity.

Fiat Nuova 500, 1957

Fiat's chief engineer Dante Giacosa, who held the position for an astonishing 40 years, was the head of the team, of which most other members are uncredited, that created the Nuova 500 in 1957. It was similar in size to the original 1936 Topolino (Italian for little mouse), but the engine was at the back, and the egg-like shape was gloriously crafted and modern. One style icon, the Vespa scooter, had already put Italy on two wheels; now the little Cinquecento gave many Italians their first taste of four. It was made until 1975, inadequately replaced by the 126, but its true spirit was revived in the new 500 of 2007.

Austin A40, 1958

In this popular and crisply styled family car, you will find the origin of the two-box compact design that would come to dominate the market with the advent of the supermini class in the 1970s. Although the A40 did not boast the one-piece hatchback rear door that would have made it a true groundbreaker, the Countryman version did offer a split tailgate that got it most of the way there. The A40 is also significant because it represented a major spread of the influence of independent car design bureaux—in this case Pininfarina—on manufacturers that had, previously, relied upon their own in-house capabilities.

Austin-Healey 3000, 1959

The Healey 100 prototype stole the 1952 London motor show as the world's cheapest 100-mile-per-hour sports car and was certainly among the most beautiful (thanks to Healey stylist Gerry Coker). Over dinner on the eve of the show, Austin's Leonard Lord and racing driver Donald Healey were deep in conversation. By the time the show closed, the car was rechristened the Austin-Healey 100: a new name had been added to Britain's roll call of sporting marques. By 1959, with a larger engine, a restyled nose, and the adoption of distinctive two-tone paint, the A-H 3000 became the ultimate style incarnation of the breed.

Cadillac Eldorado, 1959

This was the final car from the great Harley Earl and the ultimate in automotive burlesque: 20 feet long, massive tailfins soaring up an unprecedented 42 inches, and jet-age imagery accentuated by a pair of bullet-shaped turn and stoplights mounted in them. Earl said about it: "We haven't depreciated these cars, we've appreciated your mind." Frontal styling was equally distinctive with twin headlights and a double-decker grille. The 1959 cars came as two-door Coupe De Villes, pillarless four-door hardtops, and as a gargantuan Fleetwood 75 formal limousine. Best remembered, though, is the Eldorado Biarritz convertible—and especially any example painted pink.

Jaguar MkII, 1959

It was custom for Jaguar's founder and industry dynamo William Lyons to take the credit for his cars' looks. And while he certainly didn't have the time to do all the penwork, his unerring eye for great lines was what made Jaguars look so satisfying. For the MkII, he was updating an older car, the retrospectively named MkI, but his revisions to the cabin, wing line and front and rear made the predecessor appear slug-like by comparison. It was a subtly influential car: In the mid-1990s, Chrysler aped the rounded curve of the cabin windows for its new LH sedan.

BMC Mini, 1959

Alec Issigonis always railed against the idea that he ever just "styled" anything. Yet Issigonis' Mini shape, only there for its purpose of clothing what was then the most innovative, best handling, and roomiest small car in the world, is nonetheless a design classic in its profile alone. Surprisingly, close imitators were few, Honda coming nearest with its N360 and N600. Most were rear-engined and cramped, which must have made Issigonis smile wryly through his customary haze of cigarette smoke. His form-following-function aesthetic persisted in BMC's 1100 and 1800 cars, although Pininfarina did its best to civilise his design brutalism.

Chevrolet Corvair, 1960

Compared to the Cadillacs of the year before, the Corvair was almost spartan in its design. The work of General Motors designer Ned Nickles, working for Bill Mitchell, its clean and simple lines, with a prominent styling "waist" running all round the body and a deeply wrapped-around rear window, inspired a generation of car stylists in 1960s Europe. For example, just look at the NSU Prinz 4, Hillman Imp, Fiat 1300/1500, and Simca 1000. It was technically fascinating too, with an air-cooled six-cylinder engine in the back, but tricky handling made the Corvair a whipping boy for American safety campaigner Ralph Nader, leaving it forever tarnished.

Aston Martin DB4, 1961

A perfect cocktail of Anglo-Saxon manners and Italian style, this essentially English car had a body designed by Touring of Milan, one of the traditional old *carrozzerie* It was the ultimate British tourer and the first entirely new Aston Martin road car under the David Brown regime, retaining the Bulldog aura of the DB2 but boasting a 140-mile-per-hour top speed. The DB4 had a brand-new chassis and double-overhead-camshaft engine delivering 240 brake horsepower. Touring provided the svelte, fastback body style and its *Superleggera* construction system—aluminium panels on a thin tubular framework.

Jaguar E-Type, 1961

Only the second car to be included in the permanent collection of New York's Museum of Modern Art, to many the E-Type is the most beautiful automobile ever. There's something phallic about it, certainly, but it was the cool aerodynamic theory of streamlining expert Malcolm Sayer, together with the showmanship of his employer William Lyons (pictured), that created the winning formula. That sleek profile was inspired by the Le Mans–winning Jaguar D-Type, but the final Series III car of 1971, which pioneered Jaguar's awesome V-12 engine, had a softer, fatter body shape totally lacking the original E's fierce visual energy.

Renault 4, 1961

As Renault's response to the Citroën 2CV, the Renault 4 was a long time coming, making its debut 13 years after the minimalist Citroën first delivered motoring to millions of French drivers. Then again, for Renault, the car entered much new territory: It was the company's first front-drive car, although its engine was mounted longitudinally rather than transversely, and it pioneered the concept of a compact five-door hatchback with folding rear seats. The frugal 4 was so much appreciated that it eventually became the biggest-selling French car ever. But it was a basic tin can to the end in 1993, sticking with crude features, such as all-round sliding windows.

Lincoln Continental, 1961

The "clap-door" Continental is one of America's most important cars. Eschewing the fins and chrome then still popular on most domestic cars, Lincoln launched a car with clean, unadorned lines, American in scale but almost European in feel; it was slab-sided, magnificent, and unforgettable. Members of the design team included Eugene Bordinat, Don de la Rossa, and Elwood Engel. The rear-hinged rear door provided the clap-door nickname, and it became the "in" car with the rich and famous. Endorsement by the White House was great too—except that it was in a stretched Continental that President John F. Kennedy was assassinated in Dallas in 1963.

Jeep Wagoneer, 1963

You'd never call it beautiful, but the lofty Wagoneer—the work of Brooks Stevens—defined the boxy, macho sport-utility shape that, today, we take for granted in the Range Rover, Isuzu Trooper, and a whole raft of American terrain-busters from the Ford Bronco to the Chevrolet Blazer. The Wagoneer's lofty 161-centimetre height was masked not just by the waistline below the window line, but also by a full-length body crease and the ghosted outline of separate mudguards and running boards pressed into the lower side panels. Slim window pillars imbued the cabin with an airy, light-filled atmosphere.

Porsche 911, 1963

The greatest-ever sports car (to many) was drawn by Ferdinand Alexander "Butzi" Porsche (pictured), eldest son of the company founder. But it can trace its origins directly back to Hitler's Volkswagen, with which the original Porsche 356 shared its underpinnings. After nearly 50 years, today's 911 is still recognisable as a direct descendent of Butzi Porsche's 1963 slope-backed original. The image has fluctuated, though: For the 1960s and 1970s buyer, the 911 was the choice of the seasoned aficionado. By the mid-1980s, it became a yuppie icon. For some, including Porsche, that image has lingered a little too long.

Ferrari 250 GTO, 1963

This is one of the greatest sports-racing cars ever, victorious in the international GT racing championships for three years on the trot. To appreciate the front-engined V-12 GTO is to drive it, say connoisseurs, and it was supposedly capable of 180 miles per hour. Yet its swooping and purposeful two-seater coupé bodywork, designed by Sergio Scaglietti in close collaboration with Ferrari's racing department and engineer Mauro Forghieri, is just as noteworthy. It's pleasingly unadorned, apart from several very necessary air intakes, and is among the most evocative of GT profiles from a golden age of motor sport before mid-engined configurations upped the ante.

Ford Mustang, 1964

The Mustang was, in essence, a compact car with a sporty aura that captured the spirit of the baby boom era. It was also one of the fastest selling cars of all time—418,000 in 1964 alone. Brainchild of high-flying Ford executive Lee Iacocca, the Mustang was based on the floorpan of the budget Falcon range. Its crisp, pseudo-European styling came in notchback, fastback, and convertible forms, and personal Mustangs could be created with a vast palette of trim and power options. The basic, pretty shape continued unadulterated until 1968, when rivals finally caught up with their own pony cars.

Renault 16, 1965

So much of what we take for granted on, say, today's Renault Laguna was offered by the 16: five-door practicality, surefooted front-wheel drive, ride comfort, motorway mile-munching ability, and a generally chic and sophisticated character. The intrinsic appeal was in the car's overall package; the luggage accommodation was extraordinary compared to typical, contemporary family cars, even though, by today's standards, the hatchback still was absurdly high. Renault hired design consultant Philippe Charbonneaux to style this luxury saloon/estate hybrid. He'd had a hand in the original Chevrolet Corvette, and his work on the 16 endowed a highly practical workhorse with sharp-edged, arresting style.

Toyota 2000 GT, 1965

At the 1965 Tokyo Motor Show, the Toyota 2000GT was an absolute sensation—Japan's Jaguar E-Type. It looked fabulous, styled by German aristocrat and industrial designer Count Albrecht Goertz, and stood just 45 inches tall. A 150–brake horsepower twin-cam six-cylinder engine, Lotus-style backbone chassis, five-speed gearbox, rack-and-pinion steering, all-round independent coil spring suspension, and cast-aluminium wheels gave it enthusiast credentials. You couldn't actually buy a 2000GT until May 1967, and even then only its price tag dwarfed a Porsche's and reflected the fact the 2000GT was virtually handmade. Toyota sold a mere 337 and production ceased in October 1970.

Lamborghini Miura, 1966

Ferruccio Lamborghini was a tractor maker determined to rival Ferrari in the 1960s. Although he wouldn't let his young engineers build a racer, he was happy to give the go-ahead for this show-stopping two-seater borrowing mid-engined principles from the latest F1 machines. The unitary chassis with V-12 engine placed transversely behind the cockpit was clothed by Bertone, and Nuccio Bertone put his best man on the job—25-year old Marcello Gandini. A bold, sensual car that's lost none of its impact since, the eyelashes around the flip-up lights are memorable styling signatures. It is broadly acknowledged now as the first supercar.

BMW 1602, 1966

Car design utilises an international lexicon, and things aren't always as they seem. The remarkable small BMW saloon defined an apparently German style but, in fact, was largely inspired by the work of Giovanni Michelotti, a leading Italian consultant designer. He created the modern BMW look with the 1500 of 1961, an altogether bigger car, but this attractive small sports saloon brought its technical and aesthetic qualities to a wider audience. Both have the distinctive uplift to the rearmost lower corner of the rear side window that, despite emanating from Michelotti's studio, became known as the Hofmeister kink after the BMW styling head (1955 to 1975) Wilhelm Hofmeister.

Datsun 240Z, 1969

Japan's first internationally successful sports car, the razor-edged 240Z, designed by Count Albrecht Goertz (of BMW 507 fame), was destined to become a bestseller of the 1970s. What the Datsun badge lacked in romance and cachet the 240Z more than made up for with its well-balanced, muscular lines. The long bonnet, recessed headlights, and those tensioned rear haunches were all evidence that the Z took its styling cues from the Jaguar E-Type fixed-head, yet it was pure and elegant enough—aside from its gruesome wheel trims, a typical Japanese weakness—to have an appeal all its own.

Range Rover, 1970

In the Range Rover, designer David Bache created a perfectly proportioned stereotype that has been widely imitated but seldom bettered. When revealed in June 1970, there was nothing else like it—nothing combining such tremendous go-anywhere ability with great ride quality, saloon car comfort, and a level of style worlds away from Land Rover's stout practicality. Its body had a newly pressed suit crispness that, while supremely functional, exuded upper-class style. Within a year, the waiting list stretched to the horizon. It's still the only vehicle ever exhibited at The Louvre as a modern sculpture and became as potent a symbol of Britain as the classic red telephone box.

Fiat 130 Coupé, 1971

Until Paolo Martin went freelance as an independent industrial designer, he had been the unseen hand behind Pininfarina's 1970s generation of chunky designs: Rolls-Royce Camargue, the Peugeot 604, and this, his finest, the coupé version of the largest postwar Fiat model, the 130. The balance of the glasshouse, the passenger section sticking above the rest of the car, compensates for the abruptly chopped front and rear ends. In fact, every view of the car has laser-straight lines united by subtle curves. It remains a masterpiece, albeit of a style that, so far, has not been revived.

Lamborghini Countach, 1971

In its later years, the Lamborghini Countach became a kind of parody of itself, a tacky, bespoiled posermobile for anybody with excess money and vulgarity. But it wasn't always a byword for populist tack. The original, bright yellow Bertone-styled prototype of 1971, destined to supplant the Miura as Ferruccio Lamborghini's flagship ultra-car, was certainly dramatic yet remarkably pure and unadorned. Both cars were the work of Marcello Gandini, but, where the Miura was sensual and muscular, the Countach was a futuristic, knife-edged wedge. At 186 miles per hour, it was even faster than the Miura; "Countach," meanwhile, is a Piedmontese expletive like "wow," only fruitier.

Renault 5, 1972

Renault's already rich heritage of design innovation was crowned by the 5. It was designed by Michel Boué, although tragically he died aged 35 before the car even entered production. The nimble, ultra-practical, front-wheel drive, small hatchback exemplified by the 5 changed the small car market sector in one deft move. Its clean-cut two-box profile, hatchback opening down to bumper level and plastic-moulded bumpers and dashboard, set the standard all others followed. The Renault 5 is remarkably similar to modern incarnations of the top-selling supermini typified by cars today such as the Ford Fiesta, Peugeot 207, and Renault's own Clio.

Volkswagen Golf, 1974

The quintessential hatchback and a landmark design for Giorgetto Giugiaro, the Golf was as pure in its design philosophy as the Beetle, which had feathered the nest for it: a simple, reliable, truly modern and high-quality machine for the people—just like the Beetle. And, just like the Beetle, Detroit scorned. (GM's Bill Mitchell called it a "bullfrog that swallowed a box.") As with the Beetle, VW had the last laugh. Old Golfs don't perish easily, so it will be years before the rarity of original survivors highlights the car's significance. Above all, it established a standard of aesthetic clarity in its sector.

Audi 100

A harmonious large saloon that set the trend for the remainder of the 1980s and the early 1990s, the Audi 100 made aerodynamics a sales virtue; at a time of recession and high fuel prices, its slippery form gave it excellent economy for its size. The car's coefficient of drag, at 0.30, was stated on its side windows in a prominent decal, while other factors that helped its wind-cheating abilities were flat wheel trims and flush-fitting glass. The design, much of which was the work of RCA graduate Martin Smith, was austere on the inside to match its unadorned exterior.

Fiat Uno, 1983

The Fiat Uno saw Giorgetto Giugiaro's vision for the future of passenger comfort made real. A series of concept cars from his Italdesign consultancy—the Alfa Romeo Taxi in 1976, the Lancia Megagamma in 1978, and the Alfa Romeo Capsula in 1982—had been created around the idea of a tall and commanding passenger compartment against a prevailing 1970s norm of low-slung and cocooning. The Uno brought this welcome new aspect to the showroom, with deep glass and excellent headroom, giving Fiat a distinct advantage over supermini rivals such as the Ford Fiesta and VW Polo.

Renault Espace, 1984

The Espace, the pioneer and style setter of European multipurpose vehicles had a twisted genesis. It originated in the British studios of Chrysler Europe and was scheduled to be built by the company's partner Matra. But Chrysler Europe was sold to Peugeot, and the design—originally by Fergus Pollock—was refined by Matra's Antoine Volanis, the stylist who penned every Matra model from the Djet to the Rancho. Renault then stepped in to back it. Ironically, Chrysler in the United States pioneered the sector with its minivan a year earlier, but Volanis' sophisticated one-box design for seven occupants was streets ahead in the style stakes.

Ford Ka, 1996

Ford's curvy little hatchback was previewed in 1994 with a cherry-red doppelganger bearing the same name. Indeed, Ka seemed a typically silly concept car name, a tongue-in-cheek take on "car" guaranteed to make you smirk. It was the work of Chris Svensson, who showed off his ideas for how a sharp-looking, futuristic small car might look at the 1992 Royal College of Art graduation show. The Ka went on sale four years later, its cuddly curves sharpened up into new-edge ellipses and its huge plastic bumpers also forming the lower wings to create an effect, if anything, even more distinctive than the concept.

Toyota RAV4, 1997

The RAV4 represented a watershed in the march of four-wheel drive into the everyday lives of ordinary motorists. It was not the first compact SUV—sport-utility vehicle in the modern idiom: That was the 1988 Daihatsu Feroza/Sportrak. But it was easily the most successful combination of road car dynamics (thanks to its modified Camry platform), off-road ability, and high-riding driving position. A curious stylistic combination of hatchback, sports car, and 4x4, buyers loved both its looks and its road behaviour (and almost all were used on the road). Subsequent versions, and a positive armada of rivals, have diluted the RAV4's impact, but it remains a trendsetter.

Audi TT, 1999

Another car that began life as a well-crafted concept car, the TT, conceived by Freeman Thomas and Peter Schreyer, jumped the species barrier between automobile and product design. Its smooth, clean lines and defined curves are inspired by the 1930s Bauhaus design movement in Germany. It was a masterfully self-conscious exercise in consumer psychology that proved a hit with buyers. Yet the car was only made a production feasibility by technology advances in platform-sharing—essentially, and under that characteristic shape, the TT is the same car as the VW Golf and Skoda Octavia.

MCC smart, 2000

The Micro Compact Car organisation was originally conceived by Swiss watch tycoon Nicolas Hayek to rejuvenate an interest in microcars that had been absent in Europe since the austerity days of the 1950s bubble car. He intended to do that with design, scheming the prototype for an ultra-short urban two-seater that would be cheap and fun to own. The final, toy-like car, the smart, had input from his first partner Volkswagen and then from Mercedes-Benz, which brought it to the market. Pundits were unsure the innovative, colourful, and upright city car would work. Buyers in every traffic-choked European city have proven them wrong.

MINI, 2000

Any attempt to reinterpret Issigonis' engineering-led icon would be a controversial undertaking. But the last of the classic Minis, built in 2000, was woefully behind the times in every area except perky character and sparkling driving pleasure. Hence, design leader Frank Stephenson plumped for a retro feel to the new Mini, while BMW's product planners schemed the car as primarily a two-plus-two for the trendy and childless—buyers with plenty of disposable income to lavish on their Minis to customise them from a vast array of options. It proved a wise premium strategy: Within five years, sales were running at the same rate as the hallowed original.

BMW 7 Series, 2002

The BMW E65 7 Series will never grace the automotive hall of fame because, accomplished as it is, it is merely one of many large executive cars jostling in an established market sector for broadly the same, sober customers. What it will be remembered for, with its bustle-back rear end with a twin-deck boot lid, its large wheels, and its overstated visage, is stirring up huge debate—especially online—about car design. Its creator, Chris Bangle, split opinion with his cussed new direction for mainstream BMW styling. Whether deemed good or bad by critics, professional or layman, the main thing was that it was talked about. Sales, meanwhile, were notably unaffected.

Toyota iQ, 2008

Irresistible Japanese minimalism goes global in the iQ, a car for our times. With its tiny proportions and three-cylinder engines, it's designed for meek environmental impact, but the interesting part is in the thinning down of traditional elements, such as the fuel tank, differential, seats, and even the air-conditioning unit, to provide three-plus-one seating in a compact package. Like the Smart and MINI, overhangs are banished. Huge doors and wheels confound city car expectations, as does an unlikely alliance between Toyota and Aston Martin to offer a bespoke edition exclusively to existing Aston owners.

glossary

A comprehensive glossary of vehicle design terms, expressions, and techniques, written by David Browne, Course Director for Automotive Design at Coventry University. This is an updated version of material which originally appeared on cardesignnews.com.

Beltline

The line directly underneath the side windows of the car created by the junction of the **greenhouse** and the body side or **shoulder**. The position and inclination of the beltline affects the appearance and proportion of a car, as well as its character and **stance**. A car with a low beltline and tall **greenhouse** may look delicate, elegant, or modern. A car with a high beltline and shallow greenhouse will tend to look tough and mean. A *rising* beltline provides the long, fashionable wedge appearance and imparts a dynamic sense of purpose and direction.

UK English: **Waistline**

Body section

A vertical slice through a car body side that is then viewed at 90 degrees to help understand or appreciate the form. Tape lines applied across the surface show a section nicely, the trailing edge of an open front door describes it perfectly, but only at that point; body sections are rarely constant. A glance at typical body sections will reveal that most have convex main surfaces, although **creases** and **feature lines** may introduce local negative contrasts.

Body wide line

The lateral line at which the maximum width of a car can be measured (excepting door mirrors). It may be created by a **crease** or any of the main **body section** lines, but for practical purposes (in car parks, etc.) it is usually designed to be an applied bodyside protector moulding or rubbing strip. The developing trend is to avoid added bodyside protectors, with the body wide line defined by a more subtle body crease.

Bone line
(See also swage line, feature line, crease, character line):

There can be a fine line between some of these terms, and this has led to a certain interchangeability of terminology. Though not structural per se, all of the above terms have an important primary function in reinforcing body panel stiffness and reducing vibration. They will, however, be part of the *visual* structure of a car.

Their principal purpose is to variously create definition, add emphasis, visual interest, design organisation, and to direct—or even deceive—the viewer's eye. A bone line is a hard, positive only, linear peak in a car's body side, more prominent than a crease line. Relating it to the often-used "taut skin over muscle and sinew" metaphor (see **haunch**), this implies sheet metal, similarly stretched, but over something more structural. An interesting, or unique, bone line can also be a **character line**.

Bonnet

UK English term for **hood**.

Bulkhead

UK English term for **firewall**.

Cab forward

Cab forward design, coined by Chrysler and first seen on the 1987 Portofino concept car, led to the production of a family of cab-forward products, including the 1993 Dodge Intrepid and the 1994 Chrysler LH and New Yorker. The benefit to the overall **package** was space: By moving the screen, driver, and passenger forward, space was liberated for the rear compartment, and this was further enhanced by moving the (non-driven) rear wheels, and therefore **wheel arch** intrusion, backwards. One way or another, it was a pretty innovative package and style combination.

Cant rail

The structural member that usually sits squarely on top of the **B-pillar**, forming the top edge of the door frame aperture, and which may run (visually) seamlessly into the **A- and C-pillars**, an arrangement most clearly defined by glass-roofed versions of cars, such as the Mercedes E-Class.

Character line

An important **feature line** or **crease** that may be sculpted or, more pleasingly, created by the meeting of two planes on a car's surface and that gives or adds both definition and personality to the form. A character line is more fundamental and important to a design than a feature line or a crease, and the best examples may be sufficiently unique to represent that car when abstracted, e.g. Seat Altea, Mercedes CLS.

See also: **Form language, surface language**

Cheater panel

The small triangular, usually matte black–painted, surface at the base of the **A–pillar**. It generally forms the leading edge of the side glass graphic—or **DLO**—on, or just ahead of, the front door and which may usefully disguise sculptural uncertainties in this awkward, but key, conjunction of three planes. For such a small item, its contribution is surprisingly important. Functionally, if in the door, it happily provides a natural platform for external rear-view mirrors and a useful channel for the front glass drop.

Rear cheater (or **Flag** in the United States). Again, a small, usually matte black–painted, triangular panel at the base of the *trailing* edge of the rear side window or in the rear quarter panel. In the former, its function will be to create a shorter door glass, to provide a vertical channel, and to enable the window to be lowered without obstruction from the door closing and locking mechanisms. Functional considerations aside, designers will use cheaters to create the illusion of a longer and more elegant **DLO**.

Clay

Automotive styling clay is a dull, brown, grainless, wax-based material used as a finishing surface for scale and full-size exterior and interior models. Although temperature sensitive, unlike water-based ceramic clay, it doesn't dry out and cannot be fired. When preheated to around 60 degrees Celsius, it becomes very malleable and is applied as a 25-millimeter or so skin over a structure called a buck or armature. After cooling to room temperature, it is then sculpted using a variety of hand tools or computer-controlled three- or five-axis milling machines. The particular advantage of clay is that it can as easily be added to as subtracted from, and the finished product is, literally, seamless.

Dressed clays

As clay is a dull and lifeless material, clay models need a bit of help to be properly understood by decision-making non-designers. The simplest form of dressed clay—whether small-scale or full-size—is one in which the glass areas are blacked out. This can be achieved quickly and easily using black masking tape or black paint. **Shut lines**, wheels, and other areas of contrast will have been added, leaving the bare clay to represent the painted surfaces. This provides effective 3D graphic contrast, though finer nuances of the design may still effectively be camouflaged by the non-reflective clay. The next step will be to Di-Noc or paint the remaining surfaces.

Crease line

A crease is the pressed or folded line created by the meeting of two different planes or surfaces. Unlike feature lines, a crease is integral to a design, and cannot simply be *applied* to a surface, but is commonly the means of *defining* major surfaces and elevations. A crease may be positive or negative but has more inherent integrity than a **feature line**. However, a particularly strong or interesting crease in an otherwise simple surface might take on the importance of a **character line**. Two very adjacent **creases** may work together to create a **feature line**, like those seen on Giugiaro's 1974 Mk 1 VW Golf.

Crown

Crown in a panel is *compound* curvature—usually convex: In one plane, it would simply be curvature. To the engineer, crown provides inherent stiffness; to the designer it enables the control of **highlights** and **lightlines**.

The *appearance* of flatness can be achieved by the very subtle use of crown, but *true* flatness cannot be accurately controlled. A simple way of measuring crown is to compare it with an offered-up straight-edge. There is *always* considerably more crown—in any direction—on automotive surfaces than seems apparent, likely, or even possible. Glass is not considered to have crown. Glass surfaces, particularly windscreens, are to all intents and purposes, single curvature. The *principal* curvature—in plan for front and rear screens, end elevation for side glass—dominates any slight, but necessary curvature in the opposing planes.

Crumple zones

Those sacrificial front and rear ends of a car, designed to progressively collapse—or crumple—in a controlled manner, absorbing and dissipating crash forces rather than transmitting them to the more expensive mechanical parts or the occupants.

They can also make the visual consequences of a modest accident look rather alarming and give rise to uninformed speculation about the flimsiness of modern cars. Since Euro NCAP (New Car Assessment Programme) started publishing the results of its independent testing, occupant safety has become highly marketable. Yet now that manufacturers have demonstrated they can rise to the *that* challenge, NCAP has started publishing results of *pedestrian* safety tests, which may have a greater effect on the *appearance* of the front end of cars.

DLO

The expression stands for "day light opening" and is used to describe the graphic shape of a car's side glass. The DLO is the strongest and most important graphic element of a car's design, as it provides the opportunity to create a major contrasting surface that can be employed to flatter or accentuate a form.

Where there's graphic continuity, it may also include the front and/or rear screens. This notion has really only been convincingly achievable since the advent of flush glazing and bonded front and rear screens that additionally enabled non-opening pillars to be glazed over.

Down the Road Graphics (DRG)

The design features and characteristics of the front end or face of a car that enable the marque to be immediately identified from a distance.

Di-Noc

Di-Noc is a thin, prepainted—usually in silver—stretchable plastic film that is applied like a transfer—by sliding it into place off its wetted backing paper. The advantage this has over paint is that it can be simply peeled off to facilitate design changes without spoiling the clay surface.

DNA

Design DNA has become a term banded about by the automotive design fraternity and, like the term diva, popularised in the media to the extent that the true meaning and value of the expression has been lost.

The terms genetic information, hereditary character, and pedigree get to the contextual meaning—core marque values—the deep-down being of a company and how its designed products might reflect these fundamental values and connect with other products from the same company. It is *not* about the incorporation of relatively superficial styling themes, devices, or clichés, which have more to do with *brand* identity and marketing strategies: It is rather, *marque* identity, which is not the same thing at all.

The Citroën 2CV and DS are nothing alike physically, but share the same inherently innovative, clear-thinking creativity, intrigue, and fitness for purpose that was the essence—DNA if you like—of all the great Citroëns.

Feature line

A simple line in a car's body surface. The best feature lines will be sympathetic to the design of a car, but some may simply have been introduced to relieve otherwise dull or large areas of plain sheet metal. They can also be used to accentuate the form and to link, tie in, coordinate, or visually organise the loose array of items, such as door handles, vents, rear number plate recess, and front and rear lenses, etc., which appear on all cars. Any and all body panels may have feature lines—some have been known to have too many. See also **crease line**.

Fender

Fenders are those local panels that are legally required to wrap or cover road wheels, protecting the bodywork—sometimes the occupants—and other road users from spray, dirt, stones, and anything else thrown up by the revolving tyres. In their early, simplest form, they closely followed the shape of the wheel, like bicycle mudguards. Today, identifiable front fenders live on in *all* body configurations, but *rear* fenders only in three-box saloons. Integral in hatchbacks, the panel—which accommodates the rear wheel—is referred to as the rear quarter panel.
UK English: **Wing**

Firewall

The structural panel that separates the engine compartment from the passenger compartment. Principle functions include sound and heat insulation, but the firewall may also support items like the battery or screen wash bottle. Sports cars and some sedans have *rear* firewalls, though these days many are engineered into the seat backs.
UK English: **Bulkhead**

Form language (or surface language)

This can refer to the manipulation of the form of any *individual* vehicle or to the visual feel or identity that characterises and unites a manufacturer's entire *range*.

Usually, the way the principle surfaces of any car's exterior—and *interior*—are treated will help to confirm its nature or purpose. A small city car, intended to be nonthreatening and friendly, may have soft curves, generous radii, a happy face, and playful interior detailing. Sportscars' surfaces should help make them look athletic and powerful, and 4x4s will tend to be chunky and *apparently* unsubtle and unrefined.

Deployed *corporately*, surface language is a form of brand or marque identity, referring to the *manner* in which designers from different companies will treat the sculptural journey from broadly similar points A to points B.

Audi designs—epitomised by the original TT—have highly disciplined geometric surfaces and detailing. This cerebral designing characterises the whole range and creates a unified family identity. Interestingly, the organised surfaces of an Audi-designed Lamborghini could not be mistaken for the more emotive sculpture of the Ferrari 458 Italia.

Jaguarness can be traced backwards to the emotive E-Type, D-Type, and C-Type, but the sharper new XF and XJ set out to define the new way *forward*. Some form language is even afforded the significance of being *named*: Ford's graphic New Edge of the 1990s and the less convincing moving-when-standing-still Kinetic Design. BMW's controversial flame surfacing unifies its entire, diverse range.

Some early Japanese, and more recently Korean and Chinese manufacturers, with no design history of their own, have borrowed others' successful design language as a shortcut to market acceptance.

Greenhouse (or glasshouse)

The upper, glazed part of the passenger compartment that sits on the bodywork. This conjunction is referred to as the **beltline** or **waistline**. As front and rear **screen angles** have become ever "faster," and **tumblehome** more pronounced, conspiring to increase solar gain, this piece of terminology is finally coming into its own.

Hard points

Points on a **package drawing** indicating the position of component parts or extremities that cannot be moved and that must therefore be accommodated or designed around.

These include the engine, suspension, fuel tank, wheel centres, and wheelbase (and therefore inner wheel arches) pedals—maybe a whole shared **platform**—thereby exerting considerable influence on both exterior and interior designs.

With pedestrian impact legislation requiring an 81-millimetre clearance over those (literally) immovable components to allow sufficient panel deformation, some hard points—along with **headswing** clearances—have become theoretical points in space and are creating an impact of their own on the appearance of cars, particularly the front end.

Front and rear lamps, which have to comply with a range of positional requirements, could be said to be negotiable hard points, as the 1999 Fiat Multipla ably demonstrates.

Haunch

Haunch is the name given to the emphatic sculpting of the **fender** panel above the rear **wheel arches**, which alludes to skin tightly stretched over the well-toned muscles and sinews of an athlete and therefore implies power and performance. Haunches have been an essential ingredient of the generic rear-wheel drive coupé from the 1950s and are often associated with Jaguar, which has used this device as a key part of its form language since then.

Highlights and lightlines

These exist on the surfaces of all shiny objects and are key to describing and understanding form. **Lightlines** are effectively paths of reflected light that run along a surface and make it possible to understand its sculptural form without reference to its outline shape.

A **highlight** is a visible concentration of light that flares off a **lightline** at a point that is dependent on the position of the viewer. As with **lightlines**, sharp **creases** will create crisp, tight highlights, and gentler ones will generate correspondingly bigger but softer highlights. A car is not, of course, a purely static object, and as the car (or the observer) moves, both lightlines and highlights will travel along and around its surfaces. Organising this flow around a complex 3D form so that it works from any and all angles and views is hugely challenging and requires great sculptural feel and experience.

Reflections and horizon line

Any shiny surface with light falling on it will reflect both that light and any adjacent or distant objects.

In the stereotypical desert scenario, a car's upper surfaces will reflect the clear blue sky and its lower surfaces the uninterrupted expanse of sand. Where they meet creates the horizon line. This ready-made sketch or rendering formula, drawn along the DLO and/or the body sides, has been used by generations of car designers and is instinctively understood by the observer.

Because the sky and sand are featureless and the horizon line (effectively a dark **lightline**) is straight, any deviations in their reflection can only have been caused by the sculpture of the car, which they are therefore helping to describe.

Lightlines, **highlights**, and **reflections** are created under artificial circumstances, so design studios usually have a high-walled outside viewing yard where full-size models can be discreetly appraised from a greater distance, in real life surroundings, and in the cold light of day.

Hood

The exterior body panel that covers the engine compartment of front-engined cars (they're called *engine covers* on rear-engined cars) and that can usually be lifted or opened to provide access to the engine. The trailing edge is called the *hood cowl line*. Hood **shut lines** are usually on the top surface and flow neatly forwards from the inside edge of the **A-pillar**. Most Land Rovers and Saabs have signature clamshell hoods that effectively incorporate the tops of the front **fenders**, moving the shut lines (and their associated flanges) to the body sides.
UK English: **Bonnet**

Indexing

Indexing is the organizational business of lining up surfaces, features, and details in order to achieve sculptural flow and graphic continuity, but it is only necessary, or referred to, when there is a gap, or break, in physical continuity created by—for example—the wheels.

A car's body sides sculpted straight through *without* the intrusion of wheel openings, which are then surgically removed, would guarantee surface and feature line continuity and perfect indexing.

But there may be an element of **cheating** in the process—*strict* continuity of line, etc. may be *implied* and therefore *perceived* rather than actual. The trusting human eye makes the connection, and no one is any the wiser.

By contrast, the banana-shaped sills of the Peugeot 306 were clearly only considered *between* the wheel arches in both side and plan views—a device used in some sports cars to maximise visual emphasis on the wheels and therefore performance.

Indexing occurs elsewhere on cars, too. The upper and lower grilles on Audis were indexed through the bumper until Walter de'Silva joined up the dots to create the brand's bold new face. There is *some* serious and some playfully absent (on the doors) indexing on the L R Discovery 4.

Instrument panel (IP) (Also Facia, Dashboard, Dash)

The instrument panel (or IP) is a hugely important, multifunctional platform that contains information displays relating to a car's performance, well-being, and geographical location; major and minor controls; switches, etc.; heating and ventilation outlets; storage access; and, of course, the obligatory cupholder. It also *conceals* a number of functions—the passenger airbag, the air-conditioning/ventilation/screen-demisting systems and their associated trunking, as well as the important structural crossmember.

Jewellery

The collective name for those bright component parts applied to the main exterior body surfaces (grille, wheels, and painted brake callipers even), head and taillights, side repeaters, door handles, bright trim, and badges) or in the interior (sometimes switches, instruments, vents, local metallised details, etc.).

Their impact will depend on contrast with body colour. Jewellery will stand out against dark colours and be discrete against silver—though this can be a useful way of diminishing *un*attractive details.

Lighting has become *serious* jewellery, projector and LED technology enabling anything designers can dream up—a far cry from the once-obligatory off-the-shelf seven-inch round sealed-beam headlights.

Mercedes used to be the most consummate user of chrome, but used it to *define* form rather than just decorate it, turning it into a Teutonic art form with the 1963 600 limousine. (illus)

Overdone aftermarket jewellery can, in effect, turn a whole car—usually a large, black 4x4 with huge chrome wheels and spinners—into an item of bling.

Light catcher or daylight catcher

The name given to a styling device that is intended—like a **feature line**—to add surface interest but that is deliberately positioned so as to reflect light from an area normally in shadow and is typically found on a car's lower body side, door/s, or **sills**.

The introduction of an upward-facing detail in a part of the body section that would usually reflect ground tones creates bright sky reflections of the same value as those on the upper body surfaces. This simultaneously draws the eye downward, lowers the visual centre of gravity to below the wheel centres, and helps plant a car on the ground, giving it a more positive emphatic stance.

If the light catcher is long and pointed, it will also add a forward dynamic. Chrome steps on 4x4s have much the same visual lowering and toughening effect.

Joint lines

The trunk lids of some cars simply cannot be pressed in one piece because of the inherent right-angled nature of the panel, coupled with the preferred sharp undercuts associated with the design of some licence plate recesses.

The impression of a single panel is achieved by butting and laser welding a separate lower licence plate–bearing panel to the main boot pressing, but this *does* leave a (barely visible) joint line sometimes concealed by a bright strip.

Lightlines—*see* Highlights *and* Lightlines

Overhang

Those parts of a car that project forward of the front wheels and extend rearwards of the rear wheels and that incorporate the crumple zones.

The relationship between overhang and **wheelbase** is critical in achieving an overall visual balance: Too much overhang is undesirable. Fortunately, the visual perception of excessive overhang can be reduced by the judicious use of **plan shape**. Some designers argue that unequal overhangs add a certain visual dynamic, whereas a car with equal overhangs will tend to look inherently static.

Package/Package drawing

A package is the basic layout of a car. Typically, package *drawings* are delivered, via engineering, as an assembled collection of largely nonnegotiable **hard points** in the form of the car's unclothed functional contents.

This will include recommended length, width, and height; wheel centres; engine, drivetrain, and fuel tank location; screen position and angle; and maximum and minimum percentile manikin positions (with sightlines); the latter will also impact on the interior's design, as will inner wheel arch intrusion.

In 2D elevation, or 3D CAD form, this will provide the initial **underlay** over and around which a designer will have to demonstrate his **sketches** can be persuaded to fit—without loss of character. Drawn over a tens lines grid, to a stated scale, and therefore measurable, package drawings leave no scope for artistic licence.

Pillars

Pillars fulfill a number of primary functions. They are important structural members, doors are hinged off and/or close on to them, they support the roof cage and protect the occupants, and visually frame the windows. Pillars may be removed graphically by being matte blacked out or by being wrapped by the side or rear glass and by internal masking to achieve the required DLO graphic.

A-pillar (or A-post)

The upright structural support on either side of the windshield that is usually bonded to them. A-pillars invariably flow visually seamlessly into the **cantrail**. Rollover requirements are so tough these days that many A-pillars have become worryingly thick and can obscure other road users. One-box designs, which thrust the A-pillars forward into the driver's field of vision, can further accentuate this. The base of the A-pillar, where a number of planes conspire to meet, remains the most challenging area for designers to resolve satisfactorily.

B-pillar

Strictly speaking, the B-pillars of most four- and five-door (and some two- and three-door) cars are not visible until their door or doors are opened. What we refer to as B-pillars are actually the adjacent uprights of the front and rear side window frames that sit over, and hide, the actual B-pillar. The *real* B-pillar is invariably a hefty, vertical, structural member that front doors latch on to and off which the rear doors are hinged. It will also accommodate the upper front seat belt mountings.

C-pillar, D-pillar (rearmost pillars)

While an A-pillar might have elegance and a B-pillar is largely plain, functional but anonymous, a C-pillar can have *style*. Some, like BMW's so-called Hofmeister kink have become important marque signifiers. Strictly speaking, for a car with three windows along the side (i.e., estate car, SUV, or MPV), the C-pillar is the third pillar—that is the rear door pillar. The rearmost pillar is therefore the D-pillar.

Plan shape

Plan view is simply the elevational view of a car as seen from directly above. Plan *shape* refers to the amount of curvature in body sides, and particularly front and rear ends, as seen from above (i.e., in plan view).

Cars have *predominantly* constant curvature in plan, but these days this curvature will accelerate noticeably towards the front and rear ends (where it is referred to as tuck-in), leading into much more *generously* radiused corners—or in some cases, effectively, no corners at all. Clever use of plan shape—visually pulling the corners back—provides the best opportunity to disguise the greater overhangs required by ever-tougher impact testing.

Platform

It is not unreasonable to think of a platform as a latter-day chassis—a basic structural and mechanical architecture subsequently clad in the visible sheet metal of the bodywork. It is the *invisibility* of the elements of the platform—typically powertrains, suspensions, and structural pressings, such as floorpans and firewalls—that enables the widespread practice of platform sharing and the massive economies of scale to be achieved. This is common among different brands in the same group (ie VW/Audi/Seat), but the pursuit of economy leads to some surprise partnerships (Fiat 500/Ford Ka).

Screen angle

This is the angle the windshield of a car slopes back from the vertical, measured at its center line. A "faster," more acute angle traditionally signifies a sportier kind of car. The limit, however, is physical rather than legislative: As the screen angle increases, so too does the likelihood of internal refractions, 67 degrees being the angle at which laminated glass effectively starts to become opaque. The iconic Lamborghini Countach was pretty much on the limit for screen angle. The glass areas are part of a car's sculptural form, and while a screen will be substantially flat in front of the driver's eyes, double curvature may be introduced at the sides where the screen wraps round to meet the **tumblehome** of the side glass.

Shoulder and shoulder line

The shoulder line basically runs the length of a car's upper body side, where it folds over to meet the side windows, and its nature will reflect the essential character of the car. The surface between the shoulder line and the **beltline** directly below the side windows is referred to, reasonably, as the **shoulder**: amusingly, it is therefore *below* the beltline. It should not be confused with the similarly positioned **haunch**. Volvo's trademark shoulders have been developed into a marque identity characteristic, which emphasises strength—and therefore safety—a long-held Volvo byword. See also **beltline**.

Shut line

A shut line—or cut line—is the necessary clearance gap between two adjacent exterior body panels or interior trim panels, either of which may be openable. They may be identified individually as door shuts or hood shuts, and their tightness and consistency are reliable indicators of build quality. Continuity of surface and **feature lines**, and alignment of adjacent panels, is now taken for granted. Designers seize every opportunity to incorporate shut lines that will be sympathetic to a car's form and reflect its character and that will be consistent with its **surface language**.

Sill/Cill (Rocker Panel)

The visible structural member that runs between the front and rear wheel arches below the doors. Some doors overlap, and hide, their sills.

As the outline that defines the lower body, the sill is also a strong *visual* element, and its shape is quite likely to reinforce the character of a car. In the majority, the lower sill will be part of a continuing line, **indexed** through the wheel arches, running round the car. In a sports car, it may well go negative and curve down to meet the wheels. This can go badly wrong if the sill is also negative in plan view.

In most cars, the sill has to be stepped over to enter or exit. In the Mercedes A-Class, the sandwich floor construction means that the floor is level with the *top* of the sill, guaranteeing an easy exit.

Once commonly matte-blacked out, sills now tend to be body

coloured. This has led to a generation of cars with apparently deep body sides—sporting maybe, but in many instances visually heavy. Designers sometimes take the opportunity to sculpt their surfaces to achieve aerodynamically profiled sills that appear to aid airflow from the front wheels and to the rear ones.

Stance

Stance suggests attitude, intent, and ability; confers presence; and is equally identifiable whether a car is stationary or on the move. (The apparently similar term *poise* refers to a car's dynamic behaviour). Stance is largely defined by the body-to-wheel and the overall vehicle-to-ground relationships that are important in all cars, but vital on those for which attitude is critical. Wheels that fill a car's **wheel arches** in depth as well as diameter will suggest a confident stability. Wheels and wheel arches pulled out from the body sides will imply performance and even aggression, as will minimal ground clearance. Conversely, generous ground clearance is both a physical and visual requirement of an off-road vehicle.

Surface language—see form language

Swage line

Swaging is a technique in which cold metal is formed over a grooved tool or swage. In the early automotive context, the edge of one panel was swaged so that it could overlap its neighbour to create the impression of a continuous surface—usually running along the **beltline** or waistline. By the time production techniques made one-piece doors possible, the swage line had become a popular, elegant device (and a useful division in two-color paint schemes) often concealed by coachlined or chromed waist mouldings, effectively becoming, in the process, a **feature line**. Today, the term is often used generically—particularly by those with an engineering background—for any raised, continuous, pressed bodyside **crease** or **feature lines**.

Tumblehome

Tumblehome is nautical terminology. It was introduced to automotive design with the advent of curved side glass and the need to describe the convex inward curvature of the side of a car above the **beltline** or **waistline**.

 Unlike **screen angles**, the degree or amount of tumblehome is not measured. The amount of tumblehome needs to be carefully

balanced by the designer as part of the overall car **package**. Cars like the Fiat Multipla or Honda Crossroad are examples of cars with very little tumblehome, due to their emphasis on practicality and spaciousness.

Waistline —See Beltline

Wheel arches

These are essentially circular apertures in the body sides that admit the road wheels and, importantly, *frame* them. At their simplest—and often most satisfying—wheel arches appear to have been surgically cut out of the body sides. The relationship of wheel to wheel arch is critical, and designers attempt to make the former fill the latter as fully as possible. Wheel arches—and the wheels—may be emphasised by pulling out the body sides locally or by the addition of wheel arch extensions or eyebrows. Sometimes made from textured matte-black plastic, these offer the added bonus of reducing the depth of—and protecting—the painted sheet metal between the wheel arch and the top of the fender. Clever detailing on the sheet metal may be used to achieve the same result.

Wheelbase

This is the distance between the front and rear wheel centres and is a critical dimension in the quest for internal space efficiency and optimised accommodation. Successive models in all manufacturers' ranges tend to be incrementally bigger than their predecessors, but the biggest dimensional gain is invariably to the wheelbase. **Overhangs** consequently have been quietly shrinking. The wheelbase is also a critical dimension *visually*, contributing greatly to the balance and proportion of a car.

Wing—See Fender

directory

Becoming a car designer
These days almost all car designers have completed a course in vehicle or transportation design, although an increasing number of young designers are coming from industrial or product design backgrounds. This is particularly the case among those working on automotive interior design. Nevertheless, the majority of young car designers are drawn from transportation design courses, which are the first port of call for car designer recruitment.

Studying car design
Despite similar course titles, the philosophy, reputation, focus, and ultimately the fees of vehicle and transportation design courses vary widely. Different courses often emphasise different aspects of vehicle design. While one may focus on traditional drawing techniques and model-making, another may have a greater engineering focus. Some courses focus on just car design, while others may focus on other areas of transportation design, even boat design. There is no right or wrong course necessarily: All have their own advantages and limitations. The best advice we can offer is to try to choose a course that best reflects your interests and ultimately what you want to do.

Generally, courses that have the closest connections with the automotive industry offer the best chance to acquire real-world experience, whether working on a genuine design brief from a car manufacturer while at college or by attending a work experience placement within the car industry itself at a carmaker's design studio. It is very common for graduates to return to their work placement companies for full-time employment once they have graduated.

Vehicle and transportation design courses

EUROPE
France
Creapole
128 Rue de Rivoli
75001 Paris
France
Tel: +33 1 44 88 20 20
Fax: +33 1 44 88 20 22
Website: www.creapole.fr

Strate College Designers
175/205, rue Jean-Jacques Rousseau
92130 Issy les Moulineux
France
Tel: +33 1 46 42 88 77
Fax: +33 1 46 42 88 87
Website: www.stratecollege.fr

Germany
Hochschule Pforzheim
Tiefenbronner Str 65
75175 Pforzheim
Germany
Tel: + 49 7231 28 68 91
Email: mtd@fh-pforzheim.de
Website: www.fh-pforzheim.de

Italy
Istituto d'Arte Applicata e
Design—Torino
Via Lagrange 7
10123 Turin
Italy
Tel: +39 011 584 868
Fax: +39 011 584 868
Website: www.iaad.it

Istituto Europeo di Design (IED)
International Office
Via Sciesa, 14
20135 Milano
Italy
Tel: +39-0257 96951
Fax: +39-0254 68517
Website: www.ied.it

Spain
Elisava Escola de Disseny Superior
Plaza de la Merce
C/Ample 11-13
08002 Barcelona
Spain
Tel: +34 933 174715
Fax: +34 933 178353
Website: www.iccic.edu

Sweden
Institute of Design
Umea University
SE–90197 Umea
Sweden
Tel: +46 90 786 69 90
Fax: +46 90 786 6697
Website: www.dh.umu.se

United Kingdom
School of Art & Design
Coventry University
Priory Street
Coventry
Warwickshire, CV1 5FB
UK
Tel: +44 1203 631313
Fax: +44 1203 838 793
Website: www.coventry.ac.uk/csad/

University of Huddersfield
School of Design & Technology
Queensgate
Huddersfield
West Yorkshire, HD1 3DH
UK
Tel: +44 1484 473813
Email: info@huddersfield3d.co.uk
Website: www.huddersfield3d.co.uk

University of Northumbria at Newcastle
The Centre for Industrial Design
Squires Building
Sandyford Road
Newcastle upon Tyne, NE1 8ST
UK
Tel: +44 (0)191 227 4913
Fax: +44 (0)191 227 4655
Website: www.northumbria.ac.uk

Royal College of Art
Kensington Gore
London, SW7 2EU
UK
Tel: +44 171 590 4444
Fax: +44 171 590 4500
Website: www.rca.ac.uk

NORTH AMERICA
United States
Academy of Art
79 New Montgomery Street
San Francisco, CA 94105
USA
Tel: +1 415 274 2200
Email: info@academyart.edu
Website: www.academyart.edu

Art Center College of Design
1700 Lida Street
Pasadena, CA 91103-1999
USA
Tel: +1 626 396 2344
Website: www.artcenter.edu

University of Cincinnati
Transportation Design
School of Design
2624 Clifton Avenue
Cincinnati, OH 45221
USA
Tel: +1 5135566000
Website: www.design.uc.edu/ transportation

The Cleveland Institute of Art
University Circle
11141 East Boulevard
Cleveland, OH 44106-1710
USA
Tel: +1 216 421 7000
Fax: +1 216 421 7438
Website: www.cia.edu

College for Creative Studies
201 E. Kirby
Detroit, MI 48202-4034
USA
Tel: +1 313 664 7400
Fax: +1 313 664 7620
Website: www.ccscad.edu

ASIA/OCEANIA
China
Tsinghua University
Beijing 100084
China
Tel: +861062782015
Fax: +861062770349
Website: www.tsinghua.edu.cn/eng/

India
Bhopal Institute of Transportation Styling
Sanasar Chandra Road
India
Tel: +91 11 456892
Fax: +91 11 625432
Website: n/a
Korea
Hong Ik University
Sangsudong 72
1 Mapogu
Seoul, Korea
Tel: +82 02 320 1114
Fax: +82 02 320 1122
Website: www.hongik.ac.kr

Australia
Faculty of Art & Design
Monash University
900 Dandenong Road
Caulfield
East Victoria 3145
Australia
Tel: +61 3 9903 2707
Fax: +61 3 9903 2845
Website: www.artdes.monash.edu.au

Industrial design courses

EUROPE
Spain
Escuela Universitaria de Ingeniería Tecnica
Industrial (EUITI)
Universidad Politecnica
Camino de Vera, s/n
Valencia 46071
Spain
Tel: +34 96 387 74 64
Fax: +34 96 387 74 64
Website: ttt.upv.es/relint/

NORTH AMERICA
Canada
Carleton University
School of Industrial Design
3470 MacKenize Building
1125 Colonel by Drive
Ottawa, Ontario K1S-5B6
Canada
Tel: +1 613 520 5672
Fax: +1 613 520 4465
Website: www.id.carleton.ca

Humber College
205 Humber College Boulevard
Toronto, Ontario M9W 5L7
Canada
Tel: +1 416 675 3111
Website: appliedtechnology.humberc.on.ca

United States
Cranbrook Academy of Art
39221 Woodward Avenue
Box 801
Bloomfield Hills, MI 48303-0801
USA
Tel: +1 248 645 3300
Fax: +1 248 646 0046
Website: www.cranbrookart.edu

The Pratt Institute
New York
200 Willoughby Avenue
Brooklyn, NY 11205
USA
Tel: +1 718 636 3600
Fax: +1 718 636 3613
Website: www.pratt.edu

Savannah College of Art and Design
P.O. Box 2072
Savannah, GA 31402-3146
USA
Tel: +1 912 525 5100
Email: info@scad.edu
Website: www.scad.edu

ASIA
India
National Institute of Design
Paldi
Ahmedabad 380007
India
Tel: +91 79 6639692
E-mail: info@nid.edu
Website: www.nid.edu

Korea
Industrial Design Department
Seoul National University of Technology
172, Gongung2-dong
NoWon-gu
Seoul
Korea
Tel: +82 02 970 6678
Fax: +82 02 970 6667
Website: www.snut.ac.kr/eng/

Japan
Industrial Design Department
Musashino Art University
1-736 Ogawa-Cho
Kodaira—ShiTokyo
187-8505
Japan
Tel: +81 42 342 5011
Fax: +81 42 342 6452
Website: http://musabi.ac.jp/e-home/home.
html

Industrial Design Department
Tokyo University of Art and Design,
University of Tokyo
7-3-1 Hongo
Bunkyo-ku
Tokyo
113-8654
Japan
Tel: +81338122111
Website: www.u-tokyo.ac.jp

The world's car brands

Here we list the world's principal carmakers and brands, together with their headquarters locations and, where given, web address. Many may belong to a larger parent group but have their own headquarters: examples are SEAT in Spain and Skoda in the Czech Republic, both part of the Volkswagen group. It should be borne in mind that opportunities for automotive designers also exist among suppliers to the auto industry and at tuning companies, companies making motorcycles, commercial vehicles, buses and off-highway vehicles.

Abarth	Performance brand of Fiat	Turin, Italy	www.abarth.it
Acura	Luxury brand of Honda	Torrance, Calif., USA	www.acura.com
Alfa Romeo	Sports premium brand of Fiat group	Turin, Italy	www.alfaromeo.com
Aston Martin	Independent luxury sportscar maker	Gaydon, UK	www.astonmartin.com
Audi	Premium brand of Volkswagen	Ingolstadt, Germany	www.audi.com
Bentley	Super-luxury brand of Volkswagen	Crewe, England	www.bentleymotors.com
BMW	Premium carmaker	Munich, Germany	www.bmwgroup.com
Brilliance	Chinese automaker	Shenyang City, China	www.zhonghuacar.com
Bugatti	Supercar maker, Volkswagen group	Molsheim, France	www.bugatti.com
Buick	Part of General Motors	Detroit, USA	www.buick.com
BYD	Chinese maker of hybrids and electrics	Shenzhen, China	www.bydauto.com.cn
Cadillac	Luxury brand of General Motors	Detroit, USA	www.cadillac.com
Caterham	Enthusiasts' sports cars	Dartford, UK	www.caterham.co.uk
Chana	Chinese maker of small cars	Chongquing, China	
Chery	Major Chinese automaker	Wuhu City, China	www.chery.com.cn
Chevrolet	Principal brand of GM	Detroit, USA	www.chevrolet.com
Chrysler	US group controlled by Fiat	Auburn Hills, Mich., USA	www.chrysler.com
Citroën	Part of PSA Peugeot Citroën	Paris, France	www.citroen.com
Dacia	Entry brand of Renault	Pitesti, Romania	www.dacia.ro
Daewoo	Korean operation of GM	Seoul, Korea	www.chevroleteurope.com
Daihatsu	Part of Toyota group	Osaka, Japan	www.daihatsu.co.jp
Daimler	Parent company of Mercedes and Smart	Stuttgart, Germany	www.daimler.com
Dodge	Part of Chrysler group	Auburn Hills, Mich., USA	www.dodge.com
Ferrari	Supercar maker controlled by Fiat	Maranello, Italy	www.ferrari.com
Fiat	Volume car maker	Turin, Italy	www.fiat.com
Fisker	Luxury hybrid car maker	Irvine, Calif., USA	www.fisker.com
Ford	Multinational carmaker	Cologne, Germany & Dearborn, USA	www.ford.com
Geely	Major Chinese carmaker	Hangzhou, China	www.geely.com
GMC	Truck brand of GM	Detroit, USA	www.gmc.com
Great Wall	Significant Chinese automaker	Baoding, China	
Hafei	Chinese small car maker	Harbin, China	
Hindustan	Long-established Indian carmaker	Calcutta, India	
Holden	Australian brand of GM	Melbourne, Australia	www.holden.com.au
Honda	Major car and motorcycle maker	Tokyo, Japan	www.honda.co.jp
Hongqui	Chinese large car maker	Chanchun, China	www.faw.com.cn
Hummer	Extreme SUV brand of GM, facing closure	South Bend, Ind., USA	www.hummer.com
Hyundai	Major Korean group	Seoul, Korea	www.hyundai.com
Infiniti	Luxury brand of Nissan	Tokyo, Japan	www.infiniti.com
Isuzu	Japanese SUV maker	Tokyo, Japan	www.isuzu.co.jp
Iveco	Truck brand of Fiat	Turin, Italy	www.iveco.com
Jaguar	Luxury car maker, owned by Tata	Coventry, UK	www.jaguar.com
Jeep	SUV brand of Chrysler	Auburn Hills, Mich., USA	www.jeep.com
JMC Landwind	Chinese SUV maker	Nanchang, China	www.landwind.com
Kia	Part of Hyundai group	Seoul, Korea	www.kia-motors.com
Koenigsegg	Extreme supercars	Ängelholm, Sweden	www.koenigsegg.se
KTM	Lightweight sports cars, motorcycles	Mattighofen, Austria	www.ktm-x-bow.com
Lada	Major Russian firm, controlled by Renault	Togliatti, Russia	

Lamborghini	Extreme supercars, part of VW group	Sant'Agata Bolognese, Italy	www.lamborghini.com
Lancia	Premium brand of Fiat	Turin, Italy	www.lancia.com
Land Rover	Premium SUVs, part of Tata group	Solihull, UK	www.landrover.com
Lexus	Luxury brand of Toyota	Tokyo, Japan	www.lexus.com
Lincoln	US luxury brand of Ford	Dearborn, Mich., USA	www.lincoln.com
Lotus	Specialist sports cars, controlled by Proton	Hethel, UK	www.grouplotus.com
LTI	Makers of London taxi	Coventry, UK	www.lti.co.uk
Mahindra	SUV and truckmaker	Mumbai, India	www.mahindra.com
Maruti Suzuki	Major Indian carmaker	New Delhi, India	www.marutisuzuki.com
Maserati	Luxury sports cars, part of Fiat group	Modena, Italy	www.maserati.com
Maybach	Super-luxury brand of Daimler	Stuttgart, Germany	www.maybach-manufaktur.com
Mazda	Volume carmaker closely linked to Ford	Hiroshima, Japan	www.mazda.com
McLaren	Extreme sports cars	Woking, UK	www.mclarenautomotive.com
Mercedes-Benz	Principal brand of Daimler	Stuttgart, Germany	www.daimler.com
Mercury	Part of US Ford group, soon to close	Dearborn, Mich., USA	www.mercuryvehicles.com
MG	Former British brand, owned by Nanjing	Nanjing, China	
Mini	Premium small car brand, owned by BMW	Oxford, UK	www.mini.com
Mitsubishi	Volume car maker	Tokyo, Japan	www.mitsubishimotors.com
Morgan	Specialist sports cars	Malvern Link, UK	www.morgan-motor.co.uk
Nissan	Volume car maker, allied with Renault	Tokyo, Japan	www.nissan.co.jp
Opel	European brand of GM. Vauxhall in UK	Rüsselsheim, Germany	www.opel.com
Pagani	Extreme sports cars	Modena, Italy	
Perodua	Licence-build of Daihatsu models	Malaysia	www.perodua.com.my
Peugeot	Part of PSA group	Paris, France	www.peugeot.com
Pontiac	Defunct brand of GM	Detroit, USA	
Porsche	Sports car maker controlled by VW	Stuttgart-Zuffenhausen, Germany	www.porsche.com
Proton	Malaysian small car maker	Selangor, Malaysia	www.proton.com
Renault	Volume car maker, allied with Nissan	Boulogne-Billancourt, France	www.renault.com
Roewe	Premium brand of SAIC	Shanghai, China	www.saicgroup.com
Rolls-Royce	Super-luxury marque, part of BMW group	Chichester, UK	www.rolls-roycemotorcars.com
Saab	Former GM brand, owned by Spyker	Trollhättan, Sweden	www.saab.com
Samsung	Part of Renault-Nissan alliance	Seoul, Korea	www.renaultsamsungm.com
Scion	US youth brand of Toyota	Torrance, Calif., USA	www.scion.com
SEAT	Part of VW group	Barcelona, Spain	www.seat.com
Skoda	Part of VW group	Mlada Boleslav, Czech Republic	www.skoda-auto.com
Smart	Microcar brand of Daimler	Böblingen, Germany	www.smart.com
Spyker	Luxury sports car maker, owns Saab	Zeewolde, Netherlands	www.spykercars.nl
Ssangyong	SUV maker, controlled by SAIC	Seoul, Korea	www.smotor.com
Subaru	Part of Toyota group	Tokyo, Japan	www.subaru.co.jp
Suzuki	Small cars, SUVs, motorcycles	Hamamatsu, Japan	www.globalsuzuki.com
Tata	Indian truck and car maker	Mumbai, India	www.tatamotors.com
Tesla	Electric sports cars	San Carlos, Calif., USA	www.teslamotors.com
Toyota	Global No. 1 carmaker	Toyota City, Japan	www.toyota.com
UAZ	SUV and truck maker	Ulianovsk, Russia	
Venturi	Electric vehicles	Monaco	www.venturi.fr
Volga	Part of GAZ group	Niznhy Novgorod, Russia	
Volkswagen	Leading European automaker	Wolfsburg, Germany	www.volkswagen.de
Volvo	Likely to be sold to Geely	Gothenburg, Sweden	www.volvocars.com

acknowledgments

When a book approaches the subject of car design from so many different angles as this one does, it takes a pretty impressive cast of characters to ensure that everything comes together coherently and that the final product is clear and, I hope, entertaining.

So top on our thank-you list are all senior figures in the design business with exceptional talent for either promoting the cause of good design by explaining it to a broader audience, for teaching it to aspiring young designers, or for demonstrating it in the metal through the products they create.

Our particular appreciation therefore goes to the PSA Peugeot Citroën design team in Paris, led by Jean-Pierre Ploué, for the insights they allowed me into their work and their way of working; Ian Callum, architect of Jaguar's dynamic new style, kindly consented to write the Foreword, while the diary kept by Oliver le Grice, head of advanced design at Land Rover, gives a privileged insight into the working life of a top designer. Alfonso Albaisa, Marc Girard, Anthony Lo, Gordon Murray, Marek Reichman, Adrian van Hooydonk, Peter Schreyer and David Wilkie and many other designers all spared their precious time to answer our questions, either face-to-face or on the phone, and we would like to thank the students at Hoschschule Pforzheim, Umeå Institute of Design, CCS Detroit and Coventry University for submitting their work for inclusion in Chapter 12. We are especially grateful to Professor Dale Harrow, head of vehicle design at London's Royal College of Art for his essay on the importance of transportation design and its place within the world and to David Browne, course director for automotive design at Coventry, for his outstanding glossary of car design terms, surely the best ever to have appeared in print. Our thanks also go to colleagues Giles Chapman for his infallible photo library and his contributions to Chapters 15, 16 and 17, and to Eric Gallina and Simon Timm of Car Design News, for kindly allowing us to reproduce the tutorials for Chapter 13.

We owe a debt to David Downes and Salvador Roig of Magenta Systems for their generous support and guidance for digital design content and tutorials. Similarly our thanks to Alias and to Magic Car Pics who managed to pull many automotive rabbits out of hats under what where crucial time constraints.

TONY LEWIN
RYAN BORROFF
Spring 2010

index